Marketing Research for Non-profit, Community and Creative Organizations

How to improve your product, find customers and effectively promote your message

26 in 26

Neighborhood Resource Centers

26 Neighborhood Strategies in a 26 month time frame

A Grant Funded by the LSTA

(Library Services & Technology Act)

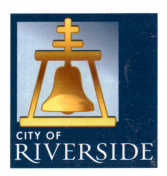

Riverside Public Library

Marketing Research for Non-profit, Community and Creative Organizations

How to improve your product, find customers and effectively promote your message

First edition

Bonita Kolb

Routledge
Taylor & Francis Group

LONDON AND NEW YORK

First published 2008 by Butterworth-Heinemann

Published 2015 by Routledge
2 Park Square, Milton Park, Abingdon, Oxon, OX14 4RN
711 Third Avenue, New York, NY 10017

*Routledge is an imprint of the Taylor & Francis Group,
an informa business*

British Library Cataloguing in Publication Data
A catalogue record for this book is available from the British Library.

Library of Congress Cataloguing in Publication Data
A catalog record for this book is available from the Library of Congress.

ISBN: 978-0-7506-8760-7 (pbk)

Typeset by Charon Tec Ltd., A Macmillan Company.
(www.macmillansolutions.com)

Contents

Preface

This book has two main purposes. First, the book has been written to educate readers on how research can be used to help their organization more effectively meet its mission by improving their product, finding new customers and developing effective promotion. Second, it will educate the reader on how to conduct the different methods of research including focus groups, interviews, projective techniques, observation and surveys.

This book will be useful for both students and existing managers of small non-profit, creative and community organizations. Many of these students and managers are drawn to working at non-profits because of their interest in the organization's mission. However, they may have limited marketing experience or education.

There are now books available on non-profit marketing that teach the reader marketing theory and practice. However, these books often only have a chapter or less on marketing research. This single chapter serves as an introduction to the purposes and methods of marketing research. However, one chapter cannot possibly provide sufficient information so that the reader is ready to plan and conduct research. The current books on non-profit marketing can help the reader gain an understanding of concepts such as product development, segmentation approaches and promotion methods. Unfortunately, the reader will not know how to conduct the research that will provide the information necessary for making marketing decisions about their product, segmentation or promotion.

What is unique in this book's approach is that it will first focus on educating readers on how research can be used in their organizations. It will then describe in detail how to conduct different research methods. To reinforce this connection the research methods will not be discussed in the abstract but will always focus on the reason the research is being conducted.

Another unique aspect of this book is its chapter on cultural considerations. Many non-profit and community organizations work with segments of the population that may not respond well to the traditional business marketing research process. Or they may be reluctant to participate because of differing cultural values. Therefore for research to be successful, the methods used often must be adapted.

While in the for-profit world it is common to refer to people who patronize a business as customers or consumers, there is no standard terminology for the non-profit world. The words that can be used include patient, client or audience depending on the type of organization. This book will use all these terms, but for simplicity sake also refers to customers and consumers.

The book starts with an introductory chapter that explains how the data that is collected from marketing research is transformed through analysis into knowledge that the organization can use to meet their mission. Chapter Two takes the reader through the steps in the research process. A unique aspect of this book is that Chapter Three is devoted to the issue of conducting research across cultural borders. This is especially important for non-profits as they often serve populations that are outside the mainstream culture. When conducting research it is crucial to start with the right research question. For this reason Chapter Four is devoted to this subject. Before starting conducting research, the organization will find useful information that has already been collected. Chapter Five explains the process for obtaining secondary or already existing data. Chapter Six explains the important process of finding the right research participants.

The reader is now ready to learn research methodology. Chapter Seven covers focus groups, which is one of the most commonly used research methods. In-depth, expert and intercept interviews are covered in Chapter Eight. Some organizations may also wish to use projective techniques and observation which are covered in Chapter Nine. Two chapters are devoted to survey research. Chapter Ten explains the process of planning the research and writing the survey questions and answers, while Chapter Eleven explains how to conduct a survey.

Finally, Chapter Twelve explains how the data is analysed and results in recommendations for actions. Of course, these recommendations need to be explained so Chapter Thirteen covers how to prepare a written and oral research report.

CHAPTER 1

Marketing research and the mission-centred organization

■ Introduction

People who manage non-profit and community organizations may have many misconceptions about marketing research. While having adopted some marketing techniques they may still have a negative view of marketing research believing it is only appropriate for businesses. This belief may be because they are unaware of the many marketing research methods that can be used by non-profit and community organizations. This unawareness is unfortunate, as adopting techniques appropriate for their organization would increase the likelihood of fulfilling their mission.

Organizations need to understand the marketing research process and how it can be adapted to meet their needs. Surveys are only one research method organizations can use along with focus groups, interviews, intercept interviews, projective techniques and observation. In addition, organizations need to appreciate the ethical and cultural considerations involved in conducting marketing research.

■ The benefits of conducting marketing research

Non-profit and community organizations are called mission centred because they are formed as the result of a desire to improve society. The organization's central purpose is to fill a need that cannot or will not be met by the for profit marketplace. While profit is not the main motivation of non-profit and community organizations they still must remain fiscally solvent to remain in operation. This is one reason many of these organizations have adopted marketing practices.

Non-profit and community organizations can be in many different fields including healthcare, the arts, social change, community development, economic revitalization and faith-based charities. All of these organizations were founded with the intention of providing assistance or promoting ideas that will improve the lives of individuals or society as a whole. Table 1.1 is from the US Tax Code and provides some indication of the wide range of activities in which such organizations engage.

Tax code	Description of organization	General nature of activities
Table 1.1 Nonprofit organizations and their purpose		
501(c)2	Religious, educational, charitable, scientific, literary, testing for public safety, amateur sports, prevention of cruelty to animals and children	Activities of nature implied by description of class of organization
501(c)4	Civic leagues, social welfare organizations, local associations of employees	Promotion of community welfare, charitable, educational or recreational activities
501(c)5	Labor, agricultural and horticultural associations	Educational or instructive, the purpose being to improve conditions of work and to improve products and efficiency
501(c)6	Business leagues, chambers of commerce, real estate boards	Improvement of business conditions for one or more types of business
501(c)7	Social and recreation clubs	Pleasure, recreation, social activities

The mission of the non-profit and community organization may be to fill a need by providing a service, a tangible good or promoting an idea. For example, the mission of an organization formed to improve public health would provide healthcare services for low-income people. The organization may also provide a tangible good by providing low-cost humidifiers for families with children with asthma. Or, rather than providing a service or good directly to a client, the organization's mission may be to influence society by promoting the idea of the importance of preventive healthcare.

Unfortunately, too often in the past non-profit and community organizations believed that to successfully meet their mission only good intentions were needed. However, a change in this way of thinking has resulted in mission-centred organizations understanding that they need to market what they have to offer to their potential clients or customers. To do so they have adopted marketing techniques such as using promotion to increase their client numbers and to design effective ad campaigns. These marketing techniques have been successfully used to reach out to those they want to serve (Hanson, 2001).

However, it is difficult to use marketing techniques successfully if the organization does not first understand their clients' needs. For example, the organization cannot design an effective ad campaign without knowing what words or images best communicate its message. Therefore, it is now time for non-profit and community organizations to understand how the process and methods of marketing research can be used to help discover the needs of those they wish to serve and then communicate their mission to current and potential clients.

EVERYONE NEEDS RESEARCH!

Why do small businesses and other types of organizations believe that marketing research is only for large corporations? Here are some myths and the response:

'I'm already doing enough research' – but is the data the right data?

'Research is only for big decisions' – research for small decisions is still useful

'I'll lose control' – research does not need to be turned over to specialists

'Market research is survey research' – there is much more to research than surveys!

'Market research is too expensive' – not necessarily

'Most research is a waste' – not if properly planned

Source: Andreasen (2002).

Question to consider: What argument would our board make against conducting marketing research?

Uses of marketing research

Mission-centred organizations must now consider adopting the research techniques used by marketing researchers. However, a marketing research effort can only be successful if mission-centred organizations first accept the fact that only their clients know what they need and want. After all there is no reason to conduct marketing research if the organization continues to insist that they already know what is best for the client. The purpose of marketing research is to help the organization learn from the potential client or customer how their needs and wants can be best be served.

Marketing is often described as consisting of the four 'P's' of price, product, place and promotion. Any business or organization must provide a product, whether a good, service or idea, that is needed by consumers. They must also price this product correctly and provide it at a location convenient to the consumer. Finally the information on the product, its price and location must be promoted using effective words and images. The purpose of marketing research is to provide the information the organization needs to determine the correct product, price, place and promotion that will motivate the potential customer. In addition, a company or organization can research the consumer's opinions and ideas and competitor actions. These issues are summarized in Table 1.2.

Table 1.2 Uses of marketing research

Issue	Purpose	Question
Product	Discover benefits provided to consumers	Why do clients use our services? How can our services be improved?
Price	Choosing price level	Should we charge for our services? What amount are our clients willing to pay?
Place	Effect of location on clients	Where is the most convenient location to provide our services? How can our location be improved?
Promotion	Effectiveness of promotion	Does our promotion motivate action? What media will reach our audience?
Consumer	Understanding our consumer	Who is the main user of our services? What non-users can we reach?
Competitor	Understanding our competitors	Why do clients use our competitor? What competitor actions could we add?

Product: How can marketing research help non-profit and community organizations with product issues? Mission-centred organizations often believe that they should not change their product as it was developed with a specific mission in mind. However, the organization should understand that while the core product may not change, the benefits the product provides can and should be adapted to what their current and potential clients might want. For example, through research, an organization helping battered women might find that besides shelter, the women need help in handling finances so that they can remain independent.

Price: Many non-profit and community organizations would not think about researching price, as their product, whether good, service or idea, is provided at no cost. However, even if the product is free there are still reasons to research price. The organization may find that the potential client is both able and willing to pay for a service that is currently being provided at no cost. If the organization received money from clients, even if only a small amount, it would mean that the organization would be less reliant on fundraising. If the organization already charges for a service, marketing research can help to determine the amount the client can and is willing to pay. Furthermore research may find that different groups of customers have different abilities and willingness to pay which means that the organization can develop pricing which meets each group's needs.

Place: Distribution, or place, refers to the physical location where the good or service is made available. Most non-profit and community organizations have limited budgets that result in their choosing a location which is affordable. However, budget should not be the only criteria. The location should also be acceptable to clients of the organization. Whether the location is acceptable can depend on distance, available means of transportation and the condition of the neighbourhood. The only means to determine what clients want in a location is through conducting marketing research.

Promotion: Promotion may be the marketing component that is most frequently researched. A good deal of money and time is spent on designing promotional material in the hopes that it will effectively communicate a message. Using marketing research before designing the campaign means that there can be less reliance on hope and more reliance on fact regarding what types of words and images communicate best.

Customers: In addition to the four 'P's' of price, place, product and promotion, the demographics and opinions and behaviour of current and potential consumers can be researched. If the organization is going to offer a product with the benefits consumers want at the right price, in the right location and communicate effectively it is important that the organization know as much as possible about their current and potential customers. This would include demographic data such as gender, age, income and education level. It would also include their opinions, values, attitudes, beliefs and consumption behaviour.

Competitors: Another use of marketing research can be to examine the actions of competitors. Competing organizations can be a useful source of ideas regarding product, price, place and promotion. Successful ideas used by competitors can possibly be adapted by the researching organization for their own use.

■ Marketing myths

There are some common myths about marketing (see Table 1.3). Many non-profit and community organizations believe that marketing consists only of the promotion of a product. While promotion is an important aspect of the marketing mix, it is only one of the four marketing components of product, price, place and promotion. After all promotion, which takes place at the end of the marketing process, can only be effective if the organization first determines the correct product, price and place.

Table 1.3 Marketing myths

Myth	Truth
Marketing is only promotion of a product	Marketing consists of a mix of product, price, place and promotion
Marketing is an occasional event	To be effective marketing must be embedded into the organization's strategic plan
Marketing can manipulate people into taking action	Marketing can only make people aware of possibilities

Another misunderstanding common among non-profit and community organizations is that marketing is an 'event' that is only conducted periodically when the time and money is available. However for marketing to be effective, it cannot be considered a single event, but rather a process that takes place on a continual basis.

An unfortunate myth held by some non-profit organizations is that marketing's purpose is to 'manipulate' the consumer into purchasing something they do not want or need. However, the truth is that it is very difficult to get anyone to do something they do not want to do – ask any parent of a teenager! After all consumers have they own tastes, personalities and desires that dictate what they will purchase. Marketing only makes them aware of possible choices.

Even if a company could manipulate someone into buying their product, there would be no long-term benefit in doing so. Both businesses and organizations depend on establishing a long-term relationship with consumers built on trust. If that trust is destroyed than the consumer will not use the services or buy the goods of the company. In addition, they will tell others about the broken trust. Any organization that wants to survive must deal honestly with consumers.

■ Defining marketing and marketing research

The four 'P's' of product, price, place and promotion are often depicted in a circle with the consumer in the middle. This depiction explains that the purpose of marketing is to provide to the consumer the right product, at the right price, sold in the right location and then promoted effectively with a message that describes the product, price and place using images and words.

Marketing

The definition of marketing provided by the American Marketing Association best describes this relationship. The definition, which can be found on the website www.marketingpower.com, states marketing is:

> the process of planning and executing the conception, pricing, promotion and distribution of ideas, goods, and services to create exchanges that satisfy individual and organizational goals.

This definition describes marketing as the planning of the total package of product, price, promotion and distribution whether the product is an idea, good or service. In addition, the purpose of marketing is to meet the needs not only of the individual but also of the organization.

Therefore marketing is not 'selling out' where the business provides whatever the consumer wants. This actually would not be possible as businesses consist of people who have certain skills and abilities that will dictate what product they can produce. Non-profit organizations are even more constrained in what they produce because they are formed with a mission of meeting a particular need. An effective marketing plan must take into account both the mission of the organization and the needs of the consumer if it is to be successful.

HOW DO YOU KNOW WHAT THE NEXT FASHION TREND WILL BE?

There is a lot non-profit and community organizations can learn from research conducted by the creative industries. According to market researchers in the fashion industry, the first step is secondary research on social trends. In-house reports, government statistics and data from academic sources are studied for information on social changes that might affect what people want from fashion.

Second, the media is used to study cultural changes. This includes both cutting-edge and mainstream TV shows, magazines and movies.

Third, the researchers hit the streets to interview the 'fashion-forward' who are the first to be knowledgeable of the newest trends.

And finally, fourth, the researchers use observational research to see what trend makers are wearing and also visit those retailers who are known for starting these trends.

Even with all these research efforts 30 to 50 percent of all new fashions that make it into a retail store are not successful. Imagine what would the failure rate would be without research!

Source: Retail Week (2004).

Question to consider: What recent failure has my organization had that could have been prevented if research had been conducted?

Definition of marketing research

People who work in community and non-profit organizations understand the importance of conducting research. However, when the word marketing is added, research may now have a negative connotation. Those employed by non-profit and community organizations may believe that marketing research is an invasion of the privacy of the consumer at worst and a nuisance at best. This opinion may result from the experience of being asked to provide information through a telemarketing survey or while shopping.

However, marketing research is a much more complex process than only conducting surveys. Marketing research is a systematic process that uses structured methods to determine the wants and needs of the consumer. The definitions provided by the American Marketing Association (AMA) may again prove useful. The AMA defines marketing research as:

> the function that links the consumer, customer, and public to the marketer through information – information used to identify and define marketing opportunities and problems; generate, refine and evaluate marketing actions; monitor marketing performance; and improve our understanding of marketing as a process.

This definition can be directly applied to the mission of non-profit and community organizations as can be seen in Table 1.4. First, the definition states that research provides information used to find opportunities and define problems. Although the non-profit and community organization is mission centred, the mission is often broadly defined. Non-profit and community organizations need to use research to determine the exact needs and desires of their potential clients.

Table 1.4 Applying the marketing research definition	
Purpose	**Application**
Find opportunities and define problems	What new services are needed?
Generate, refine and evaluate marketing actions	How can these services be provided?
Monitor the marketing process	How effective is our promotion in communicating our services?
Improve understanding	What other ways can we communicate?

For example, the mission of an organization may be to 'assist the homeless to be self-sufficient' or to 'provide arts education to low-income students.' Both of these are laudable goals, but the organization must still determine the 'how' of these missions. What exact services, goods or ideas need to be provided so that the homeless can become self-sufficient? What kind of arts education will both students and the schools welcome and how will it be delivered? Marketing research can help determine the answers.

The definition then states that the information from marketing research should be used to generate, refine and evaluate marketing actions. Once the organization has used research to find opportunities and problems, the information can be used to determine the characteristics of the product, the price of the product, the place the product will be provided and how the product will be promoted. Finally research can be used to evaluate if these choices have been correct.

KNOWING WHAT TO SAY WHEN THEY ALREADY KNOW A BEHAVIOR IS BAD

The Minnesota Partnership for Action Against Tobacco (MPAAT) wanted to give Minnesotans a message that would motivate them to quit smoking. So they held four focus groups around the state and had the participants' view and rate anti-smoking messages. What the researchers discovered is that telling smokers about the health risks was a waste of effort as smokers already had this information. Instead the participants wanted a message that would move them from awareness to action.

While the focus groups revealed that participants were well aware of the health risks to themselves of smoking, they were much less aware of the danger caused by second hand smoke. With this information, the organization decided to run ads that focused on the dangers second hand smoke presented to children along with a hot line number for help with quitting.

Additional survey research conducted after the ads were run found that over 70% of smokers who viewed the ads were smoking less around children. In addition, in the first ten months after the ads were run 5,000 calls were made to the hotline.

Source: Jarvis (2002).

Question to consider: What messages does our organization communicate to the public that should be researched for effectiveness?

■ Relationship between data, information and knowledge

The purpose of conducting marketing research is to solve an organizational problem involving the marketing mix. As described previously this problem could be about the organization's competition, their current customers or potential customers. In addition, the research could involve one of the four components of the marketing mix of price, product, place and promotion.

The problem that needs to be solved often first comes to the attention of the organization's management because of a decrease in revenue or customers. However, research should not only be used when the organization is in a crisis. A decrease in revenue or visitors is often just the symptom of the problem that has existed for some time. For example, the lack of visitors could be attributed to any number of causes that have been affecting the organization. There may be a problem with the product, such as new programming that is not attractive to the current customers. The problem may have resulted from a change in the price of admission. Even if there has been no change in price, the customer's perception about the price may have changed because of poor economic conditions.

Perhaps there are no problems with the product or the price. Rather the lack of visitors may be due to inadequate promotion. After all the visitors cannot attend an event of which they are unaware. Finally, the problem may be distribution of the product. This could include such issues as problems with the location or an inability to easily buy tickets.

Of course, all of these issues should be researched before the organization has a problem. In fact, the main purpose of marketing research is to prevent problems by learning more about what the organization's customers want and need. Therefore research should be conducted before any major changes are made in the organization regarding how they implement their mission.

This does not mean that the organization will only make changes based on obtaining prior approval of the customer. Non-profits have a mission to which they must remain true. However, conducting research and using the resulting information can actually help the organization to remain true to its mission. Often non-profit organizations will want to present programming or implement policies that may be unpopular with the public. Research should be used not to change the programming or policy but rather to determine how to better package and promote the product so that it will be acceptable.

Knowledge and recommendations for action

There is a difference between research data and the uses to which this data can be applied. Research will result in the organization obtaining data. This data will be in the form of numbers and statistics if a quantitative survey was conducted. The data can also be in the form of transcripts from interviews, lists on sheets of paper from focus groups and even drawings from projective techniques. However, the raw data is often of little use to the organization. The data needs to be turned into information and then knowledge.

For example, people may go to the doctor for a physical exam because they are not feeling well. The doctor will run various tests (research) to determine the cause of the problem. The data on the tests will be meaningless to the patient. It is the doctor's responsibility to make a diagnosis based on these results. It is this information (perhaps the tests indicate high blood pressure) that the doctor will provide to the patient. However, good doctors will go one step further. Not only will they provide information, they will also give patients knowledge regarding what they should do about the problem. After all just having the problem diagnosed does not solve anything. The doctor needs to inform patients on how to lower their blood pressure so that the problem is eliminated.

The same relationship between data, information and knowledge holds true when conducting marketing research. Too often the focus is on what method to use and once the research is completed, the researcher feels her or his task is complete. However, obtaining the data is not the end of the research process. The data must be analysed to provide the organization's management with information that they can use to solve the problem. This is the purpose of conducting research.

Relationship between data and knowledge

- Data: Raw numbers or words that have been gathered during the research
- Information: The cause of the problem
- Knowledge: What action the organization should take to solve the problem.

Critical thinking

Critical thinking can be thought of as a three-step process. The first step is identifying the pre-existing assumptions held by the non-profit organization regarding the cause of a problem or a potential opportunity. The second step is to use internal research data to challenge whether the assumption is accurate and based on reality. The third step is to explore new ideas of the actual source of the problem and its possible solution.

Unfortunately, the second step of challenging assumptions about the cause of the problem is where the critical thinking process often stops. As a result, assumptions are accepted without being questioned. The reasons for this automatic acceptance include common patterns of thought among the organization's employees and management and also the natural desire most people feel to conform.

If everyone in the organization tends to view their consumers and the external world in the same way, it is difficult for the researcher to argue against these beliefs. This is particularly true in non-profit organizations where everyone believes in a common mission. However, it is these common patterns of thought that causes the organization's problem and its solution to seem self-evident. These common thought patterns can also keep an organization from seeing opportunities that can be explored using research.

The more prevalent these common patterns of thinking are, the more important it is to challenge the assumptions. And yet, if everyone else is sure of the problem and wants to move forward with corrective action, there is a natural desire to conform to their opinion. Nevertheless, it is the responsibility of the market researcher to ask questions about whether the assumptions are based on fact, even when this is unpopular. Only after false assumptions have been eliminated can new ideas based on true facts be proposed.

Now that the initial assumptions have been dealt with and any wrong assumptions have been discarded, it is time for the final step in the critical thinking process. This is to explore new ideas regarding the problem or potential opportunity. This step in the process demonstrates why the market researcher's knowledge of the external environment and the current and potential consumers is essential. Using this knowledge shortens the process of generating and developing new ideas. This is because the researcher has already challenged many of the assumptions and has a base of knowledge about the product and consumers on which to form new ideas (Dewey, 2005).

■ Ethical and cultural considerations when conducting research

Marketing research involves asking individuals to share with the researcher their opinions and values. In addition, they are asked to reveal information on their behaviour. Because of the potentially intrusive nature of research it is important to consider how the researcher can ensure that they treat the research subject with respect. Of course, it would be the rare researcher that started to research with the intent to commit harm. However, a consideration of ethical issues before research begins can avoid unintentional problems.

Researching across cultural differences can easily result in unintentional harm. Because non-profit organizations are mission based they have an interest in reaching out to cultural groups that may not be using their services. Unless the researcher understands the cultural values of the group who are subjects of the marketing research, misunderstandings can lead to a breakdown in trust that may be difficult for the non-profit organization to repair.

Marketing research ethical issues

Simply defined, ethics is a set of guidelines that distinguishes what is right from what is wrong. While ethics are general principles, a code of conduct is a set of guidelines that spells out what is right and wrong in a specific set of activities. Because of the importance of ensuring that the rights of research subjects are respected marketing research has established codes of conduct (Market Research Society, 2006).

Guidelines for conducting ethical research

- Never conduct research where the search for truth is compromised
- Deal honestly with research subjects
- Make sure no harm results
- Communicate research findings to participants.

The first standard is that the purpose of the research itself must be ethical. It is the researcher's responsibility to ensure that the research is conducted objectively without a predetermined outcome. Researchers understand that by controlling who is asked and by changing the phrasing of a question, the outcome of a study can be manipulated. The pressure to predetermine the results may be caused by the need to have a specific outcome so that a grant may be obtained or renewed. By participating in such deceptive research, not only will the organization have failed ethically, all future research results will be suspect. It is important for both managers and researchers to remember that the behaviour of people they work with will be affected by how they behave (Barnett, 2004).

When conducting research, those working for the organization should always identify themselves accurately. They should also be honest with participants as to the purpose of the research. If this is not possible because of the research design, the information needs to be presented at the conclusion of the research.

An additional ethical issue is the responsibility to protect participants from harm. This should be of special concern to mission-centred organizations as they may be researching sensitive issues. While marketing research uses techniques that are adapted from psychology, marketing researchers are not trained as psychologists. Researchers must be careful with how questions are worded so as to minimize any emotional distress. They must also be ready to handle any distress that does inadvertently result. For example, permissible questions might be 'Have you ever been a crime victim?' or 'How did our office help you when you were a crime victim?' A question that is not part of marketing research would be 'How did you feel when you were victimized?'

Finally, the participants should have access to the research findings. Even if it is not possible to provide participants with the entire final report because of privacy issues, they should be allowed access to at least a summary of the analysis of the responses to the questions in which they participated. The organization may find that not everyone is interested, but still the offer should be made.

PROTECTING THE CHILDREN

Special care needs to be taken when conducting marketing research interviews with children. Non-profit and community organizations, along with parents and the general public, all have a stake in ensuring the protection of children. Below are some suggested guidelines from The World Association of Opinion and Marketing Research Professionals (ESOMAR):

- The welfare of the children and young people must always come first. They should experience no harmful effects for being interviewed.
- The researcher should communicate to the parents or guardians the safeguards that are in place.
- The general public must be confident that the children will be protected and there is no possibility of abuse.

Source: World Association of Research Professionals (2004).

Question: What groups do we work with that will need special protection when conducting research?

Cultural considerations when conducting research

Effective research depends on the willingness of research subjects to participate. This willingness is based on an understanding of the purpose of research and trust in the researcher. Issues that can affect this understanding and trust include the respect the organization and researcher have for the culture of the research subjects. In addition, it depends on the cultural value participants involved in the study place on privacy. Of course, having a shared language helps being able to communicate both respect and an understanding of cultural values.

Guidelines for conducting research across cultural boundaries

- Respect the culture of research subjects to build trust
- Understand the cultural values involving privacy
- Communicate in the language of the subject.

Respect: Before designing and conducting a research study that involves subjects from a different culture, it is important that the organization and particularly those involved in the research have a sincere respect for the culture. If this is not the case, the research subjects will not trust the researchers and may refuse to be involved in the research.

For many cultures trust depends on personal relationships. The idea that the researcher is only acting in a 'role' and should not be considered a unique human being might not be understood or, if understood, accepted. In this case for research to be effective the researcher must first develop and maintain a relationship with the subjects. Asking someone to 'tell me why you needed our services' might be too difficult to answer when life has held a great deal of pain and grief, unless the participant trusts the researcher as a person.

Part of respecting the culture of the participants is an appreciation of how cultures differ in their attitudes towards people in authority. In some cultures the researcher might be seen as having some level of control over the subject's life. It is important for the researcher to clearly explain the purpose and limitation of the researcher's role. If the researcher is seen as someone having authority, simple demographic questions concerning family status, address or nationality can be seen as threatening. For example, the subject may be living with a partner while still having a spouse in another country, has provided an inaccurate address to get a child into a better school district or is in the country illegally.

HOW YOU ASK CAN BE AS IMPORTANT AS WHAT YOU ASK

The Mennonites and Amish have traditional views that require staying separate from the world. The Mennonite Information Center provides information to the public on the culture and beliefs of the Mennonite and Amish communities. In addition, they help these communities by informing the public about the services and goods they might purchase.

When an organization such as the Mennonite Information Center awants to conduct research on their community, they must be careful to hire a research company that understands the challenges presented. Since the researchers must have experience working with sensitive topics, often the best researchers are those that also have a faith-based lifestyle. They then can understand the strong feelings participants might have on such subject as politics and entertainment. The company then trains the researchers on key terms and concepts that the respondents might use. Training is the key to ensuring that the survey takers get information without offending.

Source: Quinn (2001).

Question to consider: What additional training would the organization's staff need to research other cultures?

Understand: Marketing research techniques were originally derived from the area of psychology and are based on the sharing of personal information from the research subject to the researcher. It is important for the organization to understand that cultures differ in how they view sharing personal information.

The mainstream American culture is not hesitant regarding the sharing of information. People compete to get on reality and talk television shows to share there most personal secrets with the world. However, there are very good reasons why other cultures do not wish to communicate this information. If modesty or privacy is considered as important cultural values, subjects will be reluctant to provide any information that they feel should not be discussed in public. Sharing such information would bring shame upon themselves or their family.

It is important that this aspect of the subject's culture be considered when deciding upon a research method. While the researcher might feel that providing an anonymous survey form provides privacy, the subject might not trust that this is so. Instead, the research subject might see an interview as a totally unacceptable invasion of privacy. In this case a more complicated research design is necessary. The researcher might need to first hold a group meeting to explain the reasons for the research and how privacy will be respected. After trust is established than an anonymous survey might be administered.

Language: One of the more practical issues when researching across cultural boundaries is language. Effective research is dependent on clear communication of meaning between the researcher and the subject. This is difficult enough when they both share a first language. It becomes even more challenging when they do not. The best solution to this issue is for the researchers to share a common culture and language with the research subjects.

To communicate in the research subject's first language also helps to build understanding and trust. However, this is not always possible as the organization may not have access to a researcher from the necessary cultural background. In this case it is important to have someone from the subject's culture to explain the purpose of the research in their own language as this will make the subject more comfortable.

This is less of a concern when conducting surveys. Of course it will be necessary to have a survey form translated into the first language of the research subjects. In fact if there is a language issue, all written communication must be translated including not only the survey form but also any directions that are provided.

However, when conducting qualitative research much of the information is communicated orally. It is critical for the researcher to understand not just what is being said, but how it is being said. For this reason having a researcher who can communicate in the subject's language is imperative. Only using someone to interpret during the interview or focus group will result in losing too much of the meaning.

Summary

- Mission-based non-profit organizations need to conduct research to learn more about what products and services are needed by their customers. The price of the product and the place it is offered can also be researched so that they better meet the needs of customers. It is very important that promotion be researched so that that the organization knows if its message is being heard. Finally the current and potential customers and competitors can be researched.

- Unfortunately some non-profit organizations still believe in some common myths about marketing. Marketing is not only about promoting a product but rather a mix of product, price, place and promotion. In addition, marketing cannot be an occasional activity but must be a continual process. Finally, the marketing process is not used to manipulate people into actions they do not wish to take.

- Marketing is defined as planning a product that the customer wants, that is priced correctly, sold at the right location and promoted so that the customer hears the message. Marketing is providing the customer with the best the company can offer, not the least the customer will accept. Marketing research is simply learning what the customer wants so that it can be provided.

- Data is the raw numbers or words that are obtained through research. Information is the result of the analysis of the data. However, it is knowledge that leads to recommendations for action. It is the marketing researchers' skill and analysis that will result in their making recommendations that will improve the organization. The research effort is not complete without an action plan based on the findings.

- One of the responsibilities of the marketing researcher is to ensure that the research effort does no harm. Therefore careful consideration of any ethical issues is recommended before the research begins. These issues include honesty in the research effort and with the subjects involved in the research. In addition to causing no harm, research participants should be provided with information on the results of the research. The guidelines for conducting research across cultural boundaries include respect for the research participants and an understanding of their cultural values. In addition, if necessary, the research should be conducted in the group's language.

■ References

Andreasen, A.R. (2002) *Marketing Research that Won't Break the Bank: A Practical Guide to Getting the Information You Need*, Jossey-Bass, San Francisco, CA.

Barnett, T. and S. Valentine (2004) 'Issue contingencies and marketers' recognition of ethical issues ethical judgments and behavioral intentions', *Journal of Business Research*, Vol. 57.

Dewey, J. (2005) *How We Think*, Barnes and Nobles Books, New York, NY.

Hanson, J.H. (2001) 'Breaking the cycle of marketing disinvestment: using market research to build organizational alliances', *International Journal of Nonprofit and Voluntary Sector Marketing*, Vol. 6, No. 1.

Jarvis, S. (2002) 'Maximizing Effectiveness: Minn. Campaign grabs smokers by throat', *Marketing News*, 15 April.

Market Research Society (2006) 'Code of Conduct and Guidelines' online at www.marketresearch.org.uk/standards.

Quinn, M. (2001) 'Less is more; minimal marketing serves the Mennonites', *Marketing News*, 22 October.

Retail Week (2004) 'Trend spotting – follow the leader', *Retail Week*, 9 July.

World Association of Research Professionals (2004) 'Guideline on Interviewing Children and Young People' online at www.esomar.com.

CHAPTER 2

The marketing research process

- State the steps in the marketing research process and the importance of determining the research question
- Explain the different sources of primary and secondary information and research approaches
- Explore different marketing research methods available to use
- Explain how research is conducted and data analysed and reported.

Introduction

Too often nonprofit organizations believe that research only involves writing a survey form and handing it out to customers. They may also believe that such an easy task can be conducted by anyone in the organization. In fact it would not be surprising to find college interns given the responsibility for the research task. Contrary to this belief, research is a complex process that involves all levels of the organization.

If research is to be useful, management must be involved in determining the research question. After the research question has been decided, the organization must make decisions involving the research approach and method. Finally after conducting the research, the researchers must report and analyse the findings. Conducting marketing research takes time and effort, but the results will help the nonprofit organization fulfil its mission.

The marketing research process

To conduct effective marketing research, an organization needs to understand the entire research process. Understanding the process will help the organization plan their research so their efforts will not be wasted. Without planning, either the organization will not obtain enough information to justify the research cost and effort or they will obtain information, but not what is needed.

The research process can be summarized as the need to determine, decide, choose, design, conduct, analyse and report (see Table 2.1). The first step involves the organization in determining what information is needed and deciding where this information can be obtained. The organization must then choose the research approach and design the research method. Only then are they ready to conduct research. Finally, they must analyse and report the findings.

Table 2.1 Marketing research process	
Step	**Question**
Determine the research question	What do we need to know?
Decide on source of information	Where will we find the answer?
Choose the research approach	Are we looking for facts or ideas?
Design the research method	What kind of tool should we use?
Conduct the research	When, where and who will conduct the research?
Analyze findings	Do we know what the answers tell us?
Report findings	What actions should we now take?

Determine the research question

The research process starts when the nonprofit or community organization determines what information is needed. This first step involves formulating the research question. While this sounds rather scientific it simply means the organization must ask itself, 'What do we need to know that we don't know now?' There is any number of issues or problems on which the organization might need additional information. The research question might be very broad, such as who has need of the organization's services, to very specific, such as what hours should the office be open on weekends. Even intangibles can be posed as research questions, such as how music might affect the organization's customers (Spangenberg *et al.*, 2005).

Because the organization is often in a hurry to obtain information, it may be tempted to start research before spending enough time considering the problem. As a result they may jump to conclusions based on their own knowledge rather than information from their clients. For example, if the number of people volunteering is declining, the people managing the organization might conclude that it is because of hiring a new volunteer coordinator. Based on this assumption they may decide to research why volunteers are unhappy with the coordinator. This research would be wasted if it is actually the raising price of gas that has resulted in people volunteering less because they are cutting down on unnecessary travel.

In fact there are a number of possible research questions for a decline in volunteer numbers as can be seen in Table 2.2.

Decide on the sources of information

Once the research question has been determined the next issue the organization will face involves deciding the source of the information that will answer the question. Information, or data, is referred to as either secondary or primary.

Table 2.2 Sample research questions	
Issue	**Question**
Price	Has the 'cost' of volunteering increased due to travel expenses or lack of time?
Product	Do volunteers find the tasks they are given boring?
Place	Do volunteers find the organization's location inconvenient or unattractive?
Promotion	Are people unaware of the volunteer activities available?
Consumer	Why do people volunteer at any organization?
Competitor	Are our competitor's volunteer numbers growing or declining?

Secondary

Information that is already available as the result of some other organization conducting research is called secondary data. Since using already available data saves time and money, organizations should always first look for secondary data. For example, if the research question concerns what services the elderly need in rural communities, other organizations such as governmental agencies may have already conducted research. While the responses received from the research may not directly answer the organization's research question, it can still be used as a source of information and assistance in research planning. Even if the responses are not directly applicable, perhaps because the research on the needs of the elderly was done in an urban environment, the questions might be useful as a model for what can be asked.

The organization may find useful secondary data can result from studies conducted by government agencies, nongovernmental organizations, other nonprofits and educational institutions. Unlike research conducted by for profit companies, which is often proprietary, research conducted by these types or organizations is often freely available. Rather than simply searching online for studies that resulted in secondary data that the organization can use, it is better to use the assistance of a reference librarian at a nearby community or academic library.

Primary

Sometimes available secondary data may be all that the nonprofit or community organization needs to answer the research question. However, it is more likely that primary research will also need to be conducted. Primary research involves directly asking those who have the needed information.

If the organization needs to conduct primary research the next issue will be to decide who has the information that is needed. The information might need to be obtained from current clients, potential clients or other people in the community. The research might even need to involve all three groups. Once it has been determined which group has the needed information, the organization must be much more specific in determining the sample or who should be the participants or subjects of the research.

GETTING BY ON THE CHEAP

There is no reason to spend a lot of money on marketing research. After all nonprofit organizations are used to achieving goals with limited resources. The Children's Museum in Indianapolis wanted to know about the buying habits of the museum store's typical shoppers. The Museum managed to conduct a marketing study worth $25,000 for $200.

To achieve this impressive cost savings, the Museum used the students of a senior level business class at Purdue University. The students designed the research question, conducted the survey and then analysed the results. The Museum only needed to provide the $200 cost of a database containing the names of potential research subjects. The findings were so useful that they were used to design a second museum store that was opened in an Indianapolis mall.

Source: Fielding (2005).

Question to consider: Are there any local educational institutions whose students we could use to conduct research?

Research participants

The choice of who should be chosen as subjects might be based on the current or potential clients' usage pattern or demographics. In addition the psychographic profile of the client including their attitudes, values and lifestyles may be considered. For example, the organization might decide they need to have as research subjects, clients who have not used their services in the last six months as the research question concerns why client numbers are dropping. Or if the research question is about a change in procedures at the organization, clients who are frequent users might be the appropriate subjects. The organization may also determine the research sample based on demographics. They might choose as participants, male clients who are elderly or young female clients depending on the research question.

Choosing research participants is more challenging when information needs to be obtained from people who are not current or past customers. However, this is just the information needed if the organization wishes to expand to serve new groups. In this case it might be necessary to conduct the research using nontraditional methods and in nontraditional venues to obtain the needed information. In addition, the research subjects may be community members who have the information the organization needs.

Some studies, such as surveys, can be used to support a hypothesis. This hypothesis, or guess, will give the reason for the problem that the organization is experiencing. Statistical theory states that it is not necessary to ask everyone the research question. In fact the organization can be 95% or 97% certain that the answer the research obtained is correct if a randomly chosen sample consists of the correct number of participants. Other studies will use other techniques to find research subjects including purposive, convenience and snowballing where the researcher's judgment plays a role in determining who will be the participants.

FOCUS GROUPS AND FINE DINING

Most people wouldn't compare a focus group with dining out, but there are comparisons. A focus group has four stages just like a fine meal and skipping any of the stages, just like leaving out dessert, compromises the experience. What are these focus group stages and how do they compare with dining?

- Introduction: the right 'appetizer' sets the mood
- Rapport: the soup or salad prepares one for the main event
- In-depth Investigation: the main entrée which is the 'meat' of the meal
- Closure: the dessert which sends people away happy

If the meal has been excellent, the diner happily pays the bill. If the research has been successful, the organization will also feel they received value for the time and energy spent.

Source: Henderson (2004).

Question to consider: Have we conducted any research in the past that we have found 'unfulfilling' and why is this so?

Quantitative versus qualitative approaches

Once the organization has determined the research question and decided upon the secondary and primary sources of information, the next step in the process is to choose the research approach. The first decision the organization must make is whether quantitative or qualitative information is needed. The decision will be based on both the research question and how the data obtained will be used. Two other terms used to describe research approaches are descriptive and exploratory. Of course a research study can and, if possible should use both methods as they complement each other (Carson *et al.*, 2001). These terms are summarized in Table 2.3.

Table 2.3 Research studies and their use		
Method	**When to use**	**Example of use**
Quantitative descriptive	Use when details and numbers are needed	Research on customer demographics or purchase frequency
Qualitative exploratory	Use when seeking insights on opinions and ideas	Research on satisfaction or new service ideas

Quantitative: Quantitative research is useful for answering questions of fact involving what, where, who and how often. It can answer questions such as what services from the following list does the client desire, where from the following locations would be the best place to provide services, who uses the services and how often clients use the services (Daymon and Holloway, 2002).

If the organization needs to 'prove' a fact for an outside agency it might wish to conduct a quantitative survey. For example, the organization may need to determine the level of satisfaction with their services to include in a grant application. A survey of all current clients might result in a finding that 82% of clients are very satisfied. Of course, it might be impossible to survey all clients, but the larger percentage that is surveyed the more valid will be the resulting information.

Qualitative: On the other hand, if the research question asks for opinions and ideas rather than facts, the organization will need to conduct qualitative research. Qualitative research methods allow research subjects to answer questions in their own words or even in ways that do not use words. Qualitative research answers the question of 'why', such as why do customers want certain services, why do they not like the location of the current office and why do they use less services than in the past. Rather than a survey, qualitative studies use interviews, focus groups, projective techniques and observation.

Descriptive: Descriptive research is used when the research question is very narrowly focused and asks for facts that describe. Descriptive research is always quantitative and can be conducted when the organization already has information about the research question. A survey is used when the organization decides to conduct descriptive research. Descriptive research answers the questions of who, what, where and how many. For example, descriptive research is used when the organization wants to know how many people attend a performance, where they are from, what they buy and who they are.

Exploratory: Exploratory research is used when the organization has little present knowledge regarding the research question. Exploratory research is qualitative and is used when the organization needs to start from scratch by asking 'why' because there is not enough current information about the problem to conduct a quantitative descriptive survey.

Understanding the distinction between these categories of quantitative descriptive research and qualitative exploratory research is important as they have different purposes and will result in different types of data that will need different analysis.

Sometimes the organization may develop a research plan that uses both approaches. For example, the organization may be faced with the situation of wanting to add new services without being sure of what is needed by their clients. If they write a survey that provides as answers what they believe are possible services they will limit the responses of their clients. However, if they first conduct qualitative exploratory research using interviews and focus groups they may find ideas for new services that they did not consider. Then to ensure that the ideas are valid, the organization can develop and administer a quantitative survey.

Design the research method

Once the organization has decided upon the approach based on the research question and the type of information needed, the next step is to design the research method. Research methods can be divided into those used in quantitative descriptive research and those used in qualitative exploratory research (see Table 2.4). Almost everyone is familiar with the research survey used in quantitative descriptive research. However, surveys are not the most commonly used research tool in consumer marketing. The most commonly used tools in marketing research are qualitative exploratory focus groups and interviews. This is because most marketing

Table 2.4 Research methodologies

Method	Description
Surveys	Same set of predetermined questions
Focus groups	Group dynamics to draw out responses
Interviews	One-to-one in-depth discussion
Intercept interviews	Quick person-on-the-street interviews
Projective techniques	Creative techniques to get nonverbal responses
Observation	Watching people's behavior and actions

research asks the question of 'why'. Other qualitative research methods include intercept interviews, projective techniques and observation.

Surveys

Surveys are considered quantitative because the answers that result can be counted or quantified. Surveys ask questions with predefined responses such as yes or no, often or never or satisfied or unsatisfied.

The advantage of having predefined answers is that it allows a large number of responses to be quickly tabulated. The larger the number of survey responses received, the more certainty that the responses received from the research subjects are true for the group as a whole. If enough surveys are conducted, it can even be said that the answer is 'proved'.

Surveys can be personally administered or self-administered using a number of different means. Personally administered surveying methods include in-person and over-the-phone surveys. Self-administered survey methods include by mail and online. Self-administered surveys can also be left on site for current customers to pick up and complete. This is the most common means of obtaining survey information for non-profit and community organizations because the method is quite easy to administer. However, other methods such as phone or mail surveys or posting online survey forms will be necessary if the organization is trying to reach people who are not current users of its services.

The challenge in administering any survey is that people are increasingly reluctant to participate. This may be because people are too busy or because they are becoming more sensitive to the issue of privacy. Members of some cultural or ethnic groups may be even more reluctant to participate. Because of this reluctance the people that respond to the survey may not be representative of the people the organization needs to study.

Because it is difficult to convince people to respond to a survey, it is important that the survey be well designed. The questions must be written clearly and simply since if the question is confusing, the subject may not respond. In addition, the number of questions must be kept to a minimum. If the questionnaire is too long, the respondent may lose interest. The survey should also be visually attractive to encourage completion. Table 2.5 shows an example of a survey question.

Table 2.5 Example of survey question	
Question	**Answer**
Are any of the statements below reasons why you attended Brooklyn Museum's First Saturday tonight? (Please check as many as apply)	– I feel at ease with the other people here. – I came to hear the gospel choir. – I came to eat, drink and socialize. – I might meet new friends here. – I came for the movie. – I want to learn more about art. – My friends or family wanted to come. – I came for the dancing.

Focus groups

Focus groups are interviews conducted in a group setting. The moderator conducting the focus group will have a list of questions and issues that they will introduce. Rather than just ask questions, the focus group moderator uses group dynamics to draw out responses from the participants. While the moderator does have questions prepared in advance, the group will be allowed leeway in what they wish to discuss as long as it remains on the general topic.

One of the most important steps involved in designing a focus group is finding a moderator. Besides being a good listener the moderator needs to be skilled in group dynamics. The moderator's task is to keep the group on topic and to make sure that no participant dominates. In addition the moderator will encourage quieter respondents to participate.

If the organization does not have someone with the needed skill, it may be able to obtain the volunteer services of someone in the community. In fact, it is best if moderators are from outside the organization so that they can be objective since the focus group members may express negative opinions. If this happens to someone who has a strong connection with the organization he or she may take offence. If this feeling is communicated either verbally or nonverbally to the group, they will cease to provide information (see Table 2.6).

Table 2.6 Example of focus group questions	
Question	**Follow-up**
Can you give me some idea of why you think young people do not attend church?	Stephanie, what do you think?
What type of services do you believe would attract more young people?	Ben, why do you think it is hopeless to get young people to church?
Why do you believe more music at services would be attractive?	Colleen, where have you attended a service like this?
How do we communicate to young people about church services?	Sharon, you have been rather quiet, what do you think?

Interviews

The benefit of a survey is that once the effort has gone into writing the questions they can be easily reproduced and widely distributed. Even if the response rate is low, a large amount of information can still be received. Interviews may take less initial effort to design, however they will take much more effort to conduct.

Designing the interview requires deciding upon the questions to be asked and also finding the appropriate subjects. Designing the interview questions can be done relatively quickly as the number of question is smaller than in a survey. However interview research will require more time to conduct, as each respondent needs to be given sufficient time to respond. This additional time allows the researcher to explore in-depth the consumer's behaviour and motivation.

Besides the main interview questions, the interviewer will use probing follow-up questions to elicit additional information. The follow-up questioning is necessary because when first asked a question, many people will respond with what they believe to be the correct or appropriate answer. Also many people want to be polite by answering in the affirmative and with positive praise whenever possible. Additional probing questions are needed before subjects may respond with their true feelings (see Table 2.7).

Table 2.7 Example of interview question	
Interview question	**Possible follow-up responses to gain more information:**
Why do you think that young people binge drink in our town on weekends?	I see. Tell me more. Can you give an example? What else do you think? Please go on. Do you have any other ideas? Have you always felt this was true? Do you think other people feel the same?

Because of the time required to conduct interviews fewer subjects will be involved. However, although there will be fewer subjects involved, interviews provide more depth of information than any other research method. Obtaining this information is dependent on having the interview conducted by someone with the needed listening and questioning skills. In addition, choosing the research subjects to be representative of the group under study is very important. It is tempting for the nonprofit or community organization to simply choose as subjects those people who can be easily convinced to participate. Unfortunately the wrong subjects will result in the wrong information being obtained.

Intercept interviews

Interviews have the advantage of obtaining in-depth information. However they have the disadvantage of taking time to conduct, which limits the number of participants that can be involved in the research. In contrast intercept interviews involve many participants. However, each participant is only asked three or four quick questions. Intercept interviews are a useful technique when research subjects will not agree to a lengthy interview.

Many more people will cooperate if they are told that the interview will only last three to five minutes. Another advantage of intercept interviews is that they can be conducted where the subjects can be found. This is why intercept interviews are often referred to as person-on-the-street interviews.

Intercept interviews can be conducted at the organization's office. However, they can also be conducted in other venues as a means for the organization to obtain information from potential clients who are not currently being served. For example, if the organization provides sports activities for young people it might conduct intercept interviews at the local basketball court where young people congregate. Quick questions could be asked young people regarding their awareness of the organization's programme and the sports activities in which they would be interested.

Example of intercept interview questions

- What booths at the Diabetes Awareness Fair did you visit today?
- What booth did you find most helpful?
- Do you plan on making any healthy changes?

THE EVOLVING PURPOSE OF THE MUSEUM

How many purposes can a museum have? At first museums were formed to both give pleasure and to educate. A more recent purpose has been to provide an opportunity for spiritual uplift. Today's museums try to combine a bit of all three elements and have become a new public space for the community.

But how do you combine all three elements and still satisfy the purists who only come for the art? The J. Paul Getty Museum in Los Angeles used focus groups to tell them how to do it differently. The result is more information on the walls so that those new to art can easily enjoy what they see. For those who want education, there are computers which provide additional information. To help the visitor engage with what they are seeing there are laminated cards which ask challenging questions. And if they need to ponder the meaning of the art, there are now comfortable chairs instead of hard benches.

In fact their mission statement states that their purpose is not only to educate but also to 'delight' and 'inspire'.

Source: Keates (1999); Getty Museum (2006).

Questions to consider: How could we use research to determine the purpose of our organization in the minds of our customers?

Projective techniques

Projective techniques are research methods that gather information without asking for verbal responses. They are often used in focus groups as a means of encouraging communication. In addition projective techniques can be used on their own. Some simple projective techniques include word association, story or sentence completion and cartoon techniques.

Projective techniques were developed in the field of psychology but are now commonly used in marketing research. They are particularly useful when the research participant may be reluctant to discuss a subject. Even when there is no reluctance, projective techniques can create an increased level of interest and interaction in the research process. A research question of interest to the organization, such as how to redesign the waiting room to better serve clients, may not be of interest to research subjects. In this instance the researcher could provide the participants with an outline of the waiting room space along with cut outs of various pieces of furniture and ask them to redesign using these materials. This technique will obtain much more information about the potential new designs than asking verbally.

Word association is asking the participant's first response to a name, photo or event. The idea is to obtain an emotional response to an issue rather than an intellectual opinion. If simply asked their opinion many people may not be able to verbalize their feelings and will think about what is the 'right' answer. Asking only for their first 'gut level' response results in participants responding with their true feelings rather than how they think they should answer.

Another projective technique is story completion. This technique provides a means for participants to respond with a concrete rather than an abstract answer. For example, participants might be asked to finish a story on what a typical client experiences when he or she arrives at the office. This will allow an opportunity to communicate firsthand experiences without labelling them as such.

Sentence completion is an even simpler projective technique. An example would be asking participants to complete a sentence regarding the reason for the client's visit. Cartoons can also be used where the participant fills in the bubble over the character's head. This might be a cartoon of someone attending a neighbourhood meeting saying, 'I'm glad I attended because....'

Example of project word association technique

- Three words to describe your experience at our Low-Water Gardening Workshop are:
- When I think of First Community Health, the first word that comes to mind is:
- One word that I think of when someone mentions experimental theatre is:

Observation

Another research method that can be used is observation. This method records what people actually do rather than what they say they do. This is an inexpensive technique that can be easily used by nonprofits.

For example, if the organization wants to redesign the lunchroom where meals are served to the elderly they might ask clients how they want it changed. However, it might be difficult for clients to respond because it is something to which they have not given much thought. Instead the organization might have researchers watch and record how the lunchroom is being used. In this way they might find that clients tend to want to gather in small groups rather than use the large tables.

While simple to conduct, observation research still takes planning. Careful thought must be given as to the days and times the observations should be made along with what subjects to observe. In addition, as it is impossible to record all activity, the researcher must be provided with guidelines as to the type of behaviour that should be noted.

Example of project observation technique

1 Once at the community park mark your location on the map provided. Choose three 'subjects' to observe.
2 If possible please try to choose a variety of individuals, groups, couples or families.
3 Next, record where the subject is located in the park for the first time slot.
4 Also record in what activity they are engaged.
5 Repeat every 15 minutes.

Conduct the research and analyse the findings

Once the organization has determined the research question, decided the source of information, chosen the approach and designed the method, it is now ready to conduct the research. The planning stage might have taken more time than the organization had anticipated. However, the more time that is spent in planning, the more likely that the research will be successful in obtaining the needed information to answer the research question.

Decisions that need to be answered regarding conducting the research are where, when and by whom (see Table 2.8). The organization should conduct

Table 2.8 Decisions for conducting research

Where	When	Who
Location	Time of year	Organization member
Furnishings	Day of week	Professional researcher
Supplies	Time of day	Board member
Refreshments	Length of study	Community volunteer
Restroom facilities		Graduate student

the research where the research participant will be most comfortable. For current clients this might be at the organization's location or some other location with which the participant is familiar. The organization should ensure there is comfortable seating and any other furnishings that may be needed are available. If the subject will be asked to write, a desk, table or clipboard should be provided. The room should feel welcoming and not sterile so as to put participants at ease. Refreshments should be provided as a sign of hospitality and restroom facilities should be conveniently located. If the research is a focus group or interviews, a means for recording information should be available. If this is not possible or advisable, the researcher should be prepared to take notes.

The time of the research should be convenient for the research participants, not the researcher or organization. The organization should consider what day of the week and which time of the day will result in the highest level of participation. In addition the length of time the research study will take should be estimated. This may range from a few days to plan and conduct a single focus group to weeks or even months for an extensive research study.

There may be someone in the organization with the skills needed to conduct the research. If no one has the skills or needed objectivity, there are alternatives to hiring a professional. The organization may have a board member who could volunteer to conduct the research. Another alternative is for the organization to contact local colleges and universities to find if there might be a graduate student who would take on the task as part of an academic project.

EVEN ARTS ORGANIZATIONS NEED RESEARCH!

Here are some issues for which an arts organization needs research:

Problem: 'The thirty and forty something market segments are conspicuous by their absence in our audience and among our membership.'
Question: What new products should our organization offer to attract this segment?
Solution: Consumer Research

Problem: 'Attendance for the organization has been flat for the past three years while regional leisure and cultural patronage has been increasing at an annual rate of low single digits.'
Question: Why are people choosing to attend are competitors rather than us?
Solution: Competitor Research

Problem: 'Management is planning a very innovative program series for the upcoming season. The associated investment and risks are considerable.'

Question: How are we to design a promotional campaign to ensure that people hear about our new programming and respond favourably?

Solution: Promotion Research

Source: Chen-Courtin (1998).

Question to consider: What question does our organization need to research?

Analyse the findings

After the research is conducted the next step is analysing the findings. This analysis requires repeatedly reviewing the collected responses to find common themes, patterns and connections. This is a process that will take considerable time and should not be rushed. All the earlier research effort will be wasted if insufficient effort is spent in analysing the data.

Analysis of quantitative data

The analysis of statistical data from surveys involves validating the information collected, coding any open-ended questions, entering the information into a statistical software package, tabulating the responses and then analysing the findings. Validating involves examining the survey forms to ensure that the forms have been properly completed. Forms that are incomplete or confusing will have to be discarded. In addition the data should be checked to ensure that the research subjects were appropriately chosen. For example, if the research was designed to study frequent users of the organization and yet the answer to an initial screening question was that the participant was unfamiliar with the organization, this form will also need to be discarded.

Closed-ended survey questions, where responses are limited, have built in coding. The participant has either checked or circled the correct answer. This data can be directly entered into a statistical package. However if the question is open-ended and allows the participant to write in a short answer, the researchers must give each a code. For example, a single question on why the participant does not use the organization's service will receive a multitude of different answers. Careful reading will almost always find a pattern even if the exact wording is different. Answers that deal with inconvenient hours will receive one code (which can simply be a number) while answers dealing with rude staff will receive a different code.

Once the data is coded it needs to be counted, compared and analysed. While with a small survey the counting can be done manually, comparing and analysing the data will require that the answers are entered into a statistical package such as SPSS. These software packages are quite easy to use and understand, even for someone with no prior experience. The advantage of using a software package is that it can analyse data. For example, the data may reveal that many research participants felt that the organization staff was rude. It would be very helpful to learn if all types of participants felt the staff was rude or if it was only older participants. The more detailed answer will help the organization take corrective action.

Steps in analysing quantitative data

1 Validate the information collected
2 Code any open-ended questions
3 Enter the information into a statistical software package
4 Tabulate the responses
5 Analyse the findings.

Analysis of qualitative data

Because qualitative studies consist of open-ended questions and even information that provides no verbal responses, coding and analysis is a very complex task. It will take reviewing the material repeatedly to see the patterns that emerge.

As a first step, all of the researcher's tapes and notes must be collected along with any written material created by participants. All written material produced during the focus group or interview must also be retyped into one document. For example, all the responses that asked for sentence completion should be typed together. This will help when the material is analysed for common themes. These sentences will be a rich source of quotations when the final research report is created.

Before analysis can begin, if the focus groups or interviews were taped, the tapes must also be transcribed into written form. This does not mean that a word-for-word transcript must be created. Instead, while listening to the taped focus groups or interviews, the researcher types the issues raised by the participants. These issues are then coded to see if there are similar themes that are repeatedly mentioned. One method to accomplish this coding is to take the printed transcribed notes and use highlighters to colour code the responses.

Steps in analysing qualitative data

1 Collect all relevant research material
2 Transcribe into written form
3 Code for themes and issues
4 Tabulate the responses
5 Analyse the findings.

Report the findings

Of course all of the work that has gone into formulating the question, choosing the approach, designing the method, conducting the research and analysing the findings will be wasted if not communicated to those who can implement the research recommendations. The research report may be in the form of a written report, a verbal report or both.

Written report

Written reports presenting the results of research studies usually follow a familiar outline. The written report should first explain why the research was conducted. This would of course include the research question. However, it would also include a description of the issues and concerns that are currently affecting the organization and that resulted in the research question needing to be asked. Next the written report would include details on how the research was conducted. This section would provide information on the research method and the research participants.

Only after this groundwork is laid will the report explain the findings of the research along with any recommendations the researchers make based on these findings. If the reason for the research and the methodology are not explained first, the reader may not give the research findings and recommendations much legitimacy. The research findings would include any quantitative data that was gathered using charts and graphs. A written report for qualitative research would not have statistical data. However, because there are no statistics or charts, different types of visuals are used to help the client understand the findings. Some tools include quotations, photos and even videos.

Contents of research report

- Why the research was conducted
- How the research was conducted
- What the research found
- What actions should be taken as a result of the research.

Oral report

In addition to the written report, the researchers will want to prepare an oral report. This report should not attempt to duplicate everything in the written report. Instead it should summarize key points and create enough interest so that the written report will be read.

The oral report should be presented to the organization's employees and volunteers. In addition, the research can also be presented to the Board as a means of keeping them informed of the actions of the organization and as a means of moving the Board toward acting on the research findings.

While someone who has not conducted the research can assist with the writing of the report, the researchers themselves should give the oral report. If the researcher is not comfortable presenting the oral report she or he must at least be available to answer questions. Oral reports for quantitative research will rely on charts and graphs to present statistical information in an easy to understand format. A qualitative research study requires a different type of oral report. There will be more emphasis on explaining key findings using antidotes, quotes, and photos than charts and graphs. These visual aids should be created to assist in communicating this information while keeping the interest of the audience.

Summary

- The research process involves more than just conducting research. It starts with determining the research question, deciding on the source of information, choosing the right research approach and designing the research method. Only then is the organization ready to conduct the research after which they must analyse and report the findings. The first step, determining the research question, is one of the most important. The research question may involve any aspect of the marketing mix of product, price, place and promotion. In addition the research question might address current and potential customers and the competition.

- Once the research question has been determined, the organization must decide from where they can obtain the needed information. Secondary information already exists from previously conducted research. Primary information will be gathered by the organization. This information will be gathered from research subjects. Quantitative descriptive studies, if using random statistical sampling can 'prove' a hypothesis with a high level of confidence. Purposive, convenience or snowballing sampling can be used to obtain research subjects for qualitative exploratory studies. Descriptive research answers the questions of who, what, where and how many. Exploratory research answers the question of why.

- There are numerous research methods from which to choose. One of the most well known is surveying. However, focus groups and interviews are the most commonly methods used when conducting marketing research. Focus groups need to be run by an objective moderator from outside the organization. Interviews can be either lengthy in-depth interviews or short intercept interviews. Other methods are observations and projective techniques.

- The organization must consider where and when the research will be conducted. The organization must also consider who will conduct the research. After the research has been conducted the findings must be analysed. Quantitative survey data can be analysed by counting the frequency of responses or by entering the data into a software package. Qualitative data is analysed through coding for themes and issues. Once the findings have been analysed, recommendations for action will be made. A written report will explain why and how the research was conducted. In addition the findings and recommendations must be reported. In addition an oral report should be made.

■ References

Carson, D., K. Gronhaug, C. Perry and A. Gilmore (2001) *Qualitative Marketing Research*, SAGE Publications.

Chen-Courtin, D. (1998) 'Look before you leap; some marketing research basics', *ArtsReach*, June/July, p 4–5.

Daymon, C. and I. Holloway (2002) *Qualitative Research Methods in Public Relations and Marketing Communications*, Routledge Publishing, p 3–18.

Fielding, M. (2005) 'Alternate reality: not-for-profits rely on resourcefulness to achieve goals', *Marketing News*, 15 July.

Henderson, N.R. (2004) 'Focus groups: a four-course meal', *'Qualitative Reflections'*, Vol. 16, No. 4.

Keates, N. (1999) 'Why are museums so clueless?' *Arts Reach*, April.

Museum, G. (2006). 'About the Museum' online at http://www.getty.edu/museum/about.html.org/about.

Spangenberg, E.R., B. Grohmann and D.E. Sprott (2005) 'It's beginning to smell (and sound) a lot like Christmas: the interactive effects of ambient scent and music in a retail setting', *Journal of Business Research*, No. 58 Vol.58, Issue 11, p 1583–1598.

CHAPTER 3

Marketing research and cultural differences

- Define culture and discuss additional research questions that must be asked
- Explain the necessity of translation when conducting research with ethnic groups
- Understand the relevance of Hofstede's model to choosing research methodology
- Discuss ethical issues that arise when conducting research across cultural boundaries

■ Introduction

Organizations already have some knowledge about their current customers. For example, simply by looking at their customers the organization can determine certain demographic facts such as gender, age and perhaps income level based on how they are dressed. In addition the organization will have some knowledge of the media that is used by their customers, what price is considered acceptable and what places of distribution is preferred.

However, if the organization's current or potential customers are from a different ethnic group, all of these issues, even demographic, will need to be researched. The two major issues facing an organization that needs to conduct research across cultural boundaries is what additional research questions need to be asked and how the research methodology to answer these questions needs to be adapted.

■ Defining culture

Culture is the underlying values held by a group of people. These values are used as guidelines when people make decisions on how they live their lives. These decisions range from the mundane, such as what to eat for breakfast, to the important, such as what is the proper relationship between parent and child. While these values cannot be seen, the behaviours that result from these values can be observed (see Table 3.1).

Table 3.1 Cultural values and related behaviour	
Value	**Behaviour**
Modesty	How people dress in public
Religion	Attendance at religious services
Nature	Importance given to protecting the environment
Family	Who is considered related and non-related
Education	Whether children are encouraged to stay in school

Of course individual behaviours vary even within a group that is similar culturally. However, these behaviours are not random and patterns can be observed where 'most' people in a group act in a similar way.

For example, an important part of culture is religious beliefs. If a culture holds strong religious values, it is expected that certain behaviours can then be observed, such as an unwillingness to participate in certain activities on the Sabbath. People who hold religious values may also restrict their diet to certain foods and may have rules regarding the type of clothes they wear. It can also be observed that the cultural group's socialization may revolve around religious holidays and festivals. People inside the cultural group will accept this way of life as normal behaviour. This is true whether the group is the majority or a minority cultural group.

However, an important difference lies in the fact that the minority cultural group will certainly be aware of the culture of the majority group. These cultural values are communicated through the media, education system and other social institutions. This awareness is the inevitable result of having most of the people working in these institutions be members of the majority culture. On the other hand, members of the majority culture may be less aware of the values and assumptions of minority groups.

Most people do not think very deeply about how culture affects the decisions they make. In fact cultural values are learned at such a young age that they may be believed to be universal. This does not mean that everyone in the culture will base their actions on their cultural values. However, they will usually feel guilty if they do not do so. Cultural beliefs can often be uncovered by examining the common sayings of a country. Some are universal such as there are many variants on 'do onto others as you would have them do unto you.' However, many are more culturally specific such as 'Early to bed early to rise, makes a man healthy, wealthy and rise.'

Ethnocentrism

Unfortunately there are some people that believe that the decisions they make regarding their behaviour are universal and that any other decisions are not just different but wrong. This is called the self-reference criterion and leads to an outlook called ethnocentrism. It is true that everyone makes decisions based on underlying cultural values of which they may be unaware. The resulting self-reference is usually not a problem if everyone belongs to the same group. However when cultural groups interact, problems can result.

The self-reference criterion is a problem when other people's decisions about how to behave are considered abnormal. For example, for some people it is natural for an unmarried young person to leave home to pursue a career. In fact, an adult child living at home with his or her parents would be considered a fact that must be explained to friends and relatives. In other cultures the fact that an unmarried person is not living at home is the cause of gossip among the neighbours.

Ethnocentrism is the conviction that one's own cultural beliefs are superior to others. Such an attitude will certainly result in hurt feelings when communicated to members of other cultural groups. In marketing research it will lead to making assumptions about people's wants and needs that are inaccurate. As a result the organization can lose current minority culture members or find it impossible to bring in minority cultural members as new customers.

USING RESEARCH TO GAIN INSIGHT INTO CHINESE CONSUMERS

Businesses have learned that if they want to sell a product in another culture they must first spend the time and money learning everything they can about the values and behaviors of the people. Lenovo, a company that produces PC's and other technological products wanted to sell products to Chinese consumers. The company knew that discovering consumer preferences is difficult enough when you are familiar with the consumer's culture. Therefore the company established a team to undertake marketing research to discover more about the needs, wants and desires of the Chinese.

The research started even before the team left for China. The team of researchers studied photos of Chinese billboards while listening to all types of Chinese music. The team also examined Chinese consumer products. A professor was asked to teach about Chinese history and cultural differences. A Chinese exchange student was asked to describe the Chinese lifestyle and their use of technology. All of this was done so that the team would be better able to conduct research when they went to China.

Once in China the marketing research team members lived as ordinary Chinese, commuting to work on bicycles, eating in dining halls and singing karaoke in bars. While they did so they conducted observational research noting how people used technology in their everyday life. Then the researchers conducted research in consumers' homes. They not only observed the use of technology they also analyzed the fashion taste of consumers by examining their clothing and furnishings. Although an interpreter was used on these home visits, the researchers also broke down communication barriers by giving the Chinese research participants a camera, glue stick and poster board and asked them to record their actions during a typical day. The research was so successful in predicting Chinese preferences it won a gold medal in the 2006 Industrial Design Excellence Award.

Source: ZIBA Design (2006).

Question to consider: How can we use local resources to learn more about the cultural values of an ethnic groups?

Additional research questions

All customers buy products because of the benefits they provide. The organization will lose customers from ethnic groups if it does not understand what benefits they receive from using the organization's products. In addition the promotional message may need to be changed and the pricing level may need to be adjusted to attract members of an ethnic group. Even the distribution of the product needs to be considered as people from different cultural groups may shop at different types of stores. Because of these differences marketing research will need to be conducted on many more of the marketing mix components when selling to customers from ethnically different groups. Many of these questions would not need to be asked of potential customers from a similar cultural group as the answers are already known to the organization.

Examples of research question which address cultural differences

- What are the design preferences for colour and style?
- In what type of building should our office be located?
- Who makes the decision as to whether the family will use our services?
- Do family members come to appointments in groups or alone?
- What types of media do our customers use to get information?
- How much disposable income do the customers have?

Product: People buy a product for the benefits they receive from its ownership. A product consists of its 'core' benefit of what it does. In addition, a product also has its extended benefits which involve the style and image of the product. Of course, different cultural groups will have varying ideas of what they want the product to look like. This will include the colour, size and services that come with the product. For example, an organization which sponsors a clinic might decorate the waiting room to meet their own preferences without any thought of how it might appear to their clients who bring their own standards of taste.

Not only the extended product needs to be taken into consideration. Even the core benefits that a product provides may be appreciated differently depending on the needs of a group. For example, an organization may provide the benefit of English classes for immigrant groups. The organization may take for granted that people are attending the classes to learn English. In fact, learning English may be a secondary reason for attendance. The primary reason may be to establish friendships with others from the home country. The organization could use this information to attract more people from the cultural group by improving the product, such as starting a coffee hour after classes for students.

Promotion: In addition, the organization could use this information to develop a new promotional message that emphasized the opportunity for socialization at their English classes. Rather than stress the educational benefits, the organization could use quotes from participants on how much they enjoyed meeting with others after class. However, they would first need to research what media the cultural group uses to get their information. The organization may find that the best way to provide information is through flyers, rather than the traditional media. In addition they would need to know where to post these flyers.

Place: Other issues that should be researched regarding the English classes would be what would be the best location to hold the classes. The organization may need to research if potential students would prefer the classes in their own neighbourhoods rather than at the organization headquarters. Research might discover that attendance will be the highest if the classes are held at a location where community members already feel at ease, for example, a local church.

Price: Rather than just assume that the community members will be unable or unwilling to pay a fee, the organization must research the issue. They might find that potential students would prefer to pay a small fee, as a matter of pride. Unless the organization researches the question, they will have no way of knowing.

EVEN HOW YOU DONATE, CAN BE CULTURALLY DETERMINED

The United States has a tradition of charitable giving and this is no different for immigrant groups. However, the pattern of giving is different. The first generation uses their money to support relatives and even the entire village or town they left. The second generation, if they have succeeded financially, donates their money to mainstream institutions as proof that they have 'made it'. Or, they may donate to promote their groups cultural heritage through arts and education programs. What they may not do, is donate to help less affluent members of their own ethnic group. Non-profit organizations are working to change this approach to giving. To get more information on how this can be done, they will need to conduct research of these young, wealthy members of ethnic communities.

Source: Bernstein (2007).

Question to consider: Do we understand why members of different cultural groups donate to our organization?

Levels of cultural differences

There can be different levels of cultural differences between the organization and the minority cultural group. When developing the research plan the organization should keep in mind the level of dissimilarity between those running the organization and the members of the ethnic group being researched. The differences will include location and language. If the ethnic group resides in the same geographic location as the members of the organization, the research will be easier to undertake. Even though language and cultural value differences may still exist, members of the organization have probably had contact with members of the ethnic group. They will be exposed to the cultural values of the group through personal relationships or at least through the media. It will also be easier to find information on the cultural values of the group through a local association or educational institution.

Sometimes the ethnic group will speak the same language as the majority cultural group. It is easy for the organization to believe that since the groups share a language, they will also share values. However while Americans, Canadians, the British and Australians all speak English, this does not mean they share the same cultural values. Of course, research becomes increasingly difficult if the groups do not share the same language and have different cultural values.

CULTURE AFFECTS ALL TYPES OF LIFE DECISIONS

The Girl Scouts of America has 3.8 million girl and adult members. The organization was concerned about the health of America's girls so decided to do some research. They wanted to know about the health habits of all girls including Latina, African-American, and Native American. What they learned is that girls from these groups had higher rates of obesity than the general population. They also learned that they were much less likely to be involved in physical activities. Hispanic girls were much less likely to participate in sports at school, while 50% listed television viewing as their favorite activity. The Girl Scouts learned that for new Hispanic immigrants heaviness was seen as positive and was associated with wealth and success.

How did the Girl Scouts gather this information? They conducted 16 focus groups with girls in four different areas of the country. They also conducted a survey online with a sample of 2,060 girls, 400 of which were Latina. While the research was not conducted for marketing purposes, this information can be used by the marketing department to develop programs that better meet the needs of different cultural groups.

Source: Girl Scouts Research Institute (2006).

Question to consider: What information already exists on the cultural group that can be useful in making marketing decisions?

■ Translation issues when researching across cultural boundaries

When conducting research with a group who predominately speak another language, translation will be needed during several steps of the marketing research process. During the planning stage, the organization may want to conduct research on the ethnic group itself to determine how the research methodology will need to be adapted. This could be accomplished through interviews with someone who is a trusted member of the ethnic community. Of course there will be members of the ethnic group that speak the majority language, but the organization may also want to conduct research with people who do not. Therefore oral translation will be needed. In addition written sources of information may need to be translated. These sources of information could be magazines, newspapers or newsletters that are read by the community.

The organization should also consider what research material will need to be translated. This would include written material such as survey questionnaires, projective material and instructions. Also needing translation would be letters of invitation sent to potential participants for focus groups and any email correspondence. The translation issue goes beyond just hiring someone to translate the completed material into another language. There are many cultural issues that affect the choice of words used. Therefore more than a word for word translation will be needed. What also must be considered is the choice of wording so that the same idea is communicated.

An example of this issue is the choice of wording used to refer to the ethnic group as there may be several names for the same group. There may be the official government designation and also terms that are commonly used in the media. In addition, some terms will be used among the members of the group themselves. The translator will need to know which term would be acceptable to the ethnic community when used in the written material.

Oral translation may also be needed during the research process. Of course interviews and surveys given over the phone should be conducted in the language of the research participants. Focus group moderators should also speak the same language as the research participants. This is especially true when the organization is conducting exploratory research on customers' attitudes, opinions and ideas. After all it is difficult enough to communicate these concepts even when everyone speaks the same language. The researchers who conduct these method of research should be bilingual so that they can directly communicate these research findings to the organization.

In addition, translation will be needed during the analysis process. For example, the tapes of focus group proceedings or interviews will need to be typed first in the language in which the research was conducted and then translated. Any written material produced during a focus group such as lists or word association will first need to be typed in the language in which they were produced and then translated. The responses to any open-ended questions will also need to be translated and typed.

After the analysis, a final report will be prepared. Both the written report and any oral presentation will be in the language of the organization. However, it is recommended that research participants also be provided with a summary of information on the research findings. This will need to be prepared in the language of the research subjects.

Translation needs when conducting research across cultural boundaries

- Planning phase to learn more about the cultural values of the group
- Translation of all written material
- Oral translation during the research process
- Translation of research material during analysis
- Summary report in language of research participants.

Back translation

The organization needs to ensure that the translation they have commissioned is correct as it is their name that is going to be on all of the material. A translation error that offends can create distrust within the very community that the organization is trying to reach. To ensure that the translation is correct, back translation is recommended. When using this method the written material is first translated into the needed language. For example, a survey form aimed at a Russian speaking community will first be written in English. A translator will then be hired to translate the form into Russian. Rather than stop at this step, the organization will then hire another translator to translate the questionnaire back into English using the form written in Russian. The organization will then review this back translation. If the translation has been correct, the form should correctly communicate the original idea. A new approach to translation issues is to have collaboration between the translators and the researchers throughout the process (Douglas, 2007).

Translation issues can result from one of two problems. First the translator may not have had the needed ability in both languages. Translation requires a high level of proficiency, especially if the research material is using specialized terms, such as a questionnaire about hospital services. The second problem that might arise is not the fault of the translator. The English language survey form may have used colloquialisms that do not translate well. Many words and terms can not be translated literally. A questionnaire from a social services agency may refer to clients who are 'stressed out' or 'at the end of their ropes.' These terms have meanings in English that do not come from the literal translation of the words.

Back translation process

1 Write research materials in English
2 Ask translator to rewrite materials in needed language
3 Ask another translator to rewrite the materials in English
4 Review rewritten English materials to determine if they have original meanings.

HOW DIVERSE IS THE UNITED STATES?

The US continues to become more diverse. According to the 2005 American Community Survey, African-Americans are the largest ethnic group in the US. However, almost as large is the Hispanic population. The Hispanic population has grown 58% over the past decade. The largest ethnic group is Mexican followed by Puerto Ricans. Asians comprise the third largest group at 4.3% of the population, which is 12.5 million people. The largest Asian groups are the Chinese, Filipinos and Asian Indians. However, the diversity of the US is continually changing, not just growing. In the 2000 US Census, for the first time people could categorize themselves as being of more than one race. The result? A total of eighty-six different cultural groups were identified in the US!

Source: Fact Finder (2007).

Question to consider: What ethnic groups do we currently or could we potentially serve that would require research?

■ Hofstede's dimensions of culture

Many of the decisions people make everyday, including how they greet people, what they eat, and the types of clothes they wear, are made without much deliberation. After all if everyone had to carefully consider each decision, they would never make it through the day. Instead they get up and have what they consider a 'normal' breakfast, whether it is cornflakes or fish soup. This unawareness is part of the self-reference criterion. Because their choices are based on values that have been learned at a young age, they do not consider the reason why they are making a choice.

Even if the researcher accepts the fact that it is important to consider the differences in other cultures, this can be difficult because there are so many aspects of behaviour that are determined by cultural values. Of course all people have the capacity for the same basic emotions, such as love, hate, fear and courage. What differs across cultures is which of these emotions are encouraged to be expressed and which are discouraged. A model is needed to help think about these differences and similarities across cultures.

A well known cultural dimensions model was developed by Geert Hofstede. He proposed that everyone carries around mental maps in their minds of how they should act in social situations. Most people will act in accordance with their mental map. Of course they may act differently, but if they do their actions will be in conflict with their values and they may feel guilty as a result (Hofstede, 2001).

Hofstede proposed four dimensions that could be used to categorize cultures. A culture's grouping on these dimensions can then be used to predict their actions or responses to situations. These dimensions can also be used to predict how people in a cultural group will react to various research methodologies. After all the cooperation of the research participants is necessary if the research is going to be successful. The four dimensions are power distance, uncertainty avoidance, individualism versus collectivism and masculinity versus femininity.

Power distance

The dimension of power distance measures how people react to authority and how accepting they are of role differences. In all cultures there are differences in equality. Even within families, some family members will have more power than others. This power difference might be based on gender or on birth rank. At work there are also power differences. There is someone who has the authority to tell someone else what work they must perform. There are also political power differences between those in power and those who do not have any or limited input into political decision making.

The important issue is not whether these power differences are right or wrong. After all they exist to some extent in all cultures. The important issue is whether they are accepted as appropriate and natural. In fact they may even be accepted as necessary to the effective management of a home, a business or a country.

Members of a high power distance culture will believe that decisions made by those in positions of authority should be accepted. After all making these decisions is the responsibility of those in power because they have the knowledge to make the best decisions for all. Members of a low power distance culture will believe that everyone has the ability and knowledge to make decisions. Therefore those in positions of authority should listen to the opinions of even the lowest ranking members. Table 3.1 shows the highest and lowest ranking countries along with their scores. The United States is also given for comparison (Table 3.2).

Table 3.2 Power distance	
Lowest power distance countries	**Highest power distance countries**
Austria (11)	Malaysia (104)
Israel (13)	Guatemala (95)
Denmark (18)	Panama (95)
New Zealand (22)	Philippines (94)
Norway/Sweden (31)	Mexico/Venezuela (81)
United States (40)	

Uncertainty avoidance

Risk is a part of life as the future is always an unknown. Of course, it would be psychologically impossible to live life with a constant awareness that the future is both unknowable and uncontrollable. Therefore, a society will create laws and social norms that control current behaviour and religious or civic rituals to assure people about the future (see Table 3.3).

Table 3.3 Uncertainty avoidance	
Lowest uncertainty avoidance countries	**Highest uncertainty avoidance countries**
Singapore (8)	Greece (112)
Jamaica (13)	Portugal (104)
Denmark (23)	Guatemala (101)
Sweden (29)	Uruguay (100)
Hong Kong (29)	Belgium (94)
Great Britain/Ireland (35)	Japan (92)
United States (46)	

Cultures vary on how accepting people are of the idea of an unknown future full of risk. Cultures with high uncertainty avoidance will avoid new behaviours because the results are unpredictable. They accept rules that govern behaviour because they lessen anxiety. People in these cultures understand that if everyone follows the rules there will be few surprises and believe that surprises are not good. People in high uncertainty avoidance cultures will find challenges that force them to take unfamiliar actions troubling.

On the other hand cultures with low uncertainty avoidance will accept risk as a part of life. They will be interested in new experiences because the outcome might be successful. They anticipate a positive result from change rather than problems. Therefore they welcome new challenges and do not fear failure.

Individualism versus collectivism

Humans are social beings who need other people with whom to associate. These social relationships between people involve responsibility for each others welfare, which is how people survive. The importance given to social relationships differs between cultures. This differing level of importance of relationships results in different social behaviours (see Table 3.4).

If a culture focuses on collectivism, people learn to put the group's needs before their own. What is good for everyone is more important than what is good for one individual. This fact affects decisions on where people live, the career they choose and even who is considered family. In a collectivist culture, people are more likely to live at home and work at the same jobs as their parents. Even who is considered family will be different. In a collectivist culture family relationships will be much more broadly

Table 3.4 Individualism versus collectivism	
Lowest individualistic countries	**Highest collectivist countries**
United States (91)	Guatemala (6)
Australia (90)	Ecuador (8)
Great Britain (89)	Panama (11)
Canada (80)	Venezuela (12)
The Netherlands (80)	Columbia (13)
New Zealand (79)	Indonesia (14)

defined, with even non-related people considered relatives. In a way the whole cultural group is considered family and what is good for everyone in the culture is more important than what is good for the individual. As a result people tend to think and act in similar ways.

People in individualist cultures also have family relationships. However, more emphasis is placed on the needs of the individual. In an individualist culture, people make decisions on their own personal goals rather than what is good for the group. For example, an adult in an individualistic culture will take a job that will further his or her own career goals even if it means a move away from family and friends. While people will sympathize about the move, people in an individualistic culture will understand why the decision was made. In a collectivist culture such a move may seem heartless and an abandonment of family responsibility.

Growing up in an individualistic culture affects how people think about the world around them and the possible choices they can make. People are expected to have their own ideas, thoughts and plans and to pursue them. It is believed that the more people pursue the plans that are best for them the better society will be as a whole.

Masculinity versus femininity

The terms masculinity and femininity when referring to cultures, use the traditional meanings of the words. Of course there are biological differences between the genders but how these differences are accepted and reinforced varies between cultures. For example, while differences in child bearing are biological, the importance of being nurturing is cultural. Most cultures will differ on what is acceptable behaviour for males and females.

A masculine culture believes that aggression is natural for men. Therefore the members of the culture will be more accepting of aggressive behaviour. Nurturing behaviour is expected in women but considered unnatural in men. Men in these cultures are believed to be biologically fitted for leadership. As a result certain occupations are considered masculine and reserved for men. A culture is considered masculine when these role differences between men and women are reinforced. In addition the culture will be accepting of nurturing behaviour – as long the behaviour is exhibited by females.

A feminine culture does not define role differences as strictly. Men are allowed to be nurturing without being considered feminine. In such a culture women are more accepted into all types of occupations, as those that require strength, whether physical or emotional, are not seen as being fit only for men. However, a feminine culture as a whole encourages nurturing behaviour in all its members and aggression in none (Table 3.5).

Table 3.5 Masculinity versus femininity	
Highest masculine countries	**Highest feminine countries**
Japan (95)	Sweden (5)
Austria (79)	Norway (8)
Venezuela (73)	The Netherlands (14)
Switzerland (70)	Denmark (16)
Mexico (69)	Costa Rica (21)
Ireland (68)	Finland (26)
United States (62)	

Adapting marketing research to meet cultural dimensions

Marketing research methodology has been developed from psychological and scientific methods that are commonly taught in American universities. The United States as a country tends to be low power distance, low uncertainly avoidance, very individualistic and rather masculine. Therefore, it is not surprising that the traditional methods of focus groups, surveys, and interviews are all designed to work with the majority ethnic groups in the United States. However, even in the US the cultures of ethnic groups may have originated in other countries. Therefore, these cultures may be more high power distance, high uncertainty avoidance, collectivistic and feminine. For this reason the choice of both methodology and research subject needs to be considered in light of cultural differences. These differences are summarized in Table 3.6.

Power distance: Power distance, which describes how people view the importance of authority, has a direct relationship to marketing research. Research is based on the premise that the organization needs information to help it make decisions and that this information can be provided by consumers. An individual from a high power distance culture would have a problem with this premise. After all, people in positions of authority should have the knowledge to make good decisions – that is why they are in the position of authority.

As a result they would be surprised at the idea that they can provide useful information. In a focus group situation, they would defer to the opinion of the moderator, rather than state their own opinions. After all the moderator is the person in charge and therefore not to be challenged. Research interviews would have the same problem. The research subject

Table 3.6 Hofstede's cultural dimensions

Dimension	Affect on research	Needed adjustments
Power distance	Participants in focus groups and interviews will defer to researcher as a person with a position of authority.	Use techniques, such as self-administered surveys, that will allow participant to provide information anonymously.
Uncertainty avoidance	Participants from high uncertainty avoidance countries will find techniques that provide little direction threatening.	When using projective techniques more information on expectations needs to be provided. Avoid open-ended questions in surveys.
Individualism versus collectivism	Focus group participants will not want to disagree with others. Survey questions may be answered based on the opinions of the group rather than individual.	In-depth individual interviews will provide sufficient time to convince participants their views are valid and needed.
Femininity versus masculinity	Who makes the purchase decision varies based on the cost of a product and its perception as something that is bought by only men or women.	The research sample will need to be adjusted to adapt for gender differences in product purchasing.

from a high power distance country would naturally differ to the ideas of the researcher conducting the interview.

Uncertainty avoidance: Uncertainty avoidance can also play a role in the choice of research methodology. Creative tasks such as projective techniques where little direction is given, might be construed as too risky by people from a high uncertainty avoidance culture. They would want more direction on how to proceed. A lack of direction would not be seen as an exciting opportunity to share ideas but would instead produce anxiety. In fact, even open-ended questions might create anxiety for people from high uncertainty avoidance cultures.

Individualism versus collectivism: When research is planned that involves collectivist cultures, the choice of methodology is crucial. Marketing research is premised on the idea of questioning individuals who are eager to give their opinions. With research subjects from collectivist cultures it will be difficult for them to express unique opinions. In a focus group setting, they are much more likely to exhibit a tendency toward 'group think' and go along with majority opinion. Even when they do express opinions, they are just as likely to be the opinions of family members and friends, rather than their own.

Masculinity versus femininity: Of course physical aggression has no role to play in marketing research. However, some of the methodology is based on the idea of argument and even confrontation. Focus groups in particular can use argument and verbal challenges as a means to explore deeply held beliefs and ideas. In addition, whether a culture tends to be masculine or feminine will affect who is chosen to participate in research. In a masculine culture, most purchasing decisions will be made by the men in the family as it is seen proper for them to have this authority. If men are making the purchasing decision it is their opinions that must be researched. On the other hand in feminine cultures, men would be comfortable with women being involved in the purchasing decision even for expensive products such as automobiles.

■ Ethical issues that need to be considered

While the terms 'values' and 'ethics' are commonly used, some people might not have thought about the exact definition of the words. Values are beliefs about what is right and wrong that are held by an individual. These values may have been learned from family, religious groups and educational institutions. Ethics are ideas about what is right and wrong that are held by most members of a society. Of course the values of the individuals in the cultural group help determine the ethical standards. As a result ethical rules may differ between cultural groups. The issue for marketing researchers is which ethical standards do they follow, their own or the group that is being researched? What happens when the researcher disagrees with the ethical standards of the group being researched? (Murphy, 2005)

One way of examining this issue is called contextualism which argues that different ethical standards may arise from the same value. For example, a value held by many cultures is that the weak should be protected by stronger members of a society. All cultures apply this value in having ethical standards regarding the treatment of children. Marketing research is no different and there are special ethical standards that must be applied when children are research participants to protect them from harm. However, some cultures would apply these rules to other groups such as women and feel that it is improper for them to participate in research conducted by unrelated males. Researchers from other cultures may feel that this ethical standard is unacceptable. However, they still must take it into consideration when designing the research methodology by providing a female researcher. If the researcher finds this ethical rule unacceptable, it may help if they realize it comes from a cultural value they share, which is protection of the weak.

INFORMATION ON CULTURE GROUPS IS ALREADY AVAILABLE

If a nonprofit organization wants to design a new service for an ethnic community, the first step is to find what information is already available from previous research. For example, *Black Enterprise* magazine conducted a poll among its readers about the problems facing young black males in their struggle for achievement. Over 4,000 responses were received, with 39%

stating that mentoring programs were the best way to promote achievement. Any organization that planned on serving under-achieving black males should take this type of information into account. The next step? Design their own research to confirm that this national poll reflects what is needed in their community.

Source: Scott (2006).

Question to consider: What research should we conduct to confirm already existing data on a cultural group?

The dangers of stereotyping

It is human nature to group and categorize both objects and people. After all, life would be too difficult if we had to approach each new object and person as a completely unknown experience. Stereotyping is one form of mental shorthand that people use to help make sense of the world. With stereotyping a person may have learned a few facts about a single member of a group, whether football players or fashion models. The person then takes these qualities and applies them to all members of the group. Stereotyping can be either positive, such as the football player I met was smart; therefore all football players are smart. Or it can be negative, the model I met was conceited, therefore all fashion models are conceited. Both positive and negative stereotypes can be dangerous if they lead the researcher to make inaccurate assumptions about the group.

It is important to remember, that everyone stereotypes. The issue is for researchers to be aware of the stereotypical views they hold so they do not affect the research. If they do not, they may miss information because it does not fit in with their stereotypes. For example, a researcher conducting a focus group with members from a local Asian-American community may believe that all Asians are hardworking and therefore have little preference for leisure. As a result comments from focus group members about their desire for more leisure activities may be unconsciously ignored by the researchers.

Avoiding prejudice

Prejudice differs from stereotyping as it is always negative. Prejudice can be based on any human characteristic such as age, weight, sexual orientation and ethnicity. Another significant difference between stereotyping and prejudice is that prejudice does not have to be based on any actual experience with someone. Instead it is a negative belief about a group that has been learned from others with no basis in reality. While no one wants to think that they themselves are prejudiced, it is actually very easy to have a prejudiced view of a group without even being aware of doing so.

Prejudice can be active or passive. Sometimes prejudice is so strongly held it becomes a part of an individual's belief system. People with strongly held prejudices may associate with others who also hold these beliefs. They may actually seek out members of the despised group to do them harm. Prejudice can also be passive where the individual does not act on their beliefs.

Prejudice is learned early in life which is why it is sometimes unnoticed and difficult to overcome. Of course the researcher would not act on their prejudice, but even passive prejudice can be harmful to the research process. If researchers realize they have a problem with prejudice, it is best that they not be involved in research with members of the group. It will be impossible for the researcher to hide their negative feelings.

Members of groups which have experienced prejudice are very sensitive to negative attitudes.

Summary

- Culture determines how people live their lives on a day-to-day basis, from mundane to important decisions. Cultural value and beliefs are formed at a young age. Therefore people make these decisions at an unconscious level. Ethnocentrism is an outlook where people believe that their decisions are the only right ones and any other way of living is 'not normal.' If the organization is conducting research with a group that is culturally dissimilar, additional research questions will need to be asked. This is because the organization will be unfamiliar with many common elements of consumer behaviour.

- If the cultural group that is the target of research speaks another language, translation will be needed. The organization will first need to conduct secondary research and may need to have materials translated into English. In addition the research material including the research instrument and the directions will need to be translated. Oral translation should be used when conducting the research. Finally the finished report should be translated. When translation is used, the organization must ensure that not just the words, but also the meaning is translated. One way to ensure this is done is to use back translation, where a translated document is translated back into the English language to determine if the meaning is still the same.

- Culture can be categorized using the dimension of power distance, where the level of acceptance of power differentials in society is noted. Uncertainty avoidance, categorizes countries by how members strive to limit their level of risk of the unknown. How tightly members of a society feel tied to others, is measured by individualism versus collectivism. How a society scores on maintaining traditional role distinctions is measured on the basis of femininity versus masculinity. These cultural difference categories will affect the choice of research technique that will need to be used. In addition the cultural dimensions will affect who will be asked to participate in a research study.

- When conducting marketing research across cultural boundaries, the researchers must be aware of their own stereotypical views of different groups. Stereotyping, either positive or negative, results when the actions of one or two members of a group are projected onto all members of a group. Prejudice is a learned belief that attributes negative qualities to a group. These beliefs do not need to be based on a personal experience. Societal practices can differ even when they are based on the same ethical belief.

■ References

Bernstein, N. (2007) Some complain of class divide in Chinese-Americans' Charity, *New York Times*, 20 January.

Douglas, S.P. and C. S. Craig (2007) 'Collaborative and iterative translation: An alternative approach to back translation', *Journal of International Marketing*, Vol. 15, No. 1.

Fact Finder (2007) American Fact Finder, US Census, Downloaded on July 26 from http://factfinder.census.gov/home/saff/main.html?_lang=en.

Girl Scouts Research Institute (2006) The New Normal: Healthy Living Latina Girls and Overweight: Key Facts, Downloaded on July 22, 2007 from http://www.girlscouts.org/research/publications/original/latinas_and_overweight.pdfGirlScout Research Institute.

Hofstede, G. (2001) *Culture's Consequences: Comparing Values, Behaviors, Institutions, and Organizations Across Cultures*, SAGE Publications, Thousands Oaks, CA, USA.

Murphy, P. (2005) *Ethical Marketing*, Pearson Prentice Hall, Upper Saddle River, NJ, USA.

Scott, M.S. (2006) 'Can young black men be saved?' *Black Enterprise*, June.

ZIBA Design (2006) 'ZIBA Design's search for the soul of the Chinese consumer.' *Business Week*, 25 September.

CHAPTER 4

The research question

- Describe the importance of choosing the correct research question
- Explain the process of obtaining internal information through written records and interviews
- Understand the components of the research proposal
- Introduce the different types of firms that conduct research

■ Introduction

While most people are familiar with the idea of conducting research, they are much less familiar with the steps in the process that must take place before research starts. Obviously one of the most important issues, but also one that is often neglected, is the need to determine the correct research question.

The non-profit organization may first consider the need to conduct research when faced with a problem. Stating the assumptions about the cause of the problem is the start of the process of determining the exact research question to ask. These assumptions are then challenged using information that the organization already has available, such as written records. Or the information can be obtained by interviewing the organization's employees. This internal information might provide the answer to the research question. If not, the organization will proceed by writing a research proposal to conduct research. If the organization decides not to conduct the research themselves, they can hire a professional researcher.

■ The research question

Unfortunately it is not uncommon for organizations to start to conduct research without first thinking through the problem that they are confronting. Sometimes this is because they believe that the problem is self-evident. However, this belief is often based on an assumption that results from the person's role in the organization. If attendance is down, the person in charge of promotion will believe that not enough money was spent on advertising. Meanwhile the person in charge of finance may believe that there is a problem with pricing. Neither may consider the problem from the other person's perspective.

As a result of only listening to these assumptions, an organization may make a mistaken decision about the cause of a problem. If this happens the organization may design research around the wrong problem and the wrong research question will be asked. If the wrong question is asked, the data that is obtained by the research will not be helpful to the company.

As a result the time and expense of conducting research will have been wasted. Therefore, marketing researchers must carefully think through all the possible causes of a problem rather than make assumptions.

To question the assumptions people in the organization must ask themselves, 'What do we need to know that we do not know now?' To find possible issues that need to be explored, the organization should first conduct internal research. After all, the first step in solving a problem is to first explore what is already known.

Examining assumptions

There is a process that can be followed to help ensure that the organization asks the right research question. The first step in this process is for everyone involved in the organization to suggest what they believe is the cause of the difficulty. For a small organization, these assumptions can be gathered at a meeting or through informal conversations. For a large organization, a more formal approach may be needed. An individual or group will be given the responsibility for gaining input from everyone concerned. Once the ideas regarding the cause of the problem have been gathered, it is then time to challenge each assumption by conducting internal research.

Research question writing process

1   Gather assumptions about the cause of the problem
2   Conduct internal research to determine if these assumptions are correct
3   Write a research question based on the real cause of the problem.

Thinking through the research problem

The process of using internal data to clarify the research question will save the organization's time, money and frustration. Of course, it is part of human nature to want to jump to conclusions. However, it is the marketing researcher's job to make sure that these assumptions are tested before they are acted upon. For example, a non-profit theatre company may experience a decline in sales. At a weekly meeting someone might suggest that the reason for declining sales is that the ticket price is too expensive. Another member of the organization might suggest that the reason for the decline is that the play is unpopular. These assumptions may be based on personal experience rather than on facts. The first person might personally have a limited income and therefore finds the ticket prices too high. The second person who spoke at the meeting may not like the play being produced and assumes everyone else has similar taste.

It is the marketing researcher's job to first conduct internal research on these assumptions before basing a research proposal on either. A quick check of ticket sales data might find that attendance always declines during the summer, but that sales were up for the rest of the year. An interview with the theatre house manager discovers that those who attended the play loved the performance. Therefore neither of the assumptions, expensive ticket pricing or unpopular performance, seems to be the cause of the problem. If the organization had conducted research on either of these issues they would have wasted the organization's time and money. Instead, after much discussion a third assumption is proposed that the play was poorly promoted. Examining the ads for the performance might discover that the newspaper ads were poorly placed and also confusing to read. At this point the organization would not conduct further research. Table 4.1 summarize this process.

Table 4.1 Problem: declining ticket sales			
Assumption	Research	Findings	Correct
Tickets are too expensive	Box office data	Sales always down during summer	No
Performance does not appeal	Interview house manager	Audience loves play	No
Promotion was inadequate	Examine ads placed in newspaper	Ads were poorly placed and confusing	Yes Conclusion: Fix ads, No primary research

However, if all assumptions about the cause of a problem have been explored and still no reason for the problem can be found, the organization should then consider conducting primary research. Too often managers use research to find data to support a decision they have already made, rather than find information to help make a decision (Shapiro, 2004).

WRITING A PROPOSAL THAT GETS APPROVED

A well written research proposal can make the difference between the non-profit organization's management or the board approving the needed resources to conduct research or not. Why? The research won't be approved unless management believes that the benefits that will be gained by conducting the research will be greater than the costs. To ensure the proposal reassures management, the following questions should be answered:

- What are the key questions that the organization needs answered? *If you don't know what you are looking for, how can you find it?*
- Has previous research been conducted on this question? *Why approve research when it already has been conducted?*

● How will the results be used? *If you don't know what to do with the data, why gather it in the first place*?

Source: Singer (2006).

Question to consider: What type of process should we follow when writing research proposals?

■ Internal research process

An organization already has a great deal of information that can be used to identify causes of problems. This information may be part of a formal system of identifying and retaining important organizational data. Or the information may be informally retained in the collective memory of the organization. The reason for trying to find answers by using secondary data is that it is quicker as the information already exists. In addition, it is cheaper because the organization is saved the cost of conducting research.

Existing records

It may be possible that the organization has previously conducted research that will provide helpful information. However, the organization may not be aware that it exists. Non-profit and community organizations often have higher rates of employee turnover than for profit businesses. This may be because of lower pay rates or because they employ younger employees who tend not to have settled in their career. For whatever reason, research that has been conducted may be regulated to a desk drawer and forgotten when someone moves on. It is important to examine this research to determine if there is any information that is still relevant.

Even if no formal research has been conducted, data from the box office can be extremely valuable in answering research questions. This data not only provides information on the number of ticket purchasers, it also can be used to determine if there are attendance differences by day, season or type of programme. Non-profit service organizations that do not sell tickets may still have data on how many people make use of their services. This data can also be analysed to determine if usage is increasing or decreasing, or if there is a pattern of usage based on time of day or day of week.

The organization may also have a customer database available for use. Such a database is usually maintained for conducting mailings. However, it can also be used to determine where current customers live. It also might provide information on the gender of the customers. If the organization sells products in a gift shop, the sales receipts can be used to find where the purchasers live. Finally the number of website hits can prove useful data.

Sources of internal data

- Previous research
- Box office numbers
- Customer database
- Sale receipts
- Website hits

Internal data from people

The organization's employees may also be a source of information that can be used to answer the research question. For example, if the organization is large enough to have a finance department, it can provide information on usage trends based on revenue. They are in a position to know if revenue has recently changed for the better or worse. The human resource department will have information on whether it has become increasingly difficult to find employees. Those people who have direct contact with the customer are an invaluable source of information on how the organization can be improved.

If the organization has a receptionist or information desk employee, they can be a useful source of data. Part of their duties may have been to track the number of visitors and they will also be able to provide information on the most common questions that are asked. Or, they may record information on the number of complaints received.

Internal data can also be obtained by conducting interviews. These interviews can be used to learn more about the employee's view of the cause of the problem. Although more informally conducted than research interviews, the process should still be taken seriously. First the marketing researcher should prepare the questions before the interview. During the interview the researcher should make careful notes on the answers.

Sometimes even when internal information does not uncover the reason for a problem, the organization might still decide not to conduct research. This would be when answering the question costs more than the savings that would result from fixing the problem. Perhaps a museum believes that it could increase sales in the museum store if they stock additional items. If the study is going to cost the organization $2,000 but the expected increase in sales will only bring in an addition $1,000 in revenue year, there is little reason to conduct the study.

Information from company employees

- Finance: Has revenue changed unpredictably recently?
- Box office: What have customers been complaining about?
- Human resources: Have we been having a problem hiring good employees?
- Employees: Have you noticed any new groups of people using services?

Writing the question

Once the internal research has been conducted, the organization is now ready to write the research question. A research question that starts with why or how will usually result in an exploratory research methodology. Such questions are usually very broadly stated such as, 'Why do current users of our services not recommend us to their friends?' Another exploratory research question would be, 'How can we better communicate our mission to the general public?' There could be many possible answers to these questions, which is why an exploratory technique such as focus groups or interviews will be used.

Research questions which start with who, how many or how often will use a descriptive research methodology such as a survey. After all there can only be a limited number of possible responses to questions about demographic characteristics or frequency of visits.

A well written research question will be as specific as possible. It will not only provide information on what needs to be known, it will also provide information on who will provide the information. If possible it should also quantify any information on demographics, quantity of usage or price. For example, rather than state a research question as, 'How much can prices be increased?' it should be stated as, 'Will a 5% price increase negatively affect customer numbers?'

This very specific research question does not happen at the first attempt. Instead it will take many attempts before the question is specific enough (see Table 4.2). This process is best conducted by more than one person, so they can challenge each other over what is specifically being asked. A research question will start as broadly defining the question but successive rewrites will clarify the meaning. It is internal research that will help narrow the question.

Table 4.2 Research question definition

General question	Clarification
Why are customers not using our services?	What customers?
Why are current customers not using our services?	Where are they not using services?
Why are current customers not using our services at our new location?	What current customers?
Why are older current customers not using our services at our new location?	What do we mean by current?
Why are older customers who have used our services for at least five years not using services at our new location?	What do we mean by older?
Why are customers over age 65 who have used our services for at least five years, not using services at our new location?	What services are they not using?
Why are customers over age 65 who have used our services for at least five years, not using mental health services at our new location?	Final research question

■ The research proposal

When the organization decides that it is necessary to conduct research, the next step in the process to is to write a research proposal. In a large organization the proposal will be presented to management for their approval. The purpose of the proposal is to inform management of what resources will be needed to conduct the research. Management will want to know not only what question the research will answer, but also how long the research process will take, who will need to be involved and how much the research effort will cost (see Table 4.3).

Table 4.3 Components of research proposal		
Issue	**Question**	**Example**
Question	What is the research trying to find?	Community attitudes toward local parks
Participants	Who will be involved in the research?	City residents with children living at home
Method	How will we find the information?	Surveys and focus groups
Time	When will we conduct the research?	Month of June
Location	Where will we conduct the research?	Surveys in parks, focus groups in community center

However, even small non-profit organizations should write a research proposal. In this case the proposal is a planning document that will act as a roadmap to ensure that the research effort stays on track and on budget. A research proposal should, of course, state the research question. The research proposal will also state who will participate in the research. In addition it will provide information on the research method that will be used. Logistical details such as the time frame for the research process and the location where the research will be conducted must be included.

The research proposal is the game plan for the research that will be undertaken. It can be a formal many page document. However, it can also be as short as a single page. Some organizations, because they are small and in a hurry to start research, do not want to take the time to put their plans in writing. There are several very good reasons why it is worth the effort to do so. First the research proposal will keep the research on track. Once the initial enthusiasm for research has faded, it is easy for progress to stall. The proposal will remind everyone in the organization what needs to be accomplished and why. In addition, the research proposal acts as an informal contract. It states the resources, both human and financial, that are needed to accomplish the research. This is necessary so that the resources are available when needed. Finally the research proposal assigns responsibility for the various tasks that must be accomplished. The proposal can then be used to hold people accountable so that the research will be completed as scheduled (Brace and Adams, 2006).

Why a research proposal should be written

- Action plan to keep everyone on track
- Agreement on needed financial, time and staff resources
- Holds people accountable for assigned responsibilities.

Components of the research proposal

All research proposals should consist of three components. The first section discusses the problem while the second section focuses on describing the methodology. The third section will describe how the data will be analysed and the findings reported. A formal research proposal for a large scale and expensive research project will also include additional documentation in an appendix. This information might include a budget, timeline and staffing requirements.

The research proposal – problem

The first section is crucial for a formal research proposal that needs to be approved by management. All research, even when using volunteers, has costs. Unless management believes that there is a problem that is impacting the organization, they will not approve the proposal. As a result management, or anyone else reading the proposal, will first want to know that significant thought went into deciding the question that needs to be researched. The purpose of this section is to provide legitimacy to the research effort.

The introduction in this section will start with providing information on the author of the proposal. If the author has conducted previous research this should be mentioned. If not, the introduction should discuss the sources of information, whether people, books or educational experience, upon which the researchers will be relying. If someone outside the organization has requested that the research be conducted, such as a funding agency or board member, this should be explained.

The research objective should then be stated. The objective is a general statement that explains why the organization is conducting research. This is the problem that has started the organization to think about the need to conduct research. The problem could involve competitors, customers or any component of the marketing mix, such as price, product, place or promotion.

It is the objective that will be researched internally to generate the exact research question. For example, the first indication of a problem may be that a heath services provider might notice a budget shortfall due to declining revenue from customers. An internal review of the budget might reveal that customers are paying much less of the 'recommended' fee for services than they have in the past. The objective of the research will be to determine why customers are paying less.

Once the research objective has been researched internally, the clinic will know more about the cause of the problem. For example, the clinic may have learned from volunteers who staff the front desk that customers are complaining about the additional cost of public transportation to visit the clinic. This knowledge will be used to then state the research question. In this case the research question might be, 'Is the additional cost of transportation causing clients who visit frequently to pay less to use the clinic's services?'

The problem is what is first noticed by the organization. The objective is a statement of what needs to be learned. The research question is a specific statement of what needs to be known from whom (see Table 4.4).

Table 4.4 Examples of research problems, objectives and questions		
Problem	**Objective**	**Question**
Budget shortfall	To determine why customers are paying less of the recommended fee	Does the increased cost of transportation result in a client decreasing the amount they pay the clinic per service?
Decreased attendance	To increase the number of customers attending matinee performances	What type of programming would motivate increased attendance by families at matinee performances?
Competing art gallery opening nearby	To learn how to keep customers loyal	What kind of new services can be added to retain our current customers who visit at least once a month or more?
Lack of ethnic attendance at arts festival	To motivate attendance by ethnic group members	What type of promotional message should be aimed at the local ethnic community?

Once the proposal has stated the research problem and objective, it will explain the internal research that was conducted. This will include a short discussion about what was learned during the internal research. The internal information that was obtained from written records or from interviews will then be presented. The reader of the proposal should be assured that the decision to undertake marketing research was made only after considerable thought and deliberation.

The proposal will then state the final research question. It is this question that will determine the choice of research methodology and research subjects. The research question should be written as specifically as possible and should address not only the problem but also who will be asked to participate in the research. As show in Table 4.5 the research question can address the external environment, competition, current or potential customers or the marketing mix components.

Table 4.5 Sample research questions	
Issue	**Question**
External environment	How does fear of crime at our inner city location affect visits of new customers with children during the evening hours on weekends?
Competition	Are current visitors who have been visiting our gallery for less than one year now visiting the new gallery located down the block?
Current customers	What is the demographic and psychographic composition of our audience for weekday performances?
Potential customers	Which immigrant groups who have been in the community for less than one year are potential users of our job training services?
Product	What additional preventive medicine services are attractive to families with small children who are not currently using our free dental clinic?
Price	What affect will a $5.00 co-payment have on use of our services by users over the age of 70?
Promotion	Which of three new promotional messages will most motivate young people aged 11–15 to be more careful regarding disclosing personal information while online?
Distribution	Will locating the museum store near the entrance or near related exhibits increase sales of educational books to children?

The research proposal – methodology

The second section of the research proposal will contain information on the research approach, research methodology and who will be the research participants. The research approach will be either exploratory or descriptive. It is important that the research proposal explain which approach will be used so that the management of the association will understand what type of findings and recommendations will result from the research study.

Descriptive research will result in quantified facts about the organization's customers and their behaviour. In addition, when the correct number of participants is used, descriptive research can attempt to 'prove' a hypothesis. Exploratory research will provide the organization with information on the attitudes, values and opinions of current or potential customers. However, exploratory research cannot be used to 'prove' a hypothesis. Therefore sometimes analysis of the findings from exploratory research will result in the organization understanding that it will need to conduct further descriptive research before recommendations can be made.

Besides the approach, this section of the proposal will also describe the methodology that will be used to obtain the answer to the research question. Descriptive research usually relies on surveys to gather information. However, there are more choices of how to conduct exploratory research including interviews and focus groups. Projective techniques can be used either alone or with interviews and focus groups. In addition observation can be used to conduct exploratory research.

If the researchers are planning to use more than one research methodology, the reason why should be carefully explained in this section of the proposal. For example, a non-profit organization that offers exercise classes to overweight children might first plan to conduct exploratory focus group research. This research might conclude that the classes are under enrolled because parents are not aware of the programme. Before an expensive promotional campaign is undertaken, the organization might wish to conduct a survey of local parents to confirm which media is most often used so that the correct choice is made. The proposal should explain why both methods are necessary.

While as much information as possible should be provided about the research methodology, this is only a proposal and the final survey instrument, whether a questionnaire or focus group script, will not have been developed yet. Instead, general information on the type of survey that will be used, whether mail, telephone, in person or online, should be provided. In addition the number and type of questions should be stated. Details of when and where the survey will be administered should be included, even if the dates and location at this point in time are still tentative. Of course, a description of the individuals who will be asked to participate in the research should be provided. When writing the proposal, any terminology with which the reader may be unfamiliar should be explained.

Information on research methodology for surveys

- Survey method to be used
- Number of survey forms to be completed
- Dates when survey will be conducted
- Example of survey questions that will be asked
- Description of survey participants.

DON'T FORGET THE ONLINE RESEARCH OPTION

One of the objectives of the research proposal is to convince those with the power to approve the needed resources that the benefits outweigh the costs. One of the ways to cut the costs both in terms of money and time is to conduct survey research online. Online research is gaining in popularity because it is cheaper and faster than traditional delivery methods. The amount of money spent on online research has grown in the United States from $3.8 million in 1996 to $1.35 billion in 2006. In fact online research has become so popular that one-third of all US spending on market research surveys is now spent using online forms. The reason for this change is that conducting a survey online has cost savings of 15–20% over mail surveys and 30% over phone surveys.

> Does the same cost/benefit analysis hold true for qualitative research methods such as focus groups? Qualitative research methods are much more difficult to adapt online because they are heavily dependent on face to face contact. As result online qualitative research is only 1% of all spending.
>
> *Source*: Johnson (2006).
>
> *Question to consider: Does anyone in our organization have the interest or skills to use online survey software?*

The research proposal – analysis and reports

The third section of the proposal will provide information on how the research data will be analysed. The proposal will inform management how focus group proceedings or interviews will be transcribed and then coded for themes. In addition what type of software will be used for analysing survey data will be described.

The type of recommendations and how they will be reported should be explained in this section of the proposal. Research should result in recommendations for action such as changing the product, adjusting the price, targeting new customers or using new promotions. While the researchers cannot know the specific recommendations before the research, the proposal should assure management that recommendations will be made. In addition the proposal will state whether a written report, an oral report or both will be provided to management. The proposal will also state what will happen to the survey forms, focus group tapes or projective technique material after the conclusion of the research.

The research proposal – Appendices

A formal research proposal for a large scale study will require that additional information be provided to the organization. The purpose of the material is to assure the organization that those conducting the research study have the skills and abilities needed to do the job. The appendices might include resumes of those who will be involved in the research process. In addition, information on past research can be provided including samples of previous survey forms or focus group scripts. A budget might be included along with a timeline for the research.

Sample proposal timeline for survey

- Week One: Preliminary secondary research on problem
- Week Two: Write questionnaire and meet with management to review
- Week Four: Choose sample and meet with management to review
- Week Five: Test questionnaire
- Week Seven: Start to conduct survey
- Week Eleven: Analyse data

- Week Fourteen: Write report
- Week Sixteen: Present findings

NON-PROFITS A MAJOR PLAYER IN THE US ECONOMY

It is not surprising that non-profit organizations continue to adopt and adapt the management and marketing practices of business, including marketing research. Rather than a bit player in the US economy, non-profit organizations are major players. Non-profits employ 7.2% of the workforce – 9.4 million workers! They also use the services of the equivalent of 4.7 million full time volunteers. Even without adding in the volunteer workers, non-profits employee more workers then the entire construction industry (7.1 million employees).

Where do all these employees work? Most work in health care with one third in hospitals and 21% in clinics or nursing home. Other large employers are education, social assistance and membership organizations.

Source: Perry (2006).

Question to consider: Should we research what other management or marketing practices our organization should adopt?

■ The research industry

Marketing research can be conducted internally by the organization's employees or it can hire an external marketing research firm to conduct the research. The decision will depend on the skill level of the organization's employees and also the available financial resources. Even when the budget is tight, the organization may want to consider hiring externally if there is no one in the organization with the needed skills to conduct the research. There may be an inaccurate belief that using an external firm will always be expensive. Instead the organization might find that there are companies that are willing to work for a non-profit for a reduced rate.

Internal marketing departments

Marketing research can be conducted internally by the organization that needs the answer to the research question. In a very large organization there may be a specialized marketing research group within the marketing department. This would be the typical arrangement for a large corporation such as Proctor & Gamble or Coca-Cola. In a smaller organization, the marketing department employees will be responsible for handling the occasional research needs.

METROPOLITAN MUSEUM OF ART HELP WANTED AD

Want to work for the Met? The following ad was listed in the help wanted ads:

Assistant marketing research analyst
The Metropolitan Museum of Art, one of the world's finest museums, seeks a professional to assist w/monthly surveys, reports, and projections; design and implement surveys including scheduling & material prep; data inputting, tabulation & analysis; researching topics related to market strategy; Bach's or graduate deg, prefer Arts, Education, Marketing, or Business; 2–3yrs exp in art, media, or hospitality field(s); and coursework or job exp utilizing evaluation techniques. Strong data analysis, report writing, presentation and research skills necessary. Must work well with the public; handle multiple projects; work independently; & have excellent communication skills & proficiency in SPSS, Excel, PowerPoint and Word. Salary depends upon the applicant's background and exp. This position is full-time with full museum benefits. Send letter of application & resume to: E-mail to Attn: HR Dept MW-AMRA at: employoppty@metmuseum.org Equal Opportunity Employer
Source: New York Times (2007).

Question to consider: What type of research skills do our employees already possess?

Large non-profit organizations will also have specialized personnel who have the skills and knowledge necessary to conduct marketing research. The Metropolitan Opera has a large enough marketing department so that it can be divided into separate groups. General Marketing has positions in promotions, website coordinator, designers and mailing/productions administration. A separate Customer Care and Donor Relations department has a director position along with a director and manager of subscriptions and special services. A Call Center and Fulfillment Department has positions in e-marketing.

In smaller non-profit organizations marketing personnel are expected to handle a number of different marketing functions including promotion, product packaging and special events along with any research needs. In fact when an organization hires marketing personnel they may not be aware of the need to hire someone with marketing research experience. It may be the marketing employee that must explain to management why research should be conducted.

Even smaller non-profit organizations may consist of only a handful of employees who share the responsibility for marketing tasks along with all other organizational functions. Even these small non-profits must consider the need to conduct research. If they find that they do not feel confident enough to conduct research on their own, they may approach a commercial firm that conducts research who may be willing to provide services on a pro bono basis. If this is not possible they can enlist the assistance of an intern or graduate student at a local college or university.

External providers of marketing research

Sometimes organizations that have the capability to conduct research still hire an outside firm. This may be the case when the organization lacks the skills necessary to conduct research with a specific group of individuals. For example, the organization may need to conduct research with members of an ethnic group community and feel they have no one who has the needed cultural knowledge. Another group that is difficult to research can be young people. If they are not current customers of the organization, they may have no incentive to participate in the organization's planned research. For example, an opera company may wish to conduct research on how to attract young men to its performances. However, young men would be unlikely to be interested in participating in the research simply because they do not like opera. As a result the opera may find it difficult to recruit individuals to participate in the research. However, there are marketing research firms that have the expertise to handle these types of research projects. The types of external marketing research providers include advertising agencies, syndicated firms, participant recruiters and custom and full service research firms (see Table 4.6).

Table 4.6 Marketing research firms	
Firm	**Assistance available**
Advertising agencies	Provide research as one of many services
Syndicated firms	Collect data on an ongoing basis
	Specialize in products or market segments
Participant recruiters	Have established database of willing participants
	Find specific participants for study
Custom research firms	Design and conduct research studies on specific groups or industries
Full service research firms	Will design and conduct any type of research study

Advertising agencies: Advertising agencies are the broadest category of research provider. These companies provide many different marketing services. While they specialize in promotional services, they also offer research services to help clients to develop promotional campaigns. The research services they offer involve finding the best customers to target, development of an effective marketing message and the right choice of media to communicate the message.

Syndicated firms: Syndicated research firms are businesses that collect data and then sell the information to other companies. This data may be on the product preferences of a specific group of individuals, such as the consumption habits of young Hispanic women or on the use of a product, such as movie attendance. The firms collect this data on an ongoing basis and are willing to sell it to any company with the money. An example of such a company is ACNielson who collects information on television viewing along with a host of other consumer issues. This data is bought by companies to help them decide what television shows should be used to advertise their products. Anyone can buy the information that ACNielson collects right off their website.

Participant recruiters: Another type of specialized company is one that recruits research participants. This has become a growing business, especially for online survey research. For example, a company will keep a database of people who are willing to participate in survey research. If a non-profit organization needs to determine the entertainment habits of Asian-Americans, a specialized participant recruiting firm can be used. The firm will recruit the participants based on the specifications provided by the non-profit by giving the potential participants a financial incentive.

Custom and full service firms: Custom research firms are companies that will assist with every step of the marketing research project from developing the research question to presenting the findings. Some customize marketing research firms will specialize in a specific product category, such as the entertainment industry. For example, they will conduct research only for companies that work in the fashion industry or with automobile companies. Other firms specialize by market segment, focusing on researching the preferences of urban youth or the Hispanic market. By contrast full service customized marketing research firms will handle a project for any type of product or consumer market segment. While these companies may provide excellent services, their services would be financially beyond the reach of most non-profits.

Guidelines for choosing a research firm

Before signing a contract with an external provider of research the non-profit organization should consider the firm's business practices, skills and reputation. The organization should ask for references of companies for which they have conducted research. The marketing research firm should be able to supply names of other non-profits with which they have worked. If they cannot provide a name of a non-profit they have worked with, they should at least be able to provide a name of a company of a similar size and structure. These references should be checked to determine the quality of the firm's work.

If the external marketing research firm has not worked previously with a non-profit it is important that the firm understand the non-profits budgetary constraints. In addition, it is also important to discuss with the firm the nature of the non-profit's mission. The firm must understand that any recommendations that result from the research study must fall within the mission of the organization. For example, turning the church into a night-club on weekends might bring in needed revenue and meet a community need, but certainly would not fit the church's mission! The research will not focus on bringing in the most people or the most money, but rather on reaching specific audiences as determined by the mission.

When meeting with the research firm, the non-profit organization should ask detailed questions as to charges and fees. Before any agreement is reached the firm should provide a breakdown of the cost of each service that will be provided. In addition a firm date should be provided for when the project will start and when it will be completed. Vague estimates, such as 'as soon as possible' and 'it should not cost too much' leave room for misunderstandings.

The non-profit should ask who will be conducting the research. Often, the organization will speak to a representative of the firm expecting that person to conduct the research. Usually the person negotiating the deal is not the researcher. The organization should be provided with the names of the people who will conduct the research along with their qualifications and past experience. Finally the organization should ask if the firm has a code of ethical conduct for their researchers.

Guidelines for hiring research assistance

- Ask for references
- Explain organization's mission
- Get firm figures and dates
- Learn who will conduct the research.

Alternatives to hiring an outside firm

Hiring a research firm can be expensive, but it is not the only alternative if an organization feels they must have outside assistance. Many firms may be willing to provide assistance in return for acknowledgement in the organization's promotional material. In addition management of the organization should approach board members for the names of any contacts they may have who could provide pro bono services. There may be a board member who has a marketing researcher working in their own company that they may be willing to loan to the organization.

If professional assistance is not possible, the non-profit organization may turn to a local college or university for help. A graduate student in a business programme may need a project to undertake to receive their degree and may find the organization's research needs of interest. If the organization's only recourse is an undergraduate programme, they may wish to approach a faculty member who teaches a class in marketing. The faculty member may be interested in conducting the research as part of a class project. Undergraduate students often need faculty supervision. However, a senior student who has taken a class in marketing research might undertake the project as part of an internship.

Summary

- Marketing research is conducted to find information to solve a problem. The organization will already have an assumption of what is causing the problem, but they must be careful to not base research on this assumption. Before writing a research question based on a possibly faulty assumption, the organization should conduct internal research to narrow the possibilities. This internal research will be of written data that the organization has collected in the normal course of doing business. Or it will be gathered through informal interviews with the organization's employees.

- Existing records that can be researched to clarify the problem are previous research findings, box office numbers, customer databases, sales receipts, website hits and front desk employees. This data can provide information on trends in usage, sales trends and complaints. Organization employees can also be researched, including personnel in finance, box office, human resources and general staff. These employees can provide insight into changes in customer behaviour and also changes in the demographics of the audience. Using this information, the organization is now ready to write the research question.

- The research proposal is a roadmap or game plan of the research that will be conducted. The first section of the proposal will describe the research problem including the research objectives and the research question. The second section of the proposal will describe the methodology that will be employed to answer the research question. This should be as detailed as possible but there is no need to include a finished research instrument. The third section will describe how the findings will be analysed and what type of report and recommendations will be provided.

- Large organizations may have the staff available to conduct research internally. External providers of research include advertising agencies, which provide a variety of other services. Syndicated research firms collect research data, which they then sell to interested companies and organizations. Specialized recruiting agencies do not collect data, instead they provide participants. Finally custom research firms design and conduct research and also analyse and report the findings. Small non-profit organizations may be able to receive assistance on a pro bono basis through board contacts. Or, they may ask for assistance from academic institutions.

■ References

Brace, I. and K. Adams (2006) *Introduction to Market and Social Research: Planning and Using Research Tools and Techniques*, Kogan Page, Limited, Philadelphia, PA.

Johnson, B. (2006) 'Forget phone and mail: Online's the best place to administer surveys', *Advertising Age*, 17 July.

New York Times (2007) 'Help Wanted Ads', 7 April.

Perry, S. (2006) '7.2% of Americans work in non-profit groups, study finds', *The Chronicle of Philanthropy*, 7 December.

Shapiro, A. (2004) 'Let's redefine marketing research', *Brandweek*, Vol. 45, No. 25, p.20.

Singer, M.E. (2006) 'Writer's loci: Learn how to craft a winning proposal', *Marketing Research*, Fall.

CHAPTER 5

Conducting
secondary
research

Objectives

■ Explain the advantages of collecting secondary data at the start of the research process
■ Identify the necessary requirements of usable secondary data
■ Explore how organizations can use secondary research
■ Describe the secondary data sources that are available to the researcher
■ Understand the steps necessary to complete a successful online data search

■ Introduction

Few people are interested in reading about how to conduct secondary research. After all, what the reader of this book wants to know is how to conduct a survey or a focus group, not how to sit at a computer reading about other people's research. What is important to remember is that conducting primary research costs both time and money. If another organization has already studied the issue affecting the organization, why not learn from their effort? Besides published research reports, there are many sources of information, such as articles in magazines and newspapers, that will have useful information that addresses the research issue. Online sources such as blogs and websites can also be used. This secondary research can help the organization find threats and opportunities and also information on the public, the external environment and competitors.

■ Using secondary data at the start of the research process

There are two types of data that a marketing researcher can collect. Primary data is information that is collected directly from research participants, the primary source. The other source of data available to the non-profit organization is secondary data created as the result of previously conducted research. This information has already been collected through either quantitative or qualitative studies by another organization, a company or a government agency. Qualitative secondary data is also available through a number of different sources such as articles and online sources such as blogs and websites (Stebbins, 2006). The benefits of using secondary data include lowering the research costs, finding information that can help in the design of the research methodology and general background information on the issue of concern (see Table 5.1).

Save time and money

The term 'secondary' can be confusing as this is actually the first type of research that is conducted. As there is no reason to duplicate research

Table 5.1 Benefits of conducting secondary research	
Benefit	**Example**
Save time and money by providing answer to research question	Another organization has already conducted research on the same topic
Help design research methodology	Find survey questions that can be added to the organization's questionnaire
Provide background information on issue	Learn areas of concern to the public that need to be addressed in research study

that has already been conducted, the first step in gathering data is to determine what is already known. The costs of conducting primary research include the time spent recruiting participants, collecting the data, analyzing the data and reporting the findings. Using secondary data rather than conducting primary research can help the organization lower the cost of research by saving both time and money.

Of course, the organization is not going to find any data from external sources that directly addresses their organization. However, if the organization needs information on a general problem they face, the data may already exist. For example, a social services agency may need to know what sports to add to its summer programme. They may first decide to conduct a survey of all local households with children to determine what activities are preferred during the summer. While a worthwhile idea, the organization may realize that they do not have the funds for such a study. However, a larger organization may have conducted the same type of study nationally. If the organization feels that the youth they serve are similar to youth nationally, this data can be used to design their local programme. By using secondary data, the organization saves the money and time of conducting the research themselves.

WHAT DO KIDS LIKE TO PLAY? NORTHEASTERN UNIVERSITY KNOWS!

Of course faculty in academic institutions conduct research focused on their own interests. However many academic institutions have centers that focus on conducting research that will benefit the wider community. An example is Northeastern University's Center for the Study of Sport in Society. In 2002 they participated in a study 'Play Across Boston' that examined participation in after-school and summer sports and physical activity programs. What did they find?

- Boys participate in such programs twice as often as girls
- Girls favorite sports were basketball, swimming, tennis, soccer and dance
- Boys favorite sports were baseball/t-ball, basketball, soccer, swimming and football.

How did they find this data? They studied the sports offerings of 235 programs. In addition they studied the use of 230 sports complexes. This size of study could not be undertaken by a small nonprofit organization with a limited budget.

Source: Play Across Boston (2002)

Question to consider: Realistically, how much time, money and staff could we invest in a research study?

Assist in design of research methodology

Sometimes the research question needing to be answered is general in nature rather than specific to the organization such as, 'What is the primary worry of parents who enroll their children in summer camp?' The organization that runs the camp may want this information so that it can be addressed in the next year's upcoming promotional campaign. Rather than conduct research themselves, they may find an association of summer camps that has research data available on the concerns parents have about sending their children to summer camp. For example, the data may show that safety is of primary concern to parents. If the summer camp research included parents in the organization's geographic area, they may decide that they have no need to conduct their own research.

However, the organization may still decide to conduct primary research. If they do, they now know that they should include questions in their survey or focus group on the safety issue. If they had not conducted the secondary research, they might not have asked a question about an important concern shared by many parents. This would mean that their research would not have provided critical data.

Provide background information

The organization may find that there is no specific data available on the problem that they face. This may be because the problem is one of which society has only recently become aware. For example, a health care organization may have been formed to help families deal with teenagers who have undergone weight loss surgery. These teenagers must follow a strict diet and the organization may want to know how to motivate the teens to follow medical advice. Teenagers getting weight loss surgery is a relatively new phenomenon so there may be no data available from previously conducted research. However, related research topics such as why teenagers ignore medical advice will provide useful information. In addition, there may be studies on the after-affects of weight loss surgery on adults that may prove useful. The organization may someday want to conduct their own research on the needs of such families and how they can be supportive for the teenager. In the meantime secondary research will provide the organization with some insight into the issue on how to motivate their teenage clients.

■ Requirements of secondary data

The ease with which information can be found using online resources might lead an organization to believe that secondary research is easy. After all, there is a wealth of information available for free by just using an online search engine such as Yahoo! or Google. In addition, other information can be accessed using online databases. If these resources do not provide enough information, databases only available through subscription can be found at public or academic libraries.

However, the fact that there are so many available resources does not make research easier. In fact it puts the burden on researchers to ensure that the data they are using is the best available data. There is so much information available, that data can be found to support any research issue. The researcher must not only find information, they must assess whether the information is useful because it addresses the research question. However of equal important is whether the secondary data is credible, which is determined by timeliness and its source (Mann, 2005).

Data timeliness

The question as to how old can data be before it is too old to use, is not easy to answer. Of course, if a non-profit organization is faced with a problem that is the result of a new social issue, the more recently the secondary data was gathered the more relevance it will have. However, there may be occasions when historical data is needed for comparison purposes. For example, an organization that sponsors youth sports programmes may want to know if sports participation preference among urban youth has changed over time. Therefore they may look for a study that was conducted 10 or 20 years ago. However, searching for historical data is an exception, as most organizations are looking for the most recently collected data.

If a problem is common and affects many people, the organization should be able to find current research. For example, a non-profit organization that is researching the methods that are most effective in helping people quit smoking should not have a problem finding data. There are many health education and cancer research websites that will provide information. Because this is such a common problem, new methods of quitting are always being researched and the data publicized. Therefore, the researcher should use data from the most recent study.

However, if an issue is not that common, there may be less available data. For example, an arts organization may have been formed to promote and display Chinese cartoon art with a political theme. They need to know why people are interested in this art form. However, there may be little information available on people's attendance at such shows or about their attitude toward Chinese political cartoons. Therefore any information would be useful, even if it is somewhat dated.

Information source

Once timely information has been located, the researcher must verify the source of the data. The researchers must distinguish between information created specifically to be placed on a website and information that has been created for other uses and then posted on a website. For the first type of information, the researchers should check the date of the website to learn when the information was posted. It should be remembered that websites can continue to live on indefinitely. As a result just because the researcher has accessed the data today, does not mean it was not created years ago. However, it is acceptable that the website itself may have been created years ago, as long as the information it contains is regularly updated with new data (Berkman, 2004).

The most important question for the researchers to answer is who created and maintains the website. It is important to remember that anyone with a computer and software can create a webpage. Therefore, the researchers should first determine that the website was created by a reputable individual or organization. A reputable website will have a section that clearly states the name of the organization or person that is sponsoring the site. If not, the researcher must be careful. For example, an online Google or Yahoo! search will turn up many websites about the life of the Rev. Martin Luther King. One website clearly states that it is the official website of the King Center in Atlanta. The home page of a second site also shows a large photo of Dr. King. At the bottom of the page is the information that the website is sponsored by Stormfront. Only further investigation reveals that Stormfront is part of the organization White Pride World Wide; a very different source of information!

Of course, most sources of misinformation are harmless. However, the researcher should always determine that the website is sponsored by a respected organization or individual. The credentials of the people who supply the information should be prominently displayed. In addition there should be information on how a website user can contact the organization either over the phone or through email.

While the above applies to all websites, additional verification is needed when using databases that store published research studies conducted by other organizations. Just because a research study has been published as an article does not automatically make it credible. Just as for a website, the researcher should use the same process to verify the organization for which the study was originally conducted. If the researchers are unfamiliar with the organization they should check its policies regarding publishing articles. Some publications are peer-reviewed, where experts in the field first review articles before they are published. Other publications pay authors to write articles, while some will simply choose from articles that are submitted.

Articles in academic publications are almost always peer-reviewed. The researcher will have to verify the credibility of articles in other types of sources, such as magazines and newspapers, by the reputation of the publication or the author. Well-known publications, such as the *New York Times* or the *Economist* magazine, are careful about what articles they publish because they want to maintain their reputation. Other publications are not as well known. In this case the researcher will want to check the qualifications of the author.

YOU CAN'T BELIEVE WHAT YOU READ – AT LEAST NOT WITHOUT CHECKING

Wikipedia is an online encyclopedia that allows anyone to contribute to an article. This has resulted in some interesting contributed information. The fact that Wikipedia is open to contributions from anyone is a strength and weakness. One example of a fact included by someone who contributes to Wikipedia is that seal hunters, in an effort to be more humane, are now tempting seals with peanut butter and apricot jam sandwiches. However, according to B.J. Fogg, the Director of the Persuasive Technology Lab at Stanford University, people are becoming more discerning about the information they find. People using the Internet are now learning to check on the credibility of the author rather than only read the content. As a result, Wikipedia will now require authors to give their names and credentials.

Source: Song (2007).

Question to consider: Are we willing to share our research results on our website and how can we assure the public of our study's credibility?

■ Uses of secondary research

Conducting secondary research is a responsibility that is often unappreciated by management. In fact management may wonder why marketers are immersing themselves in online databases or reading articles when they could be out talking to research subjects and obtaining primary data. However, the marketing researcher will understand how the organization can use secondary research even when they are not initially considering conducting primary research. These uses include looking for threats and opportunities that affect the organization. In addition, the marketing researchers will research the public, the external environment and competitors.

Threats and opportunities

While secondary research is being conducted the researchers will uncover data on both threats and opportunities. Threats are people, events or changes that can harm the organization's ability to compete for resources and customers. On the other hand opportunities are people, events or changes that the organization can use for their benefit. Organizations cannot protect themselves from threats or take advantage of opportunities of which they are unaware.

While many other departments in the organization are inwardly focused on specific tasks, one of the responsibilities of the marketing department is to be outwardly focused. That is why it is the responsibility of marketing researchers to continually research the external environment, including people and events. When the marketing department discovers a change that threatens the organization or an opportunity of which the organization can make good use, they can then communicate this information to management. As a result action is taken to neutralize the threat or take advantage of the opportunity (see Table 5.2).

Table 5.2 Example of use of research on threats/opportunities	
Step in process	**Example**
Threat uncovered	New competing theatre is opening
Marketing department takes action	Researches and writes report detailing competitors effective promotional campaign
Management is notified	Reviews report and decides to increase promotion budget
Action is taken	Marketing department uses increase to develop new promotional campaign
Results	Loss of audience to competitor is minimized

Organizational threats can arise from changes in the social environment that results in changes in consumers' product preferences. For example, if people are working longer hours, they may be too tired to attend late night performances. As a result the organization may decide to start their performances earlier. In addition threats can arise from stakeholder groups having changes in their perception of the organization.

For example, the marketing department may find an article in the local paper critical of the organizations move to new premises. As a result they may write a letter to the editor of the paper explaining the reason for the move.

External economic changes can affect the organizations ability to raise ticket prices or fees, while changes in the legal environment, such as a raise in the minimum wage, affect the ability to balance the organizations budget. Changes in the technological area, such as increased use of email, can provide an opportunity to the organization, as sending out newsletters by email is less expensive than printing and mailing.

In addition, new competition can result in consumers no longer using the services of the organization. This competition can be direct, where a new organization offers a very similar or exactly the same product. Generic competitors offer an alternative product targeted at the same consumer market segment as the organization. These generic competitors may be another non-profit or a for-profit business. If the marketing department finds that they are faced with competition they can react by improving their product or increasing promotion. However, the organization may react to the threat by making it into an opportunity. For example, they may approach the new competitors to engage in collaborative products or promotion that results in increased customer numbers for both.

Non-profit organizations are unique in that they have many more stakeholders than just customers. These organizations also rely on financial and other support from a variety of government, business and public groups. If any of these groups should cease to be supportive or become openly hostile, it can affect the resources of the organization. Using secondary research the organization can overcome threats or take advantage of opportunities from stakeholder groups from which the organization depends upon support. For example, a public library will want to research the attitude of any newly elected member to the City Council in regard to public library funding. In addition, it will be useful for the organization to know the new City Council members past relationship with the library, not only her or his opinion of public funding. For example, in the future the library may need to gain city permission for extension of a parking lot or they may need a special event permit to hold a fund-raiser. If the Council member is unfriendly towards the concept of a publicly financed library, perhaps believing they are no longer necessary in the age of the Internet, this attitude is a threat that must be understood and overcome. On the other hand if a Council member is elected who has a close association with the library, this is an opportunity of which the library may take advantage.

There are also opportunities of which the organization may become aware through secondary research (see Table 5.3). For example, an art gallery may have noticed declining attendance. Through secondary research of articles on consumer preferences they may learn that people are increasingly feeling stressed by workplace and home demands. As a result people are staying home in the evenings to watch DVD's rather than going out for entertainment. The art gallery, rather than despair, may see this as an opportunity. They may design a new promotional message that emphasizes that an evening at the gallery, where people can enjoy not only the art, but also comfortable seating, relaxing music and a free glass of wine, is just what a stressed out person needs to relax.

Table 5.3 Uses of secondary research to find threats and opportunities

Component	Example	Threat or opportunity
Public	Consumers	New segments to target
	Stakeholders	Groups unhappy with organization
External environment	Economic	Poor economy results in less fund-raising
	Legal	New minimum wage affects budget
	Technological	Customers newsletter online
Competitors	Direct	Threat of new organization in same field
	Generic	Competition stealing customers

Researching the public

All organizations, whether non-profit or for-profit, should use research to better understand the wants and needs of their current and potential customers. Because primary research takes considerable time and effort, the organization should always start this research using secondary data. Only after the organization has learned everything it can from secondary data should it consider conducting primary research. Secondary research should be conducted on both the demographic and psychographic changes in the population.

The demographic changes that can be researched include shifts in the age of the population or the family status of the people who are living in the area. The ethnic makeup of the community may also be altering and this should be explored. In addition, any current trends in the educational level and occupational background of the population should be researched. This type of information can easily be obtained through government census data. For example, a theatre company that learns from census data that there are an increasing percentage of families living in their area may choose to add matinee performances.

Psychographic information on people's attitudes, lifestyles and values is not as easy to research as demographic information. Possible sources of information include previously conducted research studies. If these studies were conducted by businesses the information may be proprietary and not be available to the public. However, academic research or research by other non-profits or government agencies usually is available.

For example, if an organization is looking for information on the public's attitudes towards the benefits offered by children attending summer camp, the American Camping Association website has the information from a number of publicly available research studies.

Another means of researching the changing values, lifestyles and attitudes of consumers is through lifestyle publications focused on a psychographic interest group. Because these publications must have articles that appeal to their readers, they are going to focus on issues of current interest. If the organization is interested in people's attitudes towards end of life medical care, they will find a publication that addresses the issue.

The newest way to keep abreast of changes in people's attitudes and lifestyles is through reading blogs and browsing social networking pages. Blogs are usually focused on a specific topic, whether environmental issues, a specific illness or a cultural or entertainment interest. Using these online sources of information can provide insights as to how people's values and attitudes are changing on specific areas of interest to the organization.

Sources of information on the public

- Census data
- Previously conducted studies
- Lifestyle publications
- Blogs and social networking pages

Researching the external environment

Researching the external environment involves keeping abreast of news regarding the economy, legal issues and technological changes. Economic changes affects the ability of people to both pay for admission and to contribute money. For example, if the economic news is positive with the stock market rising, this might be the time to send out a fund-raising letter. Legal news can affect an organization's ability to hire, fire and pay employees. If the organization regularly brings in artists from other countries, any legal changes that affect the ability of a foreigner to get a US visa are important to understand. Finally, changes in technology can affect the way the non-profit organization presents and promotes its product. Secondary research on how other organizations use technology might reveal that other theatres now have websites where theatre goers can order their intermission drinks online.

Economic legal and technological information can be found in specialized publications. Economic news is easier to find, as many people are interested in how the economy and the stock market are performing. Such information can be found in financial publications and through other business news media. However it is also available through any general news source, whether newspaper, website or TV broadcast. While economic news can be general in nature the legal information of which the organization should be aware may be very specific. The organization will only be interested in the legal changes that most affect their type of organization. Since it is difficult to keep abreast of legal changes, the organization may need to rely on publications of their professional association for the data they need. Finally, technological changes can impact the organization either positively or negatively. These changes include the way people communicate, the way they access and use information. The best way to keep abreast of these changes is through the general media.

Researching the external environment

- Financial and business news
- Association publications
- General media

Researching competitor information

A new competitor who has opened for business or new products or promotions by current competitors can have a profound effect on an organization. Because everyone working in a non-profit is so busy, it is easy to forget the importance of keeping abreast of competitors' actions. The organization should research direct competitors who offer a similar product. The organization can do so by researching the websites of competing organizations and also by being on their emailing or mail list.

For example, theatre companies would want to research what programming other theatres are offering. In addition, they would want to keep informed about any new promotional campaigns another theatre is launching. This type of secondary research on a continual basis can provide two benefits to the organization. First if the direct competitor is located nearby, the organization's current customers might start attending the competition. However, even if this is not a concern, conducting secondary research on the competing organization's programming or promotions may provide ideas that can be implemented.

The non-profit organization should also be aware of generic competitors. These are businesses or other non-profits that offer products that may be different but that offer similar benefits. For example, a sports gym would be a direct competitor of the YMCA recreational facilities. However generic competitors would be organizations or businesses that offer other ways to keep fit, such as running or dancing. To keep abreast of what generic competitors are offering, the non-profit organization should always read the local news. For example, if there is an article about a new running club that is being formed, the YMCA may wish to contact the membership to provide information about the Y's facilities.

Researching competitors

- Websites
- Emailings and traditional promotional mailings
- Local newspapers

■ Sources of information

Quantitative secondary data are numerical data that already has been collected. Large scale quantitative studies that produce numerical data are expensive to conduct. Therefore, government offices, large corporations and academic institutions usually conduct these studies. Much of this data will be on the demographics of the population and the percentages of consumer product preferences. The data from government and academic institutions is usually publicly available. In contrast, companies usually produce quantitative data for their own use, and this information is seldom available to the public.

Government agencies, which are a good source of quantitative data, rarely conduct qualitative studies. However, academic institutions may produce qualitative research as part of internal research conducted by a professor. The professor usually plans to publish the results of the study so the information is publicly available. Corporations that conduct qualitative research rarely make the results public. Because of the lack of government funded qualitative research, the organization must gather information from sources other than published data resulting from research studies.

Quantitative secondary data

Most quantitative secondary data is from statistical survey research that has already been conducted. Common institutions that conduct this type of research and make it freely available to the public are state or federal government agencies, academic institutions and trade associations. Syndicated marketing research firms also collect quantitative data, which they then make available for purchase. While large corporations frequently conduct such research, the data is for their own use and not publicly available.

Sources of secondary data

- Government agencies
- Academic institutions
- Trade associations
- Syndicated marketing research firms

Government agencies: Government agencies often collect data on people and also social trends. Of course the largest quantitative study in the US is the Census, which is conducted every 10 years. While everyone knows about the census, not everyone is aware that the US Census Office routinely collects and analyses data on specific groups and communities. In addition, the US Department of Commerce collects data on the economic performance of the country. The Department gathers data on business activities in different areas of the country and also on specific industries. Other data are collected by agencies that are funded by the government. For example, the National Endowment for the Arts collects data on arts participation.

Academic institutions: Many academic institutions conduct research as part of their mission. An individual academic who plans on publishing the results might conduct this research. In this case the research would be available when the article is published. However, many academic institutions also have research centres that produce research. For example, the Center for Urban and Regional Policy at Northeastern University in Boston, which calls itself a 'think and do tank' conducts research on the Boston area economy.

Trade associations: These organizations are focused on specific industries or occupations and are supported by dues paid by their members. Larger associations will often conduct research that their members would be unable to conduct on their own. For example, Dance USA is an organization that was formed to support the appreciation and promotion of dance. They conduct a yearly survey on dance organizations in the US, which is available to the public.

Syndicated marketing research firms: These companies collect quantitative data which they then sell to anyone willing to purchase. These companies usually focus on an industry, such as cinema, or an area of concern, such as charitable giving.

Qualitative secondary data

Secondary data, other than statistical information, is also available to researchers. However few government agencies, trade associations or academic institutions conduct qualitative research. As a result, non-profit organizations will need to gather their own qualitative secondary data. To do so they will use general interest and lifestyle publications, business publications and online sources such as websites, blogs and social networking pages.

General interest publications: One of the responsibilities of marketing is to keep the organization aware of changes in the external environment. The best way to do so is to always read or watch the general news. This is an excellent way to hear about new competitors, changes in legislation and economic news. The marketer should analyse this information while always asking the question, 'What does this mean for my organization?'

Lifestyle publications: Many publications, whether in print or online, are targeted at groups with specific psychographic interests. Reading these publications is an excellent means of learning what is important to people who have shared psychographic traits. For example, an organization may have been formed to support environmental awareness among teenagers. Before the organization can write a promotional message that appeals to teens, they need to be aware of how language is used by young people. If they are specifically focusing on reaching young males into extreme sports, they would want to read magazines geared towards this group. By reading the same magazines, the organization will learn more about this groups' interests and how best to communicate with them.

Online sources: Blogs and social networking pages give organizations a way to learn more about the values and attitudes of different groups of people. Most blogs focus on a specific interest or concern, such as the environment, music, health care policy or which bar is the best for a rowdy night out. By participating in blogs, the organization can become aware of the preferences of individuals who are their current or potential customers. Organizations can also use social networking pages, such as

MySpace and Facebook, to find any reference to their organization and then read what is said about them.

A BLOG FOR EVERYONE

The *Chronicle of Philanthropy* provides a list of blogs about the nonprofit world that it calls Blogroll. The blogs are subdivided into the categories of philanthropy, fund raising, charity blogs, and technology. Well over one hundred sites are listed, with a blog for nearly everyone in the nonprofit world. Even the names are interesting. Some sites are educational – 'The School for Social Entrepreneurs,' some personal – 'Seth Godin's Blog,' some are alarmist, – 'Will Billanthropy Take Over the World,' some inspirational – 'Redeeming Hope' and some down right mysterious – 'Frogloop'. Browsing the sites reveals questions under discussion from the specific, such as, 'Is it possible for one man (or woman) to work full time for two-different non-profit organizations that operate on both coasts?' to the general, such as 'Who says starting a charity can't be an absolutely glamorous undertaking?'

Source: Give and Take (2007).

Question to consider: What blogs should we be reading as part of the secondary research process?

■ Secondary marketing research process

The individuals who have the responsibility for conducting secondary marketing research may be tempted to simply sit down at a computer and start surfing. They may believe that using search engines such as Google or Yahoo! are all that is involved in conducting research. However, secondary research will be more beneficial if the researcher first does some planning. Marketing researchers should start their research with a clearly defined question to answer. For example, an organization that stages magic shows for children in hospitals may want to know more about current issues on the hospitalization of children and their need for entertainment. In addition, they may want to know more about what children like to see in magic shows.

The marketing researchers then should discuss their information needs with a reference librarian at an academic, business or general library. Many academic libraries are open to members of the general public who need to conduct research. Large cities often have libraries that specialize in serving the business public, but even a small public library will have a librarian with a specialized knowledge of information sources. There is no reason to stumble around online hoping to find the right information when a skilled guide, a reference librarian, is available. Some libraries even run workshops on how to research the library's databases.

Much of the needed information can now be found online. However, not all information online is available to the general public. Some of the needed information is only available through subscription database services, which the library should have. The reference librarian will be able to inform the researcher of the best databases to use to find the needed information. For qualitative information the research librarian may be able to suggest blogs or chat rooms that deal with the subject being researched.

Using online sources of information

If the researcher is going to conduct online research using search engines. They should be aware of limitations. The sites that come from a Google or Yahoo! search will range from the pertinent to the ridiculous. In addition, different lists of sites will be obtained depending on the words used to conduct the research. Some commercial websites will deliberately use words that result in their sites being accessed even when they have little information to offer on the topic.

For this reason the researcher would be better served by searching specialized databases available through libraries, rather than search engines. These databases have pre-selected the sources of information they contain. However, even with these databases the researcher will need to try different combinations of key search words to find the ones which will bring up the most relevant information. For example, PubMed is a database of articles on health and medicine sponsored by the National Library of Medicine and National Institute of Health. A quick search using the key words 'hospice care children' brought up 182 articles, some of which were reports on research studies that had already been conducted.

Online search strategy

A serious online secondary data search is very different from surfing the Internet. A search strategy has two stages. First the researcher must determine the possible sources of information and then must construct a search strategy using key words.

Determining possible sources of information: There are so many sources of information, that classifying them can be helpful. For example, an organization may want to consider establishing a crafts workshop that would sell the items produced by local artisans. The researcher might first want to learn more about the history of different crafts. The specialized three-volume Encyclopedia of Crafts (Schribner's 2003) might be where to start. After reading this information the researchers might decide to find more data specifically on fibre arts. A search of the catalogue of available library books might provide the names of books on the subject, such as *The Age of Homespun: Objects and Stories in the Creation of an American Myth* (Thatcher Ulrich, Laurel, 2002).

However once these sources of information are exhausted, it is time to use specialized databases. These databases, which can cover subjects from accounting to zoology, are not available to the general public because there is a subscription cost. However they are available through public or academic libraries. The researcher should check with the reference librarian to find the databases that are most likely to contain information of interest. For example, ArtAbstract contains articles on arts subjects from architecture to video. However LexisNexus, which has articles from general interest newspapers, magazines and journals, might also be helpful.

The researcher must understand the difference between a scholarly article and one meant for the general public. A scholarly article will assume that the reader is another scholar already familiar with the subject area. As a result the article might not be understandable to someone without this knowledge. Scholarly articles are written by subject area specialists and tend to be long, with 15–20 pages not uncommon. An example of a scholarly article would be 'Shelia Hicks: Weaving as Metaphor' from *American Craft*.

Newspaper and magazine articles are written by journalists for the general public and require no specialized knowledge to understand the content. They tend to be shorter, many of them only a single page. An example would be 'Weaving a New Dream' in *India Today*, which is an article about how Indian textiles are being used by the fashion industry in Paris.

Constructing a search strategy: The next step is to decide how to search the databases, which will contain thousands of sources of information. The researcher needs to understand a concept called controlled vocabulary. These are the key words and phrases that are used to index information. They are often very specific to an area of knowledge. For example, when discussing weaving, the term 'fibre' is commonly used to define the craft. If the researcher is unaware of the exact terms to use in the search, trial and error may be necessary. The complaint of 'there is no information on the subject' usually means the researcher is using the wrong terms (Munger and Shireen, 2007).

Once the correct terms are understood, Boolean Operators can be used to narrow the search. For example, the term 'fibre' put into a database key word search for ArtAbstract will produce 2,335 articles. Including the word 'and' along with 'art' will result in narrowing the search to 168 articles that contain both the words fibre and art. If the researcher wishes to broaden the search, the use of a search with the words fibre or weaving along with the term art will bring up even more articles (3837) because articles with fibre or weaving along with the term art will be found. Perhaps the researcher finds that too many of these articles deal with weaving only as an art form, and not as a more applied craft. The word 'not' can be used to exclude any articles about art. This final search would use the words fibre, and weaving but 'not' art, which produces 68 articles.

Truncation is another useful tool when conducting a database search. For example, a search might be conducted on fibre but the researcher also wants to include the word fibres. Simply adding the plus (+) sign to the end of the word fibre (fibre+) will also bring up articles where the word is used in the plural form as fibres.

Sometimes the researcher will be unsure of what ending of the word should be used. In conducting more research on weaving, the researcher might want to use the key words of fibre and weaving, but be unsure if weave, or weaving, is the correct word. By typing in weav* any word that starts with 'weav' will be included.

However when conducting a general Internet search using search engines, these Boolean Operators do not function, which is why searching is a hit or miss process. However, Internet searches are appropriate when wanting to locate the websites of companies to gather competitor information.

Summary

- Before starting the process of collecting data using primary research, organizations should first conduct secondary research of already existing data. This is data already collected by other organizations including, government agencies, academic institutions and professional associations. The reasons for researching secondary data include lowering research costs, help with design of the research methodology and providing background on the issue.

- With the ability to access information online, there is no shortage of data. However, the researchers must ensure that the data is both relevant and credible. The researcher also needs to ensure that the data is not outdated. In addition, the researcher must verify the source of the data. The individual or organization must be reputable.

- The organization should research secondary data to learn about potential threats or opportunities. The organization will then take action to neutralize the threats or take advantage of the opportunities. The organization can research their current or potential customers. They can also research other stakeholders whose opinions or actions affect the organization. The organization should research the external environment including the economic news, legal issues and technological changes.

- When conducting secondary research, the organization will be able to find quantitative information that was gathered through research conducted by government agencies, academic institutions and trade associations. The organization may need to gather qualitative secondary information from general interest and lifestyle publications as well as online sources.

- The researchers should use the assistance of a reference librarian when starting their search. Specialized databases of articles and studies are available at academic and public libraries. Finding the right information online will depend on using the correct search terms, which may take trial and error.

■ References

Berkman, R.I. (2004) 'The skeptical business searcher: the information advisor's guide to evaluating Web data, sites and sources', *Information Today*, Vol.22, Issues 11, p 47.

Give and Take (2007) 'A Round up of Blogs About the Nonprofit World' *The Chronicle of Philanthropy*, Downloaded on May 15, 2007 from http://philanthropy.com/giveandtake.

Mann, T. (2005) *The Oxford Guide to Library Research: How to Find Reliable Information Online and Offline*, Oxford University Press, New York.

Munger, D. and S. Campbell (2007) *What Every Student Should Know About Researching Online*, Pearson Education, Upper Saddle River, NJ, US.

Play Across Boston (2002) Downloaded on July 14, 2007 from http://www.barrfoundation.org/resources.

Song, V. (2007) 'The Web: Does it stack up?' *The Toronto Sun*, 19 March.

Stebbins, L.F. (2006) *Student Guide to Research in the Digital Age: How to Locate and Evaluate Information Sources*, Libraries Unlimited, Westport, CT.

Thatcher Ulrich, Laurel (2002) *The Age of Homespun: Objects and Stories in the Creation of an American Myth*, Knopf Publishing Group, New York.

CHAPTER 6

Finding participants

■ Introduction

Mostly, everyone working in a non-profit organization is aware of the different methods of conducting research, such as surveys, focus groups and interviews. However, fewer people know how an organization should choose who should be included as participants in the research. It is unlikely that most people know the difference between systematic and stratified sampling or how to calculate the exact number of people that need to be surveyed to have the results statistically valid.

This lack of knowledge is understandable, as the methods of choosing participants and sampling can be very complicated. In fact entire books have been written on the issue. However, it is not necessary to have such a detailed level of knowledge to use sampling. All that is needed is a basic understanding to choose the right sampling method. While knowledge of statistical sampling is necessary when choosing participants for a study that can be said to 'prove' a hypothesis, it is not necessary to conduct useful survey research.

■ Qualitative and quantitative sampling

The quality of research findings not only depends on an appropriately chosen research question and methodology, but successful research also depends on choosing the right research participants. Even if the right research question and methodology has been chosen, if the wrong people are asked, then the findings will be useless. Research participants for qualitative and statistically valid quantitative studies are chosen very differently and the researcher needs to know how to choose for both methods.

Quantitative research methods use random selection techniques. Once the researchers have developed a participant profile, they will randomly choose the necessary number of participants from this group. In contrast, qualitative research studies use non-random sampling methods. Non-random means that each potential research subject does not have the same likelihood of being chosen. However, non-random does not mean haphazard. Thought must be given to a process of choosing participants for any research study, even the smallest qualitative focus group. If fact, it could be argued that organizations conducting small qualitative studies must use extra care when choosing research subjects as so much weight will be given to the opinions of each. One participant in a focus group of eight has much more effect on the findings, than one participant in a survey of 500 (Stewart *et al.*, 2007).

Factors when choosing participants

When developing the participant profile of who will participate in a research study, the marketing researchers should be as detailed as possible. For example, the profile should describe all the important demographic characteristics of the potential participants. The profile needs to give this level of detail, as it will be used to design a screening process for choosing participants. Just stating that the research will involve surveying young males is not detailed enough as too many questions are left unanswered. On the other hand stating research participants should be aged 21–23 years, have finished at least two years of college, work part time, and live in their own home in zip code 17701, is too specific. It would be too difficult to find enough participants that meet this profile.

There are four general issues to consider when developing the detailed description, or participant profile, for a qualitative or quantitative research study (see Table 6.1). First the researchers should decide what demographic characteristics are important. Then they will consider what psychographic characteristics should be considered. In addition, the importance of geographic location should be thought through. Finally for some research questions the potential subject's level of knowledge of the organization or issue must be considered.

Table 6.1 Sample participant profile for study on use of Senior Centre

Type	Characteristics	Example
Demographic	Age	Age 65–80 years
	Gender	Male and female
	Occupation	Retired or working part time
Psychographic	Attitude	Attracted to new situations
	Lifestyle	Busy with hobbies and interests
Geographic	Location	Resident of Lycoming County
Knowledge	Product	Currently non-users of Senior Centres

Demographic: For all research studies, one of the important factors when choosing research participants is demographic characteristics. Marketing research focuses on learning more about needs and wants, both of which are shaped by consumers' demographic characteristics such as gender, age, income, education, family stage, occupation, ethnicity and religious affiliation.

Age, income and gender may have the most direct bearing on the choice of almost all types of products and services. Other demographic characteristics may be of importance for specific types of research questions. For example, if a non-profit organization that teaches English language classes is interested in learning the opinions of specific ethnic groups, then this characteristic needs to be described in the participant profile. Stage in family life cycle may also be important in determining who should be involved in a study. The research question might be best answered by whether the participant is single, living with a partner, married with children or a single parent. For example, a botanical garden might want to know what it can do to motivate more fathers to visit along with their children. If they wish to target dads who have weekend custody, the participant profile would include the characteristics of divorced or never married fathers who have part time custody of their children.

Psychographic: It is much easier for the marketing researcher to determine a potential participant's demographic than psychographic characteristics. This is true because psychographic characteristics involve a person's attitude, lifestyle and opinions, which are not readily apparent. However, these characteristics are often more important than demographic characteristics in determining a person's product preferences. For example, a study of the use of public swimming pools might want to know why the sale of season passes has declined, as families that formerly used the pool are no longer buying passes. When designing the participant profile, the researcher might start with demographic characteristics, such as age, family status and income level. However, the reason that season tickets are not selling may have nothing to do with age, family status or income. Instead it might be psychographic characteristics such as involvement in physical activities and interest in health issues that determine who will choose to use the pool. These psychographic characteristics cannot be as easily determined as demographic characteristics. Therefore the marketing researcher will need to develop screening questions to ensure that the participants match the needed profiles.

Geographic: Geographic location varies in importance based on the type of research methodology being used. There are two issues that are involved when specifying the location where the potential participants should live. For some research studies product or organizational knowledge is necessary. As a result the potential participant must live where the product is available. With the swimming pool use study example, the potential participants should live in the geographic area of current 'pool users'. This geographic area could be determined by studying the addresses of people who have purchased pool passes in previous years.

Another relevant geographic issue involves focus groups and interviews. For these the participant must travel to the location where the focus group or interview is being held. If the location is too distant or has inconvenient transportation options, the potential participant may decline. Of course the marketing researcher could arrange to pay transportation expenses for the participants, but this would add to the cost of conducting the study.

For survey studies the potential participants may be spread over a wide geographic area. However if phone, online or mail surveys are used, the distance may not be a problem. For observational studies, location is an important consideration, as the choice of location will determine who will be observed.

Product knowledge: When developing the participant profile, the level of product or organizational knowledge and also the knowledge of the research issue must be considered. For some studies it may be important that the potential participant have no familiarity with the issue. For example, if the organization wants to develop a marketing message to convince people to buy local food, they will want to include people who have not thought about the issue. For other studies product knowledge is important. For example, if a school district wants to know why people do not make use of after school exercise programs, they need to ask people who are aware of the programs but chose not to use them.

For other research studies it may be important that the research participant be a current user of the service. These potential participants will be able to provide insight on why they are attracted to the services that are offered. Meanwhile former users may be able to provide insight into how the services can be improved. These studies do not have to include a large number of participants. For example, a few interviews of people who currently are volunteering at the organization can lead to helpful insights as to their motivation (Callow, 2004).

Incentives for participation

Another issue that the marketing researchers must consider is the potential participant's willingness to participate. Of course, just because the organization has targeted a certain group of people as being necessary to include in the study, it does not mean that the people will be interested in participating. Some motivators for participating in studies include a desire to help the community and enjoyment of the research process. If these are not sufficient motivators, a financial incentive can be used.

Fortunately, non-profit organizations have an advantage in motivating people to participate in research studies, as the organization can explain how the research will be helpful to the organization fulfilling its mission, which in turn helps the community. An organization that wants to learn how to more effectively communicate a message encouraging people to get more exercise will be able to explain to potential participants how participating in the research will help the health of the community. This is not a claim that can be made by a breakfast beverage producer who needs to know how much pulp people prefer in their orange juice.

Some people will be willing to participate in research just because they are interested in the research process. They may enjoy the fact that the organization is seeking their opinion. For a person who may feel overlooked in everyday life, it may be flattering to have their opinion listened to and recorded. While interest in the research process is an acceptable reason for participation, the organization must be careful that a participant is someone who does not repeatedly participate in research studies. This type of participant may be more interested in hearing their own voice then in giving careful thought to the research question.

There will be occasions when the organization may want to consider providing an incentive to participate. The breakfast beverage producer described above may well need to provide a financial incentive to have people participate in a focus group about beverage preferences. However, a non-profit organization may not have the funding available to pay participants. In addition, they may hesitate to provide payment feeling to do so would be in contradiction to their organizational mission.

However, incentives should not only be thought of as a form of payment. Instead they should be considered as a way to say thank you. The non-profit organization might consider offering something as simple as a t-shirt with the organization's logo that they normally sell or give away to people who make donations. If the organization sells tickets to events, they may wish to provide free attendance. These are inexpensive ways of acknowledging that the participants' time is valuable and that the organization appreciates their participation.

Why people are willing to participate

- Belief research will help others
- Interest in research process
- Financial or product incentive.

Participant problems

One issue that faces non-profit organizations when choosing research participants is to remember to not use participants that are personally known to the researchers. This is a particular problem for non-profit organizations who often have volunteers and supporters who care deeply about the organization. Because they care deeply, they may be very eager to participate in the research. However, participation by those already known to the researchers should be discouraged, as any previous relationship can bias the data that is received during the research process. For example, the participant may hesitate to voice any negative opinions in a focus group when the moderator is a friend. Although it is tempting, to use friends, because they are easier to find, research participants should have no previous relationship with the marketing researchers. There are commercial companies that recruit participants, but most non-profits will need to rely on goodwill and small thank you gifts (Saros, 2007).

Because a non-profit organization is almost always short of money and time, there may be a temptation to use participants that do not fully meet the outline of the participant profile. However, even if it takes more time than anticipated to find the right participants, this is better than saving time, by using marginally qualified participants, only to end up wasting the research effort.

The researchers should be aware that there are people who so much enjoy being involved in the research process that they seek to participate again and again. While this is usually a problem for commercial companies that pay financial incentives, it is also an issue for non-profit organizations. In the case of non-profit organizations, a person may want to participate frequently so as to be more involved with the organization. However, the problem with repeatedly using the same subjects is that they bring no new insights to the process. This is a particularly important concern when conducting interviews or focus groups.

Finally an issue to be considered is that a qualified participant may be unwilling to be involved in the research study because of the location. Focus groups and interviews do not need to be held at the organization's offices, as the location may be in a part of town that is not often frequented by the research participants. As a result they may be unfamiliar with the neighbourhood and the transportation options. In fact, focus groups and interviews should be held at a convenient location where the participants will feel most comfortable.

Problems to be avoided

● No prior knowledge
● Does not meet profile
● Too frequent participation
● Unwilling to participate because of location.

■ Qualitative sampling procedures

The three basic methods that an organization can use when selecting participants for qualitative research studies are summarized in Table 6.2.

Method	Process
Table 6.2 Qualitative sampling methods	
Convenience	1. Find location where potential participants congregate 2. Choose participants based on profile
Snowballing	1. Choose first participant to meet profile requirements 2. Ask this participant to recruit others 3. Confirm that recruited participants meet requirements 4. Contact participants with needed information
Purposive	1. Develop participant profiles 2. Create or find list of people who meet profile 3. Choose names from list 4. Invite to participate

After the participant profile has been developed the organization must choose which of the three methods, convenience, snowballing or purposive, is most appropriate. Convenience sampling uses the participants that meet the profile and are the most convenient or easy to find. Snowballing uses recommendations after the first participant is chosen. With purposive sampling, the participants who best meet the profile are chosen.

Convenience sampling

Convenience sampling is used when researchers chose as participants any willing and available individuals who meet the profile. The easiest way to use this method is to find participants at a location that will tend to attract those who will meet the profile. For example, if the research question calls for surveying the opinions of female college students, the best place to find these students is on a college campus. Once on the campus, the researcher will use their judgment when choosing which participants to include in the study.

Convenience sampling is useful when potential participants may not be eager to be involved in the research process. The other sampling methods recruit specific individuals who are then invited to participate in the research. With convenience sampling the researcher goes to a location where potential participants already congregate. This makes the selection process much simpler as the potential participant does not need to respond to an invitation but is asked to participate personally. Convenience sampling is also an appropriate method when the group of potential participants may find it difficult to travel to another location. If the elderly are involved, an assisted living centre might be a good location to find participants. For a religious or ethnic group a community centre might work well.

HOW DO YOU GET NEW IDEAS FOR A FUNDRAISER? RESEARCH!

It seems that everyone wants a unique ring tone for their cell phone, as you can purchase anything from the score to the *Simpsons* television show to the rapper 50 Cent. Over 205 million people have cell phones in the United States and over 10% of them, or 24.1 million, purchased cell phone ring tones last year.

If you knew these facts you wouldn't be surprised that the American Composers Orchestra decided to raise money by auctioning off ring tones written by famous composers including Philip Glass and Laurie Anderson. In addition they auctioned off ring tones by well known movie score composers. Research has shown that there are a lot of people who purchase cell phone

ring tones. More research would tell you if people would be willing to pay a lot for bragging rights to an original ring tone.

Source: Kazakina (2006).

*Question to consider: How do we use research to help with
planning our fundraising efforts and events?*

Snowball sampling method

As a snowball rolls down a hill, it becomes larger by gathering more
snow. Snowballing as a sampling method works similarly. With this
method the researcher first finds a single participant that closely meets
the needed profile. This participant then recruits others with similar
characteristics that also meet the profile. These participants will then
recruit others and so on until enough participants have been found.

This method is particularly useful when recruiting participants from
populations that may not be interested in participating in the research
process. This lack of interest may be due to a lack of understanding of
the purpose of the research and how it will benefit the community.
Additionally, the participants may have a reason for not wanting to be
involved in anything of an 'official' nature. For example, the potential
participants may be illegal immigrants that are worried about attracting the notice of the government. Or, they might be involved in drug use
or be in violation of their parole. Most businesses would not have occa-
sion for conducting research with such individuals, but it would not be
unusual for a non-profit to want to learn more about the needs and
wants of these individuals.

However, there are less dramatic reasons for using snowballing. It
might be that the population, such as college students or the elderly, is
unknown to the researchers. It could also be that the members of these
populations simply might not respond to an invitation to participate that
comes from the organization. With snowballing, besides choosing the
first participant to meet the profile characteristics, the researchers must
also chose someone who is trusted and respected by the other members
of the group. This participant is then asked to recruit other similar individuals for the research. Once the participants have been referred, the
organization will then confirm that they do meet the profile characteristics. The organization will then contact them with the information they
need to participate in the research process.

Purposive sampling

There will be occasions when the research question might require that
more than one group of participants be involved in the research process.

This might be true when the organization is interested in the views of users and non-users or younger and older members of the community. The recruiting of research participants can become even more complicated when multiple groups need to be recruited based on different demographic, psychographic or geographic characteristics.

Purposive sampling methodology carefully designs these multiple participant profiles. The researcher will create a list of potential participants in each category. For example, a list of current users or visitors might come from box office records, guest book signatures, email lists or client files. In addition the organization may need to recruit participants who are not current users of the organization. These lists can come from voter lists or simply from a phone book. However, organizations or associations to which the people who match the participant profile belong, can also be used. Specific individuals from each list will then be asked to participate. This can be done based on the judgment of the researcher as to who most closely matches the profile or by who is willing to participate.

Steps in the purposive sampling process

Because qualitative research uses fewer participants than quantitative research, it is critical that the correct participants be chosen. Convenience and snowball sampling are straightforward procedures where once the participant profile has been created, the choosing of participants should be fairly easy.

In contrast purposive sampling will take more effort. However, it is the most effective means of ensuring that the correct participants are included in the research study. Once the participant profile or profiles have been created the next step in the process is to determine where individuals who meet these criteria can be found. Of course the organization may have names and addresses of current or former users of the organization. While it is often appropriate to involve people who are already know to the organization as participants in the research, more often research will be used to gather information from people not currently associated with the organization. After all, current users already know and use the organization, what is needed is the viewpoint of others so that the organization might use this information for improvement.

One means of finding a group of people that fits the participant profile is through associations, social clubs, churches, service clubs or any other group that attracts people with similar interests. Most of these organizations attract people who at least have some shared characteristics. If these characteristics match the participant profile, then this organization may be a good place to recruit research participants. For example, if a city's tourism office wants to conduct research on how to make the city more 'bicycle friendly' a local bike club might be a good source of participants. After all these people not only will have the needed knowledge, they will be motivated to participate because they are interested in the city improving its 'bikeability'.

Of course, because of privacy concerns, it is not possible to simply call up and get a list of names and contact information. Instead the researcher should contact the leader of the organization to ask for assistance. Once the purpose of the research has been explained, the leader of the organization may be willing to contact the members to ask for research volunteers. For example, if the research involves the improvement of city parks for families, there might be a local school organization that would be willing to assist.

Not all of the organization's members will meet the profile; therefore a few short screening questions should be created. The local school organization members may all live in the right geographic area and be at the right family stage. However, they may not all be interested in using the public parks. This may be because they just are not familiar with the parks or it might be that they are not physically active. Therefore, when choosing participants the researcher should first ask a screening question such as, 'Do you use the city's parks?' If they answer yes, they would be included in the research. If they answered no, they would be asked 'Do you participate in other physical activities as a family?' If they answer yes, they would be included. If no, they would not as they would not have relevant opinions to share.

These questions could be included in an email or be given verbally over the phone. Once a member of the organization or association has been identified as appropriate they will be sent an invitation to participate. More participants then will be needed should be identified, because not everyone contacted will want to be involved in the research process.

Invitation to participate: Once the groups have been identified and the participants chosen and screened, an invitation to participate should be sent. This may be in the form of an email or letter. Even if the invitation is given verbally, written information should also be provided.

The invitation should give the name of the non-profit organization conducting the research along with names and contact numbers of someone who can be contacted for additional information. Because not everyone who receives an invitation may be familiar with the organization, a short description of the organization's mission should be included. The invitation should describe the purpose of the research along with the potential benefits for the community that might result from the research findings. The details of participation should be clearly explained including the time requirements, location and the issues that will be discussed.

HOW DO YOU SAMPLE THE RICH?

Bank of America wanted to know to what charities households with incomes of over $200,000 donate. They learned that while households making $1 million per year or more are only a small amount of the total population, they contributed almost 15% of all donations. Another fact they learned was that households of over $200,000 donate a larger percentage of total giving to arts and education charities.

Interesting facts, but you may wonder how Bank of America found the rich participants. Quite easily, as they only needed to use US Census data to find neighborhoods were rich people lived. They then randomly choose households from a list of everyone in the area. Proving sampling is not as difficult as it seems.

Source: Chronicle of Philanthropy (2007).

Question to consider: How could we research demographic data available on the census website to help improve our fundraising?

■ Statistical sampling

Quantitative studies do more than simply gather information on consumers' attitudes and opinions. Quantitative studies attempt to support a hypothesis, or a guess, about the source or solution to a problem. These studies can provide 'proof' by using two statistical methods. The first involves statistical sampling to choose the participants that will be involved in the study. The second is the use of statistical tests to analyse the data.

It is not necessary to understand statistics to use these methods. The following is a short summary of what is necessary to understand to determine which random sampling method to use and how to determine the size of the sample. If an organization decides to conduct a large scale statistical study, there are many sources of additional information available in written or online sources.

Census or sample

If a researcher wants to prove with absolute certainty whether a fact is true of an entire group of people, it would be necessary to ask everyone in the group. For example, if someone wants to know with 100% accuracy how many of the ten people in their workplace smoke, they would need to ask everyone. If they only asked nine, none of whom smoked, there is always the chance that the tenth person does smoke. The only way to be absolutely sure would be to ask everyone in the group, or population. When everyone in the population is asked, it is called a census.

Of course if someone wanted to know the smoking rate for the entire country, they could not afford the cost of a study that surveyed all 300 million people living in the USA. Therefore a sample would be asked. Using a sample of the population saves time and money and is the only reasonable alternative when the population is very large or when everyone in the population cannot be reached.

However with a sample, an exact answer with 100% accuracy is impossible. Two questions arise as a result of the impossibility of 100% accuracy. The first question is, 'What level of accuracy is acceptable?' and the second is 'How many people will need to asked to get this level of accuracy?'

The answer to the first question is simple, as there are already established standards such as 90%, of 95% or 97% accuracy that are used by researchers. The higher the level of accuracy that is needed, the more people will need to be included in the study. The answer to the second question is a bit more complicated and use of statistics will be necessary.

The hypothesis

A hypothesis is a guess about the cause or solution to a problem. A statistically valid survey can be used to learn whether this hypothesis can be supported. Of course the hypothesis can never be proved totally true without a census. Therefore, the researchers try to prove the hypothesis false. Because of this fact, the organization will state the hypothesis as the opposite of what is hoped to be true (since the organization is trying to prove the hypothesis wrong). For this reason it is called the null hypothesis, which is designated using shorthand as H_o.

For example, an organization may be wondering if increased fees or ticket prices will result in fewer customers using the organization. Of course, the organization is hoping that this is not true so that it can raise prices.

Sample hypothesis statement

H_o: Ten percent less customers will visit the organization if ticket prices are raised 20%.

The organization is hoping to prove this hypothesis false with a 95% of accuracy. Of course it would be nice to know with 100% accuracy, but to survey everyone in the city who is a possible user of the organization would be too expensive, if not impossible.

The target population and sampling frame

Before tackling the question of how many people need to be included in the sample to gain this level of accuracy, the issue of the population and the sample frame needs to be addressed. When the research process first starts it is not unusual to speak in generalities about asking 'people' their opinion. Just as with qualitative research, when starting to construct a sample to be included in the study, the issue of who are the people or population needs to be clarified.

Questions to clarify population

- *Geographic*: Where does the population live?
- *Demographic*: What are their common characteristics?
- *Psychographic*: What characteristics do people who use our services share?

● *Knowledge*: What level of product or organizational knowledge does this population have?

The next step is to find a list of names of the members of the population or a sampling frame. If the organization wishes to survey current or even former users, this list can be constructed internally using the organization's own records. If the population the organization needs to study are non-users, then getting the names is more difficult. Voter lists and telephone directories can be used as a starting point. Both of these can be limited to the geographic area that is needs to be included in the population. Voter lists will also have information on gender and age. Of course both types of lists will include many individuals who do not meet the population's demographic, psychographic and usage characteristics. For this reason the first questions in a survey will be screening questions that determine eligibility to participate.

Random selection methods

Once the list of population members has been created, the next task is to decide how to choose the individuals who will participate. With probability sampling there is an equal or random chance of every person in the sampling frame being chosen to participate in the research. This method eliminates any potential bias when the researcher makes the decision of whom to include in the research. Probability sampling methods include simple random, systematic and stratified (see Table 6.3).

Table 6.3 Statistical sampling methods	
Method	**Description**
Simple Random	Numbers chosen randomly from list using random number table
Systematic	Numbers chosen randomly from list using skip interval
Stratified	Certain groups chosen for specific characteristics

Simple random sampling: This sample method gives every name on the list of population members the same chance of being chosen. For example, the sampling frame that is used may be a list of 1,000 past users of the organization's services that are in alphabetical order. If everyone on the list meets the participant profile it would seem to be an easy task to choose the 200 that are needed to be included in the study. After all, they can simply choose the first 200 on the list. However, this will lead to bias in the choice as the family names of people can depend on ethnic background. The participants would be mostly those with names that start with letters early in the alphabet. A way around this dilemma is to choose the names randomly. Putting the names in a hat would be a very low tech solution. However, a better means is to use a random number table. These tables can be easily found online. The researcher takes the first digit listed in the table, which might be 634, and includes in the sample the 634 name on the sampling frame list. If the next number is 29, the researcher will do the same, and so on until all 200 names are chosen randomly.

Systematic sampling: This method is easier than using a random number table and is almost as free from bias. With this method, every name in the sample frame is given a number. Then a skip interval is calculated by dividing the total number of names in the sampling frame by the number of participants needed, or 1,000 divided by 200, which is 20. The researcher then systematically goes down the list choosing every twentieth name. To increase the randomness, an alphabetical list can first be scrambled so that people with the same list name will not be listed together.

Stratified sampling: This method is used when the researchers believe that people's responses to a research question will vary depending on their geographic, psychographic or demographic characteristics. Stratified sampling will allow the researcher to isolate groups with specific characteristics and then compare the answers to the group as a whole. The groups might be based on demographic factors such as gender, age or ethnic background. For example, an arts organization might want to know why members of the community in general do not attend performances. However, they may have a special interest in knowing more about why young people and ethnic group members do not attend. When the sample is constructed it is ensured that enough young people or ethnic group members are included. The process can start with simple random or systematic sampling. However once the participants are identified they will be reviewed and if they do not include enough young or ethnic group members, these names will be added even if that means they are not chosen randomly.

Sample size concepts

Once the sampling method has been chosen, the final step is to determine the number of people that must be included in the study so that the hypothesis can be disproved. While it is important that enough people are included, there is no reason to include more as adding additional participants increases the cost of the research. If the sampling frame of the population has been carefully chosen, a small sample can be adequately representative of the whole.

There are a few concepts that must be understood before the researcher can calculate the necessary number of participants. First, the more variation in the population the higher the number of participants required. For example, a health provider may want to know if the services they offer are meeting the needs of the community. If the community is similar demographically, such as most being mostly older, fewer participants will be needed as there will be similarity in their needs. However if the community consists of older, younger, family and single residents, more participants will be needed to ensure that enough participants of all groups are included in the study.

The second concept is the precision that is expected. This is the range between the calculated answer and the true answer that would be known only if the all members of the population were included in the study. For example, a survey question might ask what ticket prices older people are willing to pay to attend the opera, from which an average price would be calculated. The organization must decide on how large a range or interval they are willing to tolerate between the average tabulated from the survey responses and the true answer that would be known only if everyone in the population was asked this question.

A third factor that must be considered when determining sample size is the need for confidence that the research findings reflect the reality of the total population. Total accuracy requires a census of all participants. Since this is not possible, the organization must decide what level of confidence they need that the survey data accurately reflects the whole. The higher the confidence required, the larger the sample must be (Table 6.4).

Table 6.4 Factors to consider when determining sample size

Factor	Affect on sample size
Variation within the population	More variation means larger sample
Precision needed of range between given answer and true answer	Smaller range means larger sample
Confidence that research findings represent population as a whole	Higher confidence means larger sample

Calculating the size of the sample

To calculate the required size of a sample, the organization does not need to know the size of the entire population. What is needed for the mathematical formula used to calculate the sample size is the variation in the population, the acceptable range of the estimated answer from the true answer and the confidence level that the calculated answer is correct. The basic formula used for calculating the sample size needed when conducting a survey whose answers will be expressed in averages is quite simple.

Calculating the sample size

$$n = \frac{z^2}{H^2} {}^{est}Ó^2$$

In this formula, n represents the number needed in the sample. The symbol z represents the confidence level that is needed that the answer is accurate for the population as a whole. For example, these numbers, or z-scores, are 1.65 for 90% confidence and 1.96 for 95%. Other z-scores can be found online. H is the half precision or one half of the range that the average from the survey results can be from the answer that is true for the population as a whole. The symbol Ó represents the variation in the whole population, which can be estimated. Using these three numbers the needed sample size can be calculated.

For example, a theatre might be very interested in determining what annual fee to charge to belong to the 'Friends' association. Of these three numbers, the z-score is a given and does not need to be calculated by the researcher. The researcher only needs to know that the theatre wants to be 95% confident that the answer represents the whole population. In addition, the theatre company will supply the range. They might state that they want the answer to be within a $25 plus or minus range. So this leaves only the variation in the population that the researcher needs to calculate.

IT'S NOT AS DIFFICULT AS YOU THINK!

Even if the organization does know the size of the population, calculating the sample size can be easy. In fact it can be done online! All you need to know is the confidence level you require, whether 90%, 95% or even 97%. In addition you must know the range that you are willing to tolerate that the survey answer is from the true answer for the entire population. Don't believe it can be so easy? Go to http://www.surveysystem.com/sscalc.htm to use the Sample Size Calculator. It is a good way to see how the needed sample size changes when the range and confidence level.

Source: Creative Research Systems (2007).

Question to consider: What type of statistically valid survey research could be conduct?

Normal distribution and variation: To understand the variability of data it is not necessary to have an advanced knowledge of statistics. However, when discussing variability the terms parameter and statistic need to be understood. For example, if a researcher could conduct a census on how much all adults are willing to spend to join the Friends, a true mean or average could be calculated. This number is called the parameter. Of course to conduct a census is too expensive and time consuming so the researcher surveys a sample of adults. From this data is calculated a number, or statistic, which is used as an estimate of the entire population. In this case, the statistic is the average people who are willing to pay.

Perhaps the researcher wants to make sure that this statistic is an accurate estimate of the entire population so the survey is conducted a second time with a new sample. The same sampling procedure is chosen and the same number of subjects is asked the research question. However, the sample will now consist of different individuals. The researcher again calculates the statistic. If the researcher could survey every possible sample in the population, this will result multiple average answers. If all the resulting average answers were examined, it would be found that some answers occur more frequently than others.

This similarity results from the fact that members of the population have characteristics in common, which means that many people will behave in similar ways. However, there will also be some whose behaviour will vary as some people are willing to pay very little while some will be very generous. However, most people will fall somewhere inbetween. When the similarities and differences are shown visually they will result in a graph where the most commonly resulting mean is in the middle with diminishing returns or either side for numbers that are higher and lower. This is the classic 'normal' or bell distribution curve.

Fortunately most data will fit a normal distribution curve and, therefore, the variability within a population can be estimated. Normal variability is considered to be plus or minus three standard deviations away from the true value. Therefore, the researcher can take an estimated range of variability and calculate the variation. For example, the theatre may estimate that the range in acceptable fees would be from $50 for adults with limited incomes to a high of $500 for the wealthiest adults. This gives a range of $450. Since the standard deviation is plus or minus three on each side, the researcher divides the number 450 by six. This gives the variability of the population, which would be $75.

Using the example above, the sample size for the study of how much people are willing to pay annually to belong to the Friends organization can be calculated.

Sample calculation

$$35 = \frac{1.96^2}{25^2} 75^2$$

For the estimate to be 95% with a range of 25 each way and standard variability, only 35 adults from the sample frame need to participate in the survey. However, a total of range of 50 when the variation is only 450 is quite large. Perhaps the theatre would like the answer to be more accurate. They may decide to change the range from $50 to $15. Now the sample size changes to 96. If the theatre narrows the acceptable range to only 5, the sample size necessary changes to 864! Likewise changing the confidence level will affect the sample size.

Calculating sample size when estimating a population proportion: The theatre company may also be interested in calculating a proportion, such as the proportion or percentage of theatre goers who would be interested in joining the Friends organization. In this case the z-score of confidence level will be chosen and the range estimated. The confidence level might still be 95% and the acceptable range could be within plus or minus 3% of the true answer.

However, the difficulty arises when the researcher needs a number to represent variability in the population as a whole, which for a proportion is represented by the symbol π. In this case, theoretically, the vari-ation can run from 0% to 100% of the total population. But, the theatre knows that this is too wide an estimate of variability as they can estimate that at least 20% of theatre goers are interested in joining and 20% not inter-ested. Therefore the variability is set at 40% or half of 80%. The resulting sample size needed is 1,024.

Formula and calculation

$$n = \frac{z^2}{H^2}\, \pi(1 - \pi)$$

$$1024 = \frac{1.96^2}{0.03^2}\, 0.4(1 - 0.04)$$

So, to estimate a percentage of the population as being representa-tive of the entire population takes a much larger sample. Why does the proportion take such a larger sample size? The answer lies in the range compared to the variation. In the calculation involving an average, the range was 50, which is 11% of the total variation of 450 (50/450 = 0.11). However with the proportion example, the range of 6% (plus or minus 3%) compared with a possible variation of 100% in the population as a whole. Because more precision is needed to estimate within 6% than with 11%, a larger sample is needed.

Summary

- Choosing the participants for the research study is as important as determining the research question and methodology. For both qualitative and quantitative studies, the organization must determine a profile of who should be included in the research. This can involve demographic, psychographic, geographic and usage characteristics. The organi-zation may need to consider providing incentives to participate. The organization must be careful to avoid common participant problems.

- Qualitative sampling procedures include convenience when the researcher goes to a location where individuals who meet the participant profile can be found. The snow-ball method first finds one participant that meets the profile, and then that participant recruits others. Purposive sampling uses the members of clubs or associations to find individuals who meet the profile.

- Most research studies use sampling of a population rather than a census. If statistical sampling is used, it can be said that a null hypothesis is disproved. A sample is chosen from a list of the entire population. Simple random, systematic or stratified methods of choosing participants can be used. To calculate how many people will need to participate in a study to make the results statistically valid the researcher needs the variance in the population, the range that the organization is willing to tolerate between the estimated answer and the true answer and the confidence level. A larger sample is needed to have a statistically valid answer when the question calls for a proportion or percentage than for an average or mean.

■ References

Callow, M. (2004) 'Identifying promotional appeals for targeting potential volunteers: An exploratory study on volunteering motives among retirees', *International Journal of Nonprofit and Volunteer Sector Marketing*, Vol. 9, No. 3.

Chronicle of Philanthropy (2007) '31% of donations by individuals benefit the poor, study finds', *Chronicle of Philanthropy*, 26 July.

Creative Research Systems (2007) 'Sample Size Calculator' Downloaded 1 August 2007 from http://www.surveysystem.com/sscalc.htm.

Kazakina, K. (2006) 'Auction offers unique rings: Philip glass among composers crafting cell dingles', *Globe and Mail*, 27 March.

Saros (2007) 'Welcome to Saros' Retrieved 4 February 2007 from http://www.sarosresearch.com/main-index.html.

Stewart, D.W., P.N. Shamdasani and D.W. Rook (2007) *Focus Groups: Theory and Practice*, SAGE Publications.

CHAPTER 7

Conducting
focus groups

Objectives

- Introduce the advantages and disadvantages of conducting focus groups
- Describe the focus group process from planning to analysis
- Explain the steps in conducting a focus group
- Explore the importance of the moderator's role
- Discuss the handling of conflict in focus groups

■ Introduction

Focus groups are one of the most commonly used marketing research tools. The reason for their popularity is that marketing is concerned with meeting the needs and wants of people. Organizations meet these needs and wants by providing products with the benefits that people desire. Focus groups are an excellent means of obtaining this information. While non-profit organizations have a mission that predetermines their product they can still 'package' or enhance their product by providing additional benefits. Focus groups can also provide information that will assist the non-profit in finding new market segments and improving their promotional campaigns.

By conducting focus groups, the non-profit organization can learn about the thoughts, opinions, attitudes and ideas of both current and future customers. This information is then used to improve the organization's product and promotion. To make effective use of this methodology the organization needs to understand the steps in conducting a focus group and also have access to someone with the skills needed to be a moderator. A focus group may not provide a definitive answer to a problem, but what people have to say will always provide the organization with new ideas.

■ Focus group methodology

Focus groups are a qualitative research technique that uses participant interaction to uncover consumers' attitudes, opinions and values. Focus groups are considered exploratory research because an issue or problem is being explored. For this reason focus groups are often one of the first choices of research methodology when little is known about the cause of a problem. Once focus groups have been used as a first step in exploring an issue, the findings can be confirmed using a quantitative research technique such as a survey.

Focus groups are sometimes misunderstood as mere discussion groups where people just talk while a moderator listens. However, a well designed focus group conducted by a trained moderator is much more. The purpose of a focus group is to encourage participants to go beyond their first response to the issue being discussed. Interaction with the moderator and also between the group members is designed to uncover deeper insights which can be used to develop new and creative ideas for the marketing mix. In addition, these insights can then be communicated to groups within the organization to build the case for support of the marketing programme (Hanson, 2001).

Focus groups do not start with a hypothesis about the cause of a problem. Instead they are used to generate new ideas for the organization. In addition they can be used to explore reasons for an organization's problems or failures. In a focus group ideas for a new consumer segment to target, new ways of packaging a product and more effective promotion can be generated.

Purposes of conducting focus groups

- Exploring the cause of a problem or issue
- New market segments to target
- Enhancing the product to increase its appeal
- Developing effective promotional campaigns

Exploring problems: When an organization has a problem, it is tempting to try to solve the issue internally. However, the employees of the organization can only see the problem from their own viewpoint. While these insights are important it is extremely helpful to get the opinions of current or potential consumers as to the cause of the problem. For example, if attendance is falling at the annual 'Adopt an Animal Friend' fair, the organization might consider the problem to be lack of promotion or the wrong location for the event. Rather than decide these assumptions might be correct, they should ask the opinions of potential attendees. By conducting a focus group they might learn that people do not attend the Fair because they are afraid they will be made to feel guilty if they leave the event without adopting. Using this information the organization could then revise their promotion to stress that simply attending helps the organization by building awareness.

New market segments: A non-profit organization has a mission to serve the needs of the public by providing its product or service. The best way to communicate with the public is by designing a message that is targeted at a specific group. This does not mean the organization does not want everyone to use their product, it means that the limited marketing budget must be used carefully by targeting specific groups. While the organization might think in terms of targeting groups demographically, there is a growing trend to target psychographically based on shared lifestyles, attitudes or values. Focus groups can be used to learn what psychographic groups can be targeted by the organization. For example, a local history museum might discover in a focus group that people new to the community often feel disconnected from its past. The museum could target this group of new-comers with a marketing message that communicates that the museum is a perfect place to learn more about their new home.

Enhancing the product: Of course, the success of any new product or service introduced by an organization will depend on its acceptance by the potential customers. Therefore, it simply makes sense to ask these potential customers for input into the benefits the product should provide. This does not mean that the organization will only offer what the public desires. While a focus group will not determine the product, it can help the organization package the product to make it more appealing. By using ideas from potential customers, the organization has a better chance of having their product or service be successful. For example, a religious organization may have decided to offer classes to their members on the tenets of their faith. A focus group with potential attendees would not determine the content of the classes. However, it could help the organization develop the type of classes that would have the most appeal. This could involve the time and day of the classes, where they should be located, how long they should last and what other inducements, whether desert and coffee or wine and cheese, should be added. The content stays the same, but participant input will be used to package the product so it is as appealing as possible.

Developing promotional campaigns: A final purpose for having a focus group is to gain new insights as to how the organization can best communicate with the public. The non-profit organization's product will be determined by its mission, which is its reason for existence. However, the non-profit organization cannot know how to communicate their message to the public without input from those in the target market segment it is trying to reach. Focus groups can be invaluable in determining both the marketing message and how it is communicated. After all only those who are on the receiving end of the message can know what words should be used to describe the benefits of the product.

Advantages of focus groups

Quantitative research methods answer the questions of who, how many and how often. Only qualitative research answers the question of why. Focus groups are particularly useful when wanting to get beyond a participant's first answer by asking probing follow up questions. Because non-profit organizations often deal in products that have an emotional meaning, it is important to understand people's reaction to the organization and its product.

For example, an art gallery may want to know why people are not attending its opening nights. The first response they might obtain is that people do not have the time, or can not afford to attend. Being too busy or too poor to attend are both 'acceptable' answers. However if the organization wants to know even more after they have received these answers, in a focus group the moderator can continue to ask probing questions. After all people have the time and money to attend other events. Continually probing for additional responses may uncover the fact that people feel intimidated by attending an opening night as they envision they are only for the 'art' crowd. It will take a focus group to uncover this fact, as adults do not want to readily admit to feeling intimidated.

An additional advantage of conducting focus groups is that they can be combined with other research methodologies such as projective techniques. The organization may have thought long and hard over what questions to ask research participants. However, to the participants the question comes as a surprise and they may have difficulty coming up with a response. A focus group can be combined with projective techniques that provide the participants with a non-verbal means of answering a question. In addition, these techniques will help participants to think creatively and should result in more thoughtful discussions.

Advantages of conducting focus groups

- Probes issues in depth
- Interaction between participants can spark new ideas
- Combine with projective techniques

Disadvantages of focus groups

Focus groups cannot be used to prove or disprove a hypothesis. The data that a focus group collects are words and sometimes images, but not quantitative data that can be statistically manipulated. The researchers should also understand that while the information collected in a focus group can be very helpful in making decisions on what consumers to target along with product packaging and promotion ideas, they should not be the only basis for such decisions. If a focus group has provided input that suggests a drastic or expensive change to the current marketing mix, this idea should be further researched before proceeding with the change. The number of people in a focus group is too small to generalize the findings to the entire population.

Another disadvantage that is inherent in the focus group methodology is the fact that the results that are obtained depend on the skill of the moderator. A well-moderated focus group can provide useful information. However, an unskilled moderator will be unable to use follow-up questions to move beyond the participants' initial responses to uncover underlying ideas. Worse, a poor moderator may result in a group where disagreement turns into conflict and the participants will leave with a poor impression of the organization based on the choice of moderator.

Disadvantages of conducting focus groups

- Can not be used to prove facts
- Results depend on skill of moderator

**A SPANISH LANGUAGE PUBLIC TELEVISION STATION!
WHO WOULD HAVE THOUGHT OF IT?**

A focus group, that's who! The new Spanish language public television network is called V-me and is being carried by 18 stations. The network is being partially sponsored by the investment firm Baeza Group whose chairman, a Cuban-American, had searched for educational programs in Spanish for his own children. However it was the information from focus groups that encouraged the start of the venture. The focus groups found that there was a huge demand for educational programs in Spanish that was not being met by the current Spanish language stations, which mostly broadcast telenovelas. Only through asking, did the researchers learn about this new product idea.

Source: Jensen (2007).

Question to consider: What new product ideas could we explore using focus groups?

■ Preparation of focus group methodology

A well-run focus group that provides insightful information for the organization does not just happen. If an organization watches a skilled moderator conduct a focus group it may seem effortless. However as with many skilled activities, the sense of effortlessness derives from the fact that a great deal of time has gone into the design and planning of the group. The focus group process involves three stages of preparation, conducting and analysis (Stewart *et al.*, 2007).

The process of planning a focus group starts with a meeting between the researchers and management. At this meeting they will decide who should participate in the research and also decide who should moderate the group. The next step in the preparation would be to decide what issues should be covered during the group and then to write a focus group script. Conducting the focus group involves preparation of the facility and any additional material or techniques that will be used. Once the facility and materials are prepared, the focus group will be conducted. Immediately after concluding the group, the moderator will gather and label all written information produced during the group. The analysis stage of the focus group methodology involves transcribing the tapes and organizing the written information. Once this has been completed, the moderator will code the information for themes. After the themes have been analysed, the moderator will write the report and make a presentation (see Table 7.1).

Table 7.1 Focus group methodology process	
Stage	**Task**
Preparation	Discuss issues
	Decide participant profile
	Choose moderator
	Write focus group script
Conducting	Prepare facility
	Prepare materials and techniques
	Moderate proceedings
	Collect and organize data
Analysis	Transcribe information
	Organize written data
	Code for themes
	Write report
	Make presentation

Focus group preparation

The first step in the focus group preparation process is to hold a meeting with everyone who is concerned. The importance of this meeting cannot be over emphasized, as everyone who has a stake in the outcome of the research should be involved in the planning. While the research question may already have been determined, it is now necessary to decide exactly what issues should be discussed in the focus group.

For example a focus group on attitudes toward neighbourhood redevelopment might be designed to address the research question on how neighbourhood safety can be improved. This general question then might be broken down into subject areas of perceptions of safe and unsafe neighbourhoods, the ideal safe neighbourhood and what steps should be taken to make neighbourhoods feel safer. This progression of issues would be designed to start the focus group participants with a subject they know, their own neighbourhood. It would progress to the more challenging topics that require the participants to describe an ideal neighbourhood. Finally, it would ask the most challenging question of how these changes could be implemented in their own neighbourhood (see Table 7.2).

All of the above questions will be general, so follow up questions will need to be asked. In addition the questions should start with the easiest and then progress to the more difficult. It is also important that the questions stay focused. Management may want to include in the focus group more topic areas then can be covered in the session and may give the researcher a long list of question topics. However an hour long focus group session with eight participants does not result in eight hours of discussion, but only one. In addition the focus group topics must be related. If a focus group is to be successful, it cannot jump from one topic

Table 7.2 Topics areas stated as questions

Topic	Question
Current status of safety in neighbourhood	What places in your neighbourhood feel unsafe?
People and perception of safety	What types of activities make you feel unsafe in your neighbourhood?
The ideal neighbourhood	How would you describe how a neighbourhood makes you feel safe?
Neighbourhood improvement	What change would make your neighbourhood feel safer?

to another. It takes time to develop the rapport that makes the participants willing to discuss challenging issues.

After the focus group discussion topics have been chosen, the next step in the process is to develop the participant profile. Because fewer participants will be involved in a focus group methodology than in a survey, it is especially important that the correct participants be choosen.

Choosing an appropriate moderator is also important. A larger organization may have someone on staff that can perform this function. However it may be necessary to recruit someone from outside the organization to perform this task. If the funds are available the organization can hire a professional moderator. If not, a board member may have access to a company that would be willing to provide a moderator on a pro bono basis. If these options are not available, the organization may wish to contact a nearby educational institution to determine if they have someone on staff who is willing to provide assistance.

The final step is to write the focus group script. This is the plan for how the group will proceed from the initial greetings to the conclusion. A focus group usually involves three stages of building rapport, probing and closing. The first stage is used to introduce the members to the subject and then present them with an easy to answer question. The focus group moderator will then ask more challenging questions. The focus group will move on to a concluding question. Once the script has been prepared, it will be reviewed by management to ensure it adequately covers the topics under discussion (see Table 7.3).

Conducting the focus group

Once the planning of the focus group has been completed, the researchers can move to the next steps. This will include finding a location that is convenient for the participants. In addition the participants must be greeted and made to feel welcome. Only then will the moderator be ready to conduct the focus group.

Table 7.3 Sample focus group script for Senior Center Project		
Stage	**Tasks**	
Building rapport	Purpose: To relax and bond group and to connect group to subject. Method: Welcome and general discussion Question: What is your opinion of Senior Centers? Technique: Hand out cards asking participants to write down the first three words that come to mind when they hear 'Senior Center.'	
Probing	Purpose: To uncover information useful to answering research questions Method: General discussion followed by projective techniques Question: Why do you currently not make use of the activities at Senior Centers? Technique: List negatives on sheets of papers Question: If you could design the activities program for a center, what type of activities would you include? Technique: Ideas generated by participants will be listed on large pieces of paper. Each participant will then be given a gold, silver and bronze sticker to use to vote for their favorite ideas. Question: If you could build a new Senior Center, what would it look like? Technique: Show participants photos of different styles of buildings and have them chose that they find most attractive.	
Closing	Purpose: To move group towards closure Method: General discussion followed by projective technique Question: How should the Senior Centers promote to non users? Technique: Ask participants to complete an advertisement for the Center by listing the benefits, such as fun, health, social, etc.	

Focus group location

A large for-profit corporation or a marketing firm may have a special facility just for conducting focus groups. This facility would have a reception room where participants would be greeted. A separate room with projective equipment for showing video clips, electronic whiteboards and other high tech equipment would be available. Attached to the focus group room, would be an additional room that would be used for viewing the focus group through a one-way window. This room would be used by management to watch the focus group as it was being conducted.

However, there is no need to have such a specialized facility. In fact such a facility, by being so professional, may intimidate some participants. A focus group can be held in any location where eight to ten people can be comfortably seated. In fact, the researchers should consider holding a focus group at the location that is most convenient for the participants. This could be a community centre, church or even a restaurant. If any technical equipment is needed this can be brought in from other locations.

Besides convenience, another reason for conducting the focus group at a location that is known to the participants is that it builds trust and shows respect. For example, research about preventing street crime would need to be conducted using disenfranchised youth as participants. The organization needs the ideas of these youths much more than the youths need to be involved in the research. Conducting the focus group at a community sports facility demonstrates to the participants that their 'world' and therefore their views are respected and will be taken seriously. Another example of the importance of location deals with ethnic participants who are not citizens. They may be uncomfortable in a focus group held in a corporate setting in an office building. No matter how hard the organization tries to make them feel at ease, the setting may be too reminiscent of official government authority. The elderly are another group that needs special consideration when the location is chosen, as travel may be difficult.

The moderator will arrive early to ensure that seating is available. The seating should be placed around a table if the moderator will be using projective techniques that require writing. Refreshments should be available even if it is just water and a sweet treat. The refreshments are a way of welcoming the participants and also provide a common activity that helps to bring people together. The researcher should have a supply of large pieces of paper, various markers and also pens. Large pads of self-stick paper should be available that can be placed on any wall surface, written on and then easily removed. If any special materials are needed for projective techniques there should be adequate copies available. The researcher should have a recorder for taping the proceedings. Digital recorders eliminate the need for switching tapes when the time has been used up. They are small and unobtrusive and even inexpensive ones have excellent sound quality.

Greeting the participants

Once the room has been prepared the moderator is ready to greet the participants. Making the participants feel both welcome and at ease is critical to the success of a focus group. The welcome should be sincere as without the willingness of the participants, the research would be impossible. It is also important that the moderator help the participants feel at ease. Although, the moderator might have been through the focus group process numerous times, it may very well be a new experience for the participants. The moderator should inform them of the seating arrangements, the availability of refreshments and the location of the restrooms.

Once all the participants are seated, introductions should be made. Depending on the situation, only first names or both first and last names, may be used. The moderator should now explain the purpose of the research and the topics that will be covered. The moderator should also explain that the proceedings will be taped, but that the tapes and any other material produced will only be used by those involved in the research. In addition, participants should be reassured that no names will be used in the final report so all information will be held in confidence. Finally, the moderator should inform the participants that they can receive a summary of the findings of the research if they are interested.

**FOCUS GROUP RESEARCH IS TAKEN SERIOUSLY
AT McDONALD'S**

McDonald's serves over 26 million customers a day in the United States alone. So when they introduce a new product, success can mean a huge increase in profits and failure can mean an equally huge loss. Therefore McDonalds has a year long, four stage process of conducting focus group research before a new product is introduced. Why do they take so long? McDonalds knows that it has to get beyond the participant's first response. After all, if you ask someone if they want to eat healthier food, of course the answer will be yes. However McDonalds has learned that only 10% of the participants will actually eat healthier food. Therefore McDonalds continues to research to learn exactly how to package a healthy salad so that it will be bought.

Source: Warner (2005).

Question to consider: What issues do we need to discuss in a focus group because our customers do not give us a true answer?

Focus group stages

The moderator is now ready to start the focus group. A focus group usually lasts from one hour to ninety minutes. The first few minutes will be used in building rapport. The most time will be spent asking probing and follow-up questions. The focus group will then move to the closing stage.

Building rapport: The first part of the focus group is used to build rapport between the moderator and the participants. The first questions asked should be easy ones that pertain to experiences or knowledge all of the participants share. Starting the focus group with challenging questions may intimidate the participants and result in less interaction throughout the remainder of the group session.

It is the moderator's responsibility to encourage active participation while at the same time not making any of the participants feel pressured to speak. This is the 'art' that the moderator performs that may not be understood by others. The moderator must watch and assess the facial expressions of any quiet group members to gauge when will be the right time to encourage them to speak. By keeping the early questions easy to answer and non-threatening and encouraging everyone to speak, the moderator prepares the participants for more challenging questions later in the focus group.

Probing: After the initial stage of the focus group, the moderator will move to more probing questions. These are questions that ask the participants to explore more deeply their attitudes, opinions and ideas. In addition probing questions ask participants to imagine a reality different in some way from what they experienced. These questions do not just ask 'why', they also ask 'what if'. This probing stage will take up most of the time of the focus group. These questions, because they are challenging, may require follow-up questions to clarify the participant's meaning.

Sample probing questions

- Tell me more?
- When did you start to feel this way?
- What do you mean by unhappy?
- Can you clarify what you mean when you say 'frequently?'
- How do the employees make you feel 'good'?

During the probing stage the moderator may use various methods to help the participants articulate their ideas including showing products and developing lists. In addition, projective techniques can be used during the focus group. It is very helpful if the moderator has an assistant to help with these tasks. By using an assistant, the moderator can continue to focus on the discussion without distraction.

Interaction can be used to uncover additional information while maintaining interest. If the focus group is discussing a product, the moderator may have a sample available to view. For example, the focus group might be asked to address how to increase membership in the 'Friends' organization. One issue to be discussed would be what type of gift should be offered for membership. Having sample gifts available for the participants to examine will help prompt answers.

The product could also be the layout of the clinic's waiting room that the organization is considering changing. In this case showing a computer projection of the layout would be helpful. Another example of where showing a product would be helpful is when a focus group is being used to judge the community reaction to a controversial new artist. A short video clip of the artist's work could be shown to the participants rather than have the moderator attempt to explain the work.

When ideas are being discussed during the focus groups, they can be listed on large sheets of paper for everyone to view. The reason for this technique is so that the participants have a reminder of what has been said. The lists can then be organized to summarize comments by themes. The moderator can then ask if anything of importance is missing. Another useful technique is for the moderator to ask the participants to prioritize what is listed. This can be done by giving the participants different colour labels to place by the items they consider first, second and third in importance. This not only provides valuable insights; it also gets the participants up and moving. If the participants cannot or do not wish to move, the assistant can place the stickers on the items. Finally, these lists will be useful for the moderator when using analysing the proceedings.

Projective techniques, which allow nonverbal responses, can also be used to assist the participants in answering the questions. Standard projective techniques include word association, sentence completion and card sorts. Simple projective tasks, such as asking the participants to write down the first three words they think of when the organization's name is mentioned, are excellent ways to have everyone participate and start the conversation flowing. However, the moderator can develop her or his own task. Using the example of the focus group on redesigning the clinic's waiting room, the participants could be given a blueprint and cutouts of various types of furniture and asked to create their own floor plans.

During the focus group not only will the moderator interact with the participants, the moderator will also encourage interaction between members. The moderator can do so by asking participants to respond to each other's questions.

Sample questions to encourage interaction

- Do you agree with what Kim has just said?
- Have you also had this experience?
- What do you think of the idea?
- Would you suggest a different solution than Sean's?

The moderator will use these techniques to encourage everyone to become involved. However, the moderator should never push participants to speak when they seem uncomfortable. Even though the conversation should always be non-threatening, a question may have resulted in an unpleasant memory that the participant does not wish to share. A moderator is not acting as a psychologist trying to have participants share thoughts and memories that are troubling or painful. The purpose of a focus group is research, not therapy.

The moderator should also be aware of the possibility of conflict between the participants. While a conversation may become intense, it should never be allowed to cross the line into anger. It is the moderator's responsibility to watch for signs of personal animosity between the participants and defuse it immediately. The moderator can do so by first acknowledging the feelings. After the moderator has acknowledged that the participants have strong responses to the topic, the participants are reminded that the purpose of the focus group is to provide helpful input. If the moderator does not diffuse the anger, the other participants will feel uncomfortable and stop participating.

Closing: With about 10 minutes remaining in the focus group, the moderator will move to the closing stage. The moderator will use this time to gather final thoughts or ideas. The closing stage also allows the participants to disengage from what may have been an intense experience. This time should also be used to thank the participants for their assistance. Besides just general thanks, the moderator should mention one or two of the ideas that were generated during the group that the organization may find particularly useful. The participants should leave with the feeling that the time and effort they have contributed has been helpful. Finally, the moderator will remind the participants that they may get a summary of the research findings if they wish. The only task remaining is for the moderator to collect and label any written material that was produced during the focus group process.

**ARE ALL GIVERS EQUAL? FOCUS GROUPS WERE
USED TO LEARN THE ANSWER**

It is becoming increasingly popular to donate to charities using direct payment where an amount is taken directly from the givers bank account at regular intervals. Researchers wanted to know more about the attitudes of people who chose this method. To do so, ten focus groups were held with participants drawn from the donor lists of five different types of charitable organizations. The participants were paid a $50 incentive for participation.

What was learned was that even among those that elect to support a charity on a continuing basis, the motivations varied. Some were motivated by an active commitment to the organization. While others continued to support the organization simply because they hadn't gotten around to canceling the direct debit!

Source: Sargeant (2005).

Questions to consider: How can we use a focus group to learn more about our donors' behaviour?

■ Choosing a moderator

The success of a focus group is dependent on the skill of the moderator. Of course, it is important to have the right research question and the correct participants. But even when these factors are present, if the moderator is unskilled, the focus group will not obtain the needed information. However, a skilled moderator will be able to obtain useful information even if the research question is too broad or poorly stated and the participants not as motivated as would be desired.

The characteristics of successful moderators include both inherent personal traits and skills that have been learned. The personal traits that are necessary in a moderator include interest in the research process, curiosity about people's ideas, adaptability and empathy. The skills of a successful moderator include knowledge of research methods, the topic under discussion and group dynamics. In addition they must be able to analyse and report the findings.

Personal traits

Some of the characteristics that determine whether a person will be a successful focus group moderator are inborn and can not be learned. It is easy to be interested and enthusiastic the first time someone runs a focus group. However, it is more difficult for the tenth or one hundredth focus group. For this reason the moderator must be interested in the process of research. If this is true, the moderator will approach each focus group with enthusiasm.

Successful moderators are interested in people's ideas. This is actually a different trait than being interested in people. The moderator is not a therapist who is going to explore the life stories and feelings of the participants. The personal life of participants is only relevant in regard to how it affects their attitudes and opinions about the product. Instead the moderator wants to learn more about their ideas. In fact too much emphasize on the emotions of the participants can lead moderators into situations they are not trained to handle.

Successful moderators need to be adaptable to whatever situation arises during the research process. While moderators must come to the session with a script prepared, they must also be able to change their approach as needed. For example, a focus group might have been planned to discuss what activities a teen centre should provide. However, the community leaders who are in the focus group might argue that unless something is first done to reach out and build trust with troubled youths, a teen centre will not be utilized no matter what activities it offers. The moderator must then focus the discussion on how this trust can be established.

Finally, moderators must be able to emphasize with the focus group participants. Empathy includes both understanding and compassion. At times the focus group participants will be from a community or practice a lifestyle with which the moderator is unfamiliar. The moderator must be able to look past the differences to understand the common elements that bind all people together. Particularly when working with non-profit human services organizations, moderators may work with individuals who have problems, such as with substance abuse or violence. The moderator must be able to look with compassion on those whose personal issues have led them to make poor choices. Wise moderators knows their own limits and does not work with populations with which they can not emphasize.

Personal traits of a successful moderator

- Interest in research process
- Curiosity about people's ideas
- Adaptability
- Empathy

Needed skills

Interest, curiosity, adaptability and empathy are inborn personal traits that can be enhanced, if present, but cannot be learned. Moderators can learn the other needed skills. First, successful focus group moderators should know about other available research methodologies. They should understand the uses and limitations of all qualitative and quantitative techniques. This knowledge is necessary so that focus group moderators will know when they are being asked to conduct research that is better handled by another technique. For example, an organization that provides free meals delivered to the elderly might decide they need a focus group to determine what food items are preferred. However this task, which does not require in-depth discussion, can be handled best by use of a survey. If a moderator does not understand what technique is best for each situation, they will find themselves in focus groups that are not successful because the technique is the wrong choice.

Successful focus group moderators will familiarize themselves with the research topic under study. This knowledge will help ensure the success of a group because the moderator will be familiar with any terminology used by focus group participants. They will also be better able to explore any underlying issues that the participants may be skirting. For example, a focus group on arts attendance might find the participants stating that they do not attend because they can not afford the ticket price. The moderator should already be aware that the organization has low priced tickets and also that most people will give a high price as a reason for non-attendance. With this knowledge the moderator will continue to probe even after receiving the first response, to get at the underlying reason for non-attendance.

It is essential that the moderator be skilled in group dynamics. A successful moderator will understand that disagreement is part of the focus group process. If everyone during the focus group session is in agreement, nothing new will be learned. Successful moderators are not frightened of conflict. Instead they know how to use disagreement to discover ideas without allowing disagreement to degenerate into conflict. The moderator will keep the group focused on the ideas and never allow personal attacks.

Finally, in addition to the skills necessary to conduct a group, the moderator must also have the ability to analyse and report the findings. With other methodologies the tasks of conducting the study and analysing the findings can be separated. The person who writes a survey form does not need to be the person who analyses the statistical results. However with focus groups it is not enough to have someone else listen to the tapes and analyse what was said. The insights of the moderator are critical to understanding the findings. How people respond to a question even their silences, provide critical insights that help to answer the research question.

Skills needed by a successful moderator

- Knowledge of research methods
- Knowledge of the topic under discussion
- Skill in group dynamics
- Ability to analyse and report

BE CAREFUL WHAT YOU PUT INTO THE REPORT

The US States of Vermont and New Hampshire have long been rivals. However, the rivalry became more heated after a remark made by a consultant hired by the Lake Champlain Regional Chamber of Commerce in Vermont. The consultant had been hired to develop a brand identity for the city of Burlington, Vermont. To do so, the consultant held focus groups where participants were asked about their perceptions of both New Hampshire and Vermont. One comment made by a participant was that New Hampshire was, 'nice-looking but rather drab state with little to do, no hub of civilization, just somewhere to pass through'.

Unfortunately the remark became public and was soon in the newspapers and online. As a result the vice president of the Lake Champlain chamber had to publicly apologize and state that the people of Vermont love the people of New Hampshire. People's frank opinions are exactly what you want in a focus group. However, they are for private analysis, not public consumption.

Source: Zezima (2007).

Question to consider: How do we ensure the confidentiality of research findings?

■ Handling group conflict

While a focus group moderator should not be afraid of disagreement, it is their responsibility to never let disagreement cross the line into conflict. There are two possible sources of conflict within a focus group. The first source of conflict is inappropriate behaviour by group members. This might include participants who try to dominate the group by continually talking and participants who believe they are experts on the topic. The second source of conflict is inherent in the group process itself (Puchta and Jonathan, 2004).

Handling difficult participants

While it would be wonderful if every participant was an emotionally mature adult whose only purpose in attending the group was to further the cause of research, this will not be the case. If it were true, there would hardly be any need for a group moderator. However, in every focus group there will be participants that will require extra attention. Two of the most common sources of conflict are the incessant talker and the group expert.

Incessant talkers usually have a strong need for attention. If not control-led, they will tend to dominate the other participants and cause feelings of resentment. A skilled moderator will become aware of the presence of such a participant early in the process. These participants usually tend to spend more time talking even when first introducing themselves to the group. During the group they will insert themselves in the conversation even when others are making important comments. Once moderators become aware of that a participant is an incessant talker, they must step in to redirect the conversation when necessary. They will need to kindly but firmly interrupt the talker with a simple statement such as, 'Thanks for the interesting idea but I am going to ask Maria to first finish her comment. And then let us hear what others think'. The moderator will need to continue to use this technique as incessant talkers rarely have the self-awareness to understand they are dominating the conversation.

Sometimes participants will take on the role of group expert. They will assume that only they know the right answer to any question. This type of participant will even tend to correct the ideas of other participants. If the expert speaks in a knowledgeable manner, the other participants may defer to their judgement and stop providing their own insights. Or, the other participants may start to feel resentful and argue with the self-proclaimed expert. The moderator's responsibility is to provide support that all participants' opinions are equally welcome and valid. A statement such as, 'Joe thanks for your thoughts, but Maria's opinions are also important; Maria can you tell us more?' may need to be used.

Group formation and conflict

All groups go through predictable stages. This process is inherent in how people communicate and interact socially and can not, and should not, be avoided. For this reason the moderator should have some knowledge of group dynamics. One of the most common theories was developed by studying the formation of work groups. However, it is also useful in understanding how focus group dynamics work. The Tuckman model describes four stages of group development; forming, storming, norming and performing.

Forming: According to this model all groups start with the forming stage. During this period the group members, who are strangers, make quick judgements about each other. This is a predictable and necessary step so that they can make decisions on how to treat each other. During the forming stage each participant will decide who they like, who they dislike, who they trust and who they do not trust. These decisions are based on past interactions and may have no bearing on the present reality.

The moderator can help the group through this stage by relating a positive characteristic about each participant and why they were chosen to be part of the group. The goal would be to reinforce the legitimacy of each participant's involvement in the process while still allowing people to form their own opinions of the other participants.

Storming: During the storming stage the group members will state strong opinions that may be in disagreement with the opinions of others. A participant in fact may attempt to argue with someone of whom they have a negative opinion. That participants have strong feelings and opinions is a positive sign that the focus group could result in new and interesting findings. However, all participants must feel that the moderator is in charge of the situation and will diffuse any disagreement that may escalate.

Norming: Moderators handle this stage by not getting caught up in the conflict themselves. The moderator handles the storming stage by acknowledging and even thanking all arguing participants for their ideas. The moderator then reminds the participants of the larger purpose of the group and refocuses the discussion at the proper emotional level. They use their skill to move the group to the norming stage where everyone understands the limitations that will be placed on individual members.

Performing: Once all the participants understand that the moderator will not let the conversation degenerate into personal animosity, the group enters into its performing stage where the real work of the focus group can be accomplished.

Stages of group dynamics

- Forming: Participants meet and make snap decision about each other based on past experiences
- Storming: Snap decision can result in argumentative behaviour
- Norming: Moderator establishes behaviour limitations through example
- Performing: Group can now get to work on task.

Summary

■ Focus groups are used to learn about current and potential customers' opinions, attitudes and ideas. They can be used to explore problems, find new market segments and improve the product and its promotion. Focus groups have the advantage of allowing the researcher to probe issues in depth. The interaction between participants can result in new and creative ideas. The disadvantages of focus groups are that the results cannot be used to prove facts and are dependent on the skill of the moderator.

■ The focus group process involves a preparation stage where the issues, participants and moderator are decided upon. A focus group script is then written. Conducting a focus group involves preparing the facility, preparing the needed materials, moderating the group and collecting the data. After the focus group the tapes are transcribed, the written data is organized and then coded. Finally, the report is written and an oral presentation is made.

■ Before the focus group begins, an appropriate location must be chosen. The actual moderating of the group will go through the stages of building rapport, probing and closing. During the probing stage questions will be used to encourage participants to explore their ideas more fully.

■ A successful focus group depends on a skilled moderator. The needed personal traits of a moderator include an interest in the research process, curiosity, adaptability and empathy. The skills a moderator needs are knowledge of research methods, the research topic and group dynamics. In addition the moderator must be able to analyse and report findings.

■ Disagreement within a focus group can help to generate ideas. However, this disagreement should not be allowed to escalate into group conflict. A moderator must know how to de-escalate conflict and also how to handle potentially disruptive group members.

■ References

Hanson, J.H. (2001) 'Breaking the cycle of marketing disinvestment: Using marketing research to build organizational alliances', *International Journal of Nonprofit and Voluntary Sector Marketing*, Vol. 6, No. 1, p 33–49.

Jensen, E. (2007) 'Public television plans a network for latinos', *The New York Times*, 7 February.

Puchta, C. and J. Potter (2004) *Focus Group Practice*, SAGE Publications, Thousand Oaks, CA.

Sargeant, A. and L. Woodliffe (2005) 'The antecedents of donor commitment to voluntary organizations', *Nonprofit Management and Leadership*, Vol. 16, No. 1.

Stewart, D., P.N. Shamdasani and D.W. Rook (2007) *Focus Groups: Theory and Practice*, SAGE Publications, Thousand Oaks, CA.

Warner, M. (2005) 'You want any fruit with that big mac?' *The New York Times*, 20 February.

Zezima, K. (2007) 'A friendly interstate battle of online one-upmanship', *The New York Times*, 29 June.

CHAPTER 8

Interviews

- Describe the uses of interview research and its advantages and disadvantages
- Explain the difference between in-depth, expert and intercept interviews
- Clarify the different types of interview questions and the uses of each
- Introduce the issues involved in recruiting and screening participants
- Explain the interview process and the skills needed by an interviewer

■ Introduction

Most organizations will be aware that surveys and focus groups can be used to conduct marketing research. Organizations that provide social services will certainly know that interviews can also be used to learn more about the needs of their clients. However, most organizations have not considered using interviews for marketing research. In fact, marketing research interviews can be very useful and worth the investment in time, effort and money when the organization is faced with a serious problem, such as a lack of customers, and they have no idea why.

It is true that an in-depth one-on-one interview takes a skilled interviewer and, therefore, might not be a methodology that is available to small organizations. However, all organizations can have their own personnel conduct expert interviews to learn more about their competition and then adjust their marketing mix accordingly. In addition, intercept interviews can be conducted by anyone with an outgoing personality and these will provide the organization with insights that can be confirmed with other research techniques.

■ Uses and rationale of interview research

Interview research consists of the researcher asking questions of a single participant. In-depth interviews provide the researcher with the opportunity to explore a single topic in depth. Expert interviews provide a means of gathering factual information, while intercept interviews allow the researcher to quickly gather multiple viewpoints. There are different uses for each of these types of interviews.

Uses of interview research

In-depth interviews are used when the researchers need to explore consumer behaviour and attitudes in depth. The researcher will be able to gain insights that a short conversation would not be able to produce. The insights from interviews can be used to better understand a current problem that is confronting the organization. For example, an organization that is seeing a decline in volunteers and contributions from the community may use interviews to get a clearer understanding of the reason for this decline.

Expert interviews can be used to gather factual knowledge about the cause of a problem. This includes information from other organizations that have faced a similar difficulty. For example, if a non-profit organization that serves the artistic community has seen a decline in the use of its services among young artists they may want to interview the management at other similar organizations to determine if they are also facing this problem.

While in-depth interviews can be used to gain insights from consumers into the cause of a problem and expert interviews are used to learn factual knowledge about the problem. Intercept interviews can be used to generate hypotheses. The hypothesis can then be supported or disproved using quantitative research. For example during the intercept interview process, many participants may be asked why the number of artists using the organization's services is declining. Many may state that the cost of living space in the area is driving young artists out of the city. Therefore, the hypothesis might be that the reason for the decline in the use of services by artists is the transportation cost to travel to the organization's location. This hypothesis could then be proved or disproved using survey research (see Table 8.1).

Table 8.1 Learning more about problems using interviews		
Type	**Use**	**Example**
In-depth	Gaining insights into customers behavior or attitudes	Why do you not use our organization's services?
Expert	Obtaining factual knowledge about the source of a problem	Is the number of people using your organization's services declining?
Intercept	Developing hypotheses for use in quantitative research	Why do you think people are not using the organization?

Advantages of using interview research

All research methodologies have their own unique advantages that make them useful for different situations. However each has disadvantages of which the researcher should also be aware. One of the skills a researcher must have is the ability to choose the methodology that will work best for obtaining the answer to each research question.

The advantages of interview research include the ability to probe in depth a single topic without distraction by the comments of other participants. Interview research also allows the participants time to express their ideas more fully. Because an interview only involves two people, it can be held at various locations. In addition, interviews can be used to obtain factual data.

Advantages of interview research

- Provides researcher time to probe insights free from distraction
- Provides participants time to express themselves
- Can be conducted at different settings
- Can be used to gather factual data

Provides researcher with time: One of the major advantages to interview research is that it provides the researcher with the time needed to get at underlying reasons for consumer behaviour and attitudes. In addition, this time will be free from distraction by the comments of other participants. This is especially important when discussing topics of a confidential or sensitive nature. For example, a social services organization that provides beds for homeless teens may want to know why fewer teens are using their services. When first asked the question a teen may respond with bravado, explaining he or she does not need help. It may take repeated probing questions to get at the real reason, which may range from something as simple as the teen using a new facility with more comfortable beds to a more complex reason such as fear for their safety when they stay at the organization's facilities. The interview process gives the researcher the time needed to explore in depth a single topic. However to make use of this time the researcher must be trained to listen (Rubin, 2005).

Provides participants with time: Sometimes participants want to answer the researcher's question but are not sure of the reasons for their own behaviour motivation. Interview questions ask participants to explore their reasons for use of a product and service. However, most people do not take the time to think about the reason for a decision until prompted to do so. For example, a small regional theatre may wonder why local residents do not attend while tourists with similar demographic and psychographic characteristics, do buy tickets. The first response a local resident might make is that they are 'too busy'. Participants might need time to think about what 'too busy' actually means since they find time for other activities. The underlying reason might be that they do not take the time find out what the theatre offers. They may state that if they were aware of what the theatre offers, they might then agree that they would find time to attend.

Conducted at different locations: Because an interview only involves one researcher and one participant at a time and does not need any specialized facility or equipment they can be held at the location that is most convenient for the participant. An interview can even be held in the home of the participant, which can be useful if the participant is unable to travel. An interview can also be held at a place of employment, which is convenient for expert interviews when the researcher wants to minimize inconvenience. Finally intercept interviews can be held in any public place where the participants can be found.

Used to gather factual data: Not all research involves the ultimate consumer of the non-profit organization's product. Some research is conducted with experts to gather background information on the organization's problem. In addition the organization might conduct interviews with personnel from competing organizations. This research is not designed to gain insights into behaviour but to gather facts. Interviews work well as an expert is more likely to respond to the request for information in person than through a written survey. After all, the expert has nothing to gain from the research process other than helping a colleague with a problem.

Disadvantages of interview research

Of course, there are disadvantages to any research methodology. For interview research these include the need to have a skilled researcher conduct the interview. Another disadvantage is that as the interviewer is exploring the reasons for behaviour each interview, just as each participant, will be unique. This makes comparison of results difficult. Since interviews take longer to conduct, the researcher will have findings from fewer participants to analyse. Because of these limitations, interviews are not used routinely to conduct research but when the organization faces a critical problem for which they have no idea of the cause.

Disadvantages of using interview research

- Requires researcher skilled in interview techniques
- Unable to make comparison between findings
- Fewer participants means less findings to analyse

Requires skilled researcher: An interview is used when the organization is at a loss about the cause of a problem. Because it is difficult to obtain information on underlying causes of behaviour, a skilled interviewer is needed. This person must have previous experience in interviewing from working either in the social sciences or marketing. An interview is not just a conversation, rather the interviewer is acting as a detective looking for clues and then probing more deeply when they are revealed. To find these clues the researcher must repeatedly ask for clarification of statements made by the participant. They must ask for this clarification without frustrating the participant. In addition the interviewer must be careful not to lead the participant to any specific answer. A skilled interviewer keeps the conversation on the research topic while at the same time following up on ideas presented by the participant. This is a skill that must be learned.

Makes comparisons difficult: Each interview will be unique, as the interviewer follows up clues to the underlying reasons for a problem. The interviewer may find that after conducting a number of interviews, different reasons have arisen in each. This does not mean that the research has failed, but does make comparisons of the data difficult. It will take additional analysis to find a common theme when the individual reasons differ. For example, a free dental clinic may be exploring why they have such a high number of cancelled appointments. Interviews with clients might have revealed a problem with public transportation, a discomfort with the neighbourhood where the clinic is located, and the cost of getting to the clinic. While different, additional analysis might reveal that all of these reasons relate to the clinic's location.

Small number of participants: While interviewing can provide valuable insights, the requirements of the methodology will limit the number of interviews that can be conducted. First the potential participant must be willing to give up the time to be questioned on a topic which might not be of much interest personally. This will limit the number of people who will be willing to participate in interviews. Also using a skilled interviewer, if the organization does not have one on staff, will be expensive. As a result there will be less findings to analyse and upon which to base recommendations.

BEFORE YOU WRITE THE MARKETING MESSAGE USE INTERVIEWS TO LEARN WHAT SHOULD BE SAID

An organization that wanted to develop a social marketing campaign to discourage youth violence realized that they did not know what to say to young people. So they conducted in-depth interviews with middle school students to learn more. The organization's goal was to learn what young people see as the benefit of violent behavior and, also, who would be an effective spokesperson for the anti-violence marketing campaign.

They learned through interviews that young people believe violence is needed to protect themselves and their families. Interestingly, although the youths participated in violent acts, they did not see themselves as violent. As the result of the interview research the organization developed a marketing message that encourages youth to 'rise above' violence.

Source: Bell-Ellison *et al.* (2007).

Question to consider: Do we have a promotional message that could be improved using interview research?

■ Types of interviews

There are three types of interviews that researchers can conduct. The first is the in-depth interview between a researcher and research subject that lasts for as long as an hour. The second type is an expert interview between the researcher and someone who has special knowledge that pertains to the research question. Finally, intercept interviews are short two to five question interviews that are quick to conduct and, therefore, can involve many more participants than in-depth interviews.

Interview stages

Each of these types of interviews has a unique process but also contain some common elements (see Table 8.2). Interviews usually have an opening stage where the researcher explains the reason the interview is being conducted. During this stage there will also be a conversation about the logistics of the interview including the time it will take. The participant will also use this stage to explain that all information will be held confidential and while findings will be reported, no names of interviewees will be divulged. This opening stage of the interview is used to build trust and establish rapport.

Table 8.2 Interview research process	
Stage	**Purpose**
Opening	Explain purpose of research
	Describe logistical details
	Assure participant of confidentiality
Questioning	Ask a series of prepared questions
Probing	Ask follow-up questions based on responses
Closing	Thank participant for participation
	Reassure participant of confidentiality

The questioning phase of the interview process will use predetermined questions designed to elicit information that will help answer the research question. The researcher will have developed these questions with the assistance of the management of the organization. There should only be a short list of questions so that the interviewer will have enough time to ask each. The probing stage is where the researcher will develop and ask unique questions based on the answers to predetermined questions. The interview may actually move back and forth between the questioning and probing stages as new topics are introduced. The closing stage is where the researcher thanks participants for their time, again reassures them about confidentiality and asks for any questions the participant might have about the interview process that has just completed.

In-depth interviews

An in-depth interview is conducted by a researcher with a single participant. The interviewer will be held at a location that is free from distraction so that both the researcher and the participant can concentrate on the research question. The interview will open with the interviewer thanking the participant for arriving and explaining the purpose of the interview (Table 8.3).

Table 8.3 In-depth interview process

Stage	Tasks and questions
Opening	Researcher thanks participant Researcher explains purpose of interview and interview process
Questioning	Why do you choose not to volunteer for the 'Clean Streams Initiative'? What benefits would you want from the volunteer experience?
Probing	If answer to question one is 'too busy' possible questions include: 　What activities are you involved in? 　Why do feel these are worth your time? 　Do you see a way that these activities could be combined with volunteering? If answer to question two is 'fun' possible questions include: 　What do you mean by fun? 　What activities do you consider fun? 　How do you think volunteering could be made more fun?
Closing	Researcher asks for any additional comments (enough time should be left as participants may suggest interesting ideas such as using 'MySpace' to promote the organization)

After the opening stage, the interviewer will first ask prepared questions. The prepared questions will be written to specifically address different aspects of the research question. For example an organization may have recently begun to have difficulties recruiting young volunteers for their annual cleanup of local streams. The research question might be: 'Why are students at the local university not volunteering for Spring Clean up?' A meeting of the organization management may reveal a number of issues. The organization may know that their marketing message on the volunteer opportunity is being communicated to students and yet they are not getting volunteers. They may guess that students are worried about the time commitment and are too busy to volunteer. As a result the organization may want to know what students consider a reasonable time commitment. They may also want to know what benefits students perceive they receive from volunteering.

A direct question as to the length of a volunteer commitment is a simple question that can be handled with a survey. Instead the questions prepared for the interview will cover why students do not volunteer and what benefits would attract volunteers. Only a few questions will be prepared. At first if may seem these questions will not fill an hour long interview. However, each prepared question will lead to additional probing questions. The prepared questions are general in nature with the probing questions being more specific. These probing questions cannot be prepared as they will depend on the answer received from the participant. As a result, each interview may discuss in depth a different topic, which is why interviews are not comparable. After the probing questions, the interviewer will close the interview by giving the participant a chance to offer any additional comments on topics that were not addressed during the interview.

Expert interviews

Most research focuses on obtaining data from current or potential participants. After all it is these participants that will be the users of the organization's product. Therefore information is needed to adjust the product packaging along with the pricing, promotion and distribution to ensure that the product meets the needs and wants of the consumer.

Expert interviews are usually used early in the research process when the organization needs to know more about a problem. Sometimes the organization needs information that the customer cannot provide. For example, the organization described above, the 'Clean Stream Initiative' may wonder if other organizations are having the same problem recruiting college students as volunteers. They also may want to know how college students spend their free time. Some of the answers to these questions might be learned through secondary research. However, the organization might want information that is very specific to their issue (Table 8.4).

Table 8.4 Expert interview process	
Stage	**Tasks and questions**
Opening	Researcher thanks participant
Questioning	If questioning other organizations ask: Have you had difficulty recruiting student volunteers? Why, or why not, do you believe this is true? If questioning university officials ask: In what type of activities do students participate? If students engage in volunteer activities, what motivates them to do so?
Closing	Thanks and I will pick up the check for lunch

The method of obtaining this information is through interviewing the experts that have the knowledge. In the example above, the organization may decide to interview someone responsible for recruiting student volunteers at another organization. They may also decide to interview the person responsible for student activities at the local university.

These expert interviews will have a different structure. Because the purpose of the interview is to gain factual information, probing questions are not used. Instead the interviewer will rely on prepared questions. There may be a temptation to treat an expert interview casually. After all, the person being interviewed may be considered a colleague and, in fact, may be know to the researcher or even be a friend.

However, the researcher should treat the interview seriously. After all, they are taking valuable time that the expert could put to other uses. Because the researcher wants to minimize the time commitment that is being asked from the expert, the researcher must keep the interview as short as possible. The opening stage would simply be spent thanking the expert for their time. Another way to thank the expert, and to make use of free time, is to conduct the interview over lunch or coffee with the researcher picking up the check. The prepared question stage would be simply asking the expert factual questions. Closing would be a simple 'thanks'.

Intercept interviews

Intercept or person-on-the-street interviews are short, focused interviews consisting of only two to five open ended questions. The entire interview should only take two to three minutes. The purpose is not to obtain in-depth information but rather many responses to a specific question than could be obtained through in-depth interviews.

The intercept interviews are held in the location where the participants normally can be found. This interview method is essential when participants are unwilling to participate in a lengthy interview. Because probing questions will not be used, the researcher does not need to be a skilled interviewer.

To conduct intercept interviews the researcher will first approach people that meet the participant profile. The opening stage will consist of researchers introducing themselves on a first name basis and explaining for whom they are working. The researcher will also inform the potential participant of the purpose of the interview, the amount of time that the interview will take and ask permission to start the interview. Once the prepared questions are asked, the researcher will quickly thank the participant for their time and look for another potential participant.

DO YOU NEED A SEPARATE MARKETING MESSAGE FOR LGBT YOUTH? INTERVIEWS FOUND THAT YOU DO

Researchers knew that lesbian, gay, bi-sexual and transgender youth smoke at higher rates. What they did not know was why and what to do about it. A purposive selection method was used to choose LGBT youth to interview. These in-depth interviews allowed researchers to learn that many of the youths did not know anyone that didn't smoke and couldn't image how they could avoid smoking. However they also ascribed positive qualities to people who didn't smoke including better personal appearance and higher self-esteem. The researchers were then able to use this information to develop an anti-smoking message designed specifically to target LGBT youths.

Source: Remafedi (2007).

Question to consider: Why type of interviews could we conduct to learn more about our customers?

■ Preparing interview questions

Interviews use open ended questions to obtain information from participants. An open ended question does not provide the participant with any already selected answers from which to choose. Probing questions are always open ended, but not all open ended questions are probing.

When writing interview questions the researcher can chose from among descriptive, causal and consequence questions. Descriptive questions ask the participant to describe their behaviour. As long as the question is not perceived as invasive or threatening, these are the easiest questions for the participant to answer. Causal questions ask why a behaviour takes place. These questions are more challenging for participants to answer as they may not have given the issue much thought. To answer the question the participant must think about his or her motivation for taking a particular action. Consequence questions ask the participant to describe what happens as the result of an action. While causal questions ask participants to consider why they take an action, consequence questions force participants to consider their feelings after they take an action. These are the most difficult questions to answer.

Descriptive questions

Descriptive questions ask participants to describe their behaviour. They ask questions using the words of 'what', 'when', 'where', 'how often' and 'with whom'? What do they do not ask is 'why'. For example, participants might be asked what services they use, when they use the organization's services, where they saw the ad for the organization, how often they visit the organization and with whom they share the experience. All of these are simply questions to answer and are usually asked early in the interview. They are also necessary to set the stage for the later more probing causal and consequence questions.

Interviews should never consist of only descriptive questions. Interviews are an expensive research methodology that limits the number of people who can be involved. These types of descriptive questions could be just as easily be answered in a survey form, saving the organization money.

Descriptive questions

- What services do you use at the clinic?
- How often do you visit the free clinic?
- Who accompanies you on the visits?
- When is the most convenient time for you to visit?
- Where would you prefer the clinic to be located?

Causal questions

A causal question is designed to uncover the reason, or causes, of a behaviour. They are almost always probing questions because they require the participant to take the time to consider why they perform behaviours that are usually routine. Using the example of the descriptive questions given above, the causal questions would ask for the motivation behind the behaviour. The management of the organization might assume that someone visits the clinic because of ill health. However a causal question might reveal other motivations.

Causal questions

- Besides the obvious reason that you need health care, what other benefits does a visit to the clinic provide?
- Why do you always bring family members to the clinic?
- Why do you find evening hours to be inconvenient for visits?
- Why would a downtown location be more convenient?

Consequence questions

Descriptive questions ask the participant to describe their behaviour. Causal questions ask the participant the motivation for engaging in the behaviour. Consequence questions ask the participant how their feelings or attitudes change as a result of a behaviour. This form of probing question will require participants to consider aspects of their behaviour of which they may be initially unaware. These questions are important because they can provide information as to the benefits that people receive from using the product. Even if participants cannot answer the question as to why they engage in a behaviour a consequence question might uncover the motivation. For example, a participant may be unable to articulate why they frequently visit the clinic. However when asked how they feel after a visit they may respond that they feel that someone cares about them. This lets the clinic know that patients are visiting for the psychological benefits along with the physical benefits received from the visit.

Consequence questions

- How do you feel when you return home after a visit to the clinic?
- How easy is it for you to follow the directions the doctor has explained?
- What would you want changed on your next visit?

WHY ASKING QUESTIONS IS NOT AS SIMPLE AS IT SEEMS

At first the nonprofit organization might believe that interviewing is easy. After all, you only need to ask questions and listen to the answers! But it is not as easy as it seems. First people knowingly lie, they unknowingly lie, they change their minds, and they become confused. Below are ten reasons why getting a straight answer from a participant is not easy:

1 Factual questions sometimes elicit invalid answers
2 The relationship between what respondents say they do and what they actually do is not always very strong

3 Respondents' attitudes, beliefs, opinions, habits, and interests often seem to be extraordinarily unstable
4 Small changes in wording sometimes produce major changes in the distribution of responses
5 Respondents commonly misinterpret questions
6 Answers to earlier questions can affect the respondents' answers to later questions
7 Changing the order in which response options are presented sometimes affects respondents' answers
8 Respondents' answers are sometimes affected by the question format
9 Respondents often answer questions even when it appears they know very little about the topic
10 The cultural context in which a question is presented often has an impact on the way respondents interpret and answer questions.

No wonder asking questions isn't as simple as it first seems!

Source: Foddy (1995).

Question to consider: Which of our customers might give us untruthful answers in an interview?

■ Recruiting and screening participants for interviews

Because very few participants are needed for most interview research, there may be less concern over finding appropriate participants. After all, if an organization only needs to interview five or six participants, they may believe that it will be easy to wait to the last minute as these few people can be easily found. However, the opposite is true, the fewer the participants involved in a research study the more important it is to find the correct participants as each participant's input into the study is heavily weighted.

Another reason for researchers to spend more time considering the necessary participant profile is the fact that it is harder to recruit participants for interview research. A focus group is a much more stimulating event where the participant has the opportunity to meet and interact with others. An in-depth interview will involve a private discussion with only one person. In addition the participant may not find the topic of as much interest as the researcher. Why should they want to give up on hour or more of their day? As a result, finding and recruiting the appropriate participants will be challenging.

Therefore the organization may wish to consider incentives when recruiting participants for in-depth interviews. As the non-profit organization will not be able to afford a large incentive it cannot be the only motivating factor for participation. The potential participant must also have at least some altruistic motivation. However, the incentive is a way of acknowledging and thanking the participant for their assistance (Denzin and Lincoln, 2005).

Developing the profile

Whether the research will be an in-depth, expert or intercept interview study, the first step in the methodology is to develop a participant profile. This profile will help keep the researchers focused on finding the right participants when they become discouraged and want to recruit someone who is only marginally qualified. With in-depth or intercept interviews one of the first issues will be based on usage and whether they want to include current users, past users or non-users in the study. The researchers can decide to choose participants from more than one group. If this is the case they will need to determine the proportion of each.

The researcher will then need to decide on the demographic characteristics that are important to consider when developing the profile. Such characteristics as age, gender, income, ethnicity, religion, family status and educational level may, or may not, be relevant to the study. For example the organization may decide that income and ethnicity are important demographic factors to include in the profile. The next question will be if the organization wants to limit the participants to a specific income level or ethnic group or if the organization wants to ensure that the participants are representative of all possibilities (Table 8.5).

Table 8.5 Sample participant profile for community park interviews

Characteristics	Participant profile description
Usage status	One half of the participants should be current users, defined as visiting the park at least once a month in at least two seasons of the year. One half of the participants should have not visited the park in the last two years.
Demographic characteristics	Household with child or children under the age of 16. Household can be headed by single parent, couple or other relatives. Income level should be below $25,000 a year.
Psychographic characteristics	Family should value time spent together and be reasonably active, defined as some family members participating in an outside physical activity such as team sports or solitary activities such as walking or gardening.

Psychographic characteristics will also be part of the profile. The organization must decide if the lifestyles, values and attitudes of the participants need to be considered. While age and psychographic characteristics are often related, this is not always true. Young people can have a conservative view of life and or be very sedentary in their habits. Meanwhile older people can have a very liberal view of life and have very active lifestyles.

Screening for in-depth interviews

After the profile has been developed the next issue will be where to find the participants. If the participants are to be current users of the organization, membership information, box office records, guest book sign-in forms or client files can be used. If the participants are to be non-users the organization may have to rely on snowballing, which uses referrals.

The organization will need the names of more participants than will be required at this stage in the recruitment process, as there will be referrals of people who do not meet the profile. In addition names will be referred of people who meet the profile but who are unwilling to participate. It is better to start with too many names than to continually go back and find more.

Once the organization has the names of potential participants they will need to be screened. This screening process can be done by mail, online, in person or over the phone. The purpose of the screening is to ensure that the potential participant meets the profile. A short form should be developed to ensure that all relevant questions are asked. The completed form can then be used to explain why certain people who were referred were not selected to be participants.

When conducting the screening process, the researcher should not inform the potential participant of the 'right' answer that will include them in the study. This is to ensure that people answer the questions truthfully and not just so they will be included. If participants are not selected to be included it is not necessary to explain exactly why, but just to say that while the researcher appreciates their interest, their assistance will not be needed.

Sample screening questions for study on park usage

- Are there children under the age of 16 who are living in your household?
- Is the total income for your household below $25,000 a year?
- Can you name an activity that you do together as a family?
- Does anyone in your family enjoy outside activities such as sports?

Screening participants for expert interviews

Expert interviews are conducted to obtain factual information about the causes of a problem. Researchers, especially those involved in non-profit organizations, may want to save time by simply talking to anyone that is willing to participate. However, careful thought in regards to who should be involved in the expert interviews will save time in the long run.

The researchers should consider the need to speak to someone at an organization who offers a similar product or service. For the example above, the organization conducting a study on park usage by low-income families might contact the parks department in another city for information. However, the organization might also focus on other organizations that serve the same group but with a different product. In this case the organization might contact someone at the local zoo to find if they have been successful in attracting low-income families. Finally the organization may want to speak to someone who is familiar with how to attract families to use an organization's services. In this case it might be a very different type of organization that is contacted such as an advertising agency.

Organization chosen for expert interviews on park usage research study

- *Product knowledge*: Other parks department
- *Market segment knowledge*: Zoo that attracts low-income families
- *Problem knowledge*: Advertising agency

The screening process will consist of finding the correct person with whom to speak. This may involve calls to the personnel department of the organization to determine who has the needed knowledge. The expert should then be contacted first by mail or email. This will explain the purpose of the research and the reason the organization is seeking their expertise. If the person's name was received from a mutual acquaintance this should be mentioned. This written communication will give legitimacy to the request for an interview. While it would be wonderful for the recipient of such a letter to respond immediately, it is more likely that this written communication will need to be followed up with a personal request.

Screening for intercept interview

The profile for intercept interviews will concentrate on usage and demographic characteristics. While psychographic characteristics are also considered, they are difficult to assess when only conducting a two to three minute interview. Intercept interviews are unique as they are held where the participants are already congregating as the result of an activity. For example, when wanting to conduct intercept interviews of park users, they are conducted in the park. This automatically screens for usage. The participant profile for intercept interviews would describe their demographics based on what can be physically observed.

Participant profile for park user study

- Park users
- Family groups
- Children to be young teens or younger
- With at least one supervising adult

The screening process for intercept interviews has limits. It is difficult in such a short time period to establish enough trust to ask personal question, such as income level. A substitute question on occupation can be used as occupation and income are usually closely related. Participants would find it easier to discuss their jobs than their financial situation.

The screening can be done visually with no questions needing to be asked. The researcher simply approaches a family group that meets the criteria and asks permission to conduct the interview. At the end of the interview they can ask the question about occupation. Even though some participants may not meet the criteria, the researchers may still find this interview data of interest.

BUSINESS + PHILANTHROPY = SUCCESS

Microsoft executive John Wood left his job to found Room to Read a charity that builds libraries and sponsors scholarships for girls education in the developing world. Has he been successful in his goals? Well, his libraries are expanding faster than Starbuck's franchises. His goal is to open 30 libraries a week. How does he do it? By using business techniques of internal accountability and external marketing. He has 'branded' Room to Read as a trusted name for those who want to help education in the developing world. Why? Because he knew that people want return on their investment, even when they are donating to charity.

Source: Donnan (2007).

Question to consider: How can we use research to learn how we can 'brand' our organization?

■ Interview logistics

Once the planning, recruiting and screening have been completed, it is time to consider who will conduct the interview, when they will be conducted and the best location for the interviews. First the organization will need to have a skilled interviewer to conduct the research. The organization must then plan the time for the interviews that is most convenient for the participants. Finally, the place where the interview will be held will depend on the type of interview being conducted.

Abilities needed by interviewers

There are both personal characteristics and learned skills that most be possessed by an interviewer to ensure that a successful interview takes place. The personal characteristics include patience and a sincere interest in people. A successful interview takes time as the researcher must first gain the trust of the participant. In the early stage of the interview the researcher and participant may engage in conversation that is only tangentially related to the research topic. While always keeping the interview topic in mind, the researcher must be willing to spend the time to gain the trust of the participant. A researcher will also need a sincere interest in people. For at least an hour researchers must focus all of their attention on one person. They then must have the same intense interest in the next research participant.

The interviewer will need excellent communication skills. This includes both verbal and non-verbal communication, as probing questions will challenge the participant to discuss issues of which they may not be aware. Interviewers will need to be skilled in reading the body language of the participant so that they know when to probe for more information and when they need to back off.

Abilities needed by interviewers

- *Patience*: To establish rapport
- *Interest in people*: So each participant feels valued
- *Excellent communication skills*: To gain the needed information

Location for the interviews

The location chosen for the interviews will depend on the type being conducted. In-depth interviews can be held at the office of the organization, the home of the participant or a neutral third location. Expert interviews are usually held at the office of the expert or else at a neutral location. Intercept interviews are held where the participants can be found.

In-depth interviews: In-depth interviews need to be held at a location free from distractions so that both the researcher and the participant can concentrate on the conversation. The location is usually an office at the organization. However this might be a problem if it is difficult for the participant to travel. In this case the interview might be held in the participant's home. However, while convenient for the participant, conducting an interview in the participant's home might involve frequent interruptions from family members.

A more common reason for not conducting the interview at the organization's office is that some participants might find the situation intimidating. Participants who are members of groups or communities that feel disenfranchised may feel that they cannot express themselves freely. This is because they may put the researcher in a position of official power. As a result they might limit their responses to what they feel should be said, rather than what they truly believe. The best way to eliminate this issue is to conduct the interviews at a location that is comfortable for the participants because the location is associated with an institution they trust. This institution might be community centre, business such as a store or restaurant, a school or a church. The choice of this location also demonstrates respect for the community or group to which the participants belong.

Expert interviews: These interviews are usually conducted at the expert's place of employment so that the time commitment is minimized. There may be situations when the expert may wish to have the interview conducted elsewhere so that they may speak more freely. For example, a researcher working with a dance company with attendance problems may want to speak to someone who works at another local dance company. This person may feel uncomfortable speaking about his or her own organization's problems where others may overhear. Therefore the interview should be arranged for a neutral site such as a restaurant. At this location the person can also be offered coffee or lunch.

In addition expert interviews can be conducted over the phone or even via email. Expert interviews usually do not involve communicating information at an emotional level. For this reason technology can be used without the worry of missing information communicated through body language. In addition telephone or online interviewing is necessary when the expert does not live in the local area.

Intercept interviews: These interviews are always conducted at the location where the participants who match the profile can be located. If the interviews are to be of the organizations current customers, then they are conducted on site. For example, they may be conducted in the waiting room of a clinic, the entrance to a gallery, the lobby of a theatre or even a public place such as park or beach. If the organization wants to interview people who are not current users of the organization, they then must decide where these potential users can be found. For example, if a library wants to interview young male teens who do not use their services during the summer, they may consider conducting the interviews at the local basketball or soccer fields.

Location choices for types of interviews

- *In-depth*: Researcher's office, participant's home, neutral location
- *Expert*: Expert's office, neutral location, telephone, online
- *Intercept*: Organization's premises, public place where participants congregate.

Summary

■ Interviews allow the researcher to communicate to one person at a time on the marketings issue or problem. This methodology allows the researcher to gain insights into behaviour, gather factual information or develop hypotheses. The advantages of interviews include the length of time they provide, the flexibility as to location and ability to gather facts. However they require a skilled interviewer, the findings will not be comparable and fewer participants will be involved.

■ In-depth interviews, conducted with a single research participant, go through four stages of opening, questioning, probing and closing. Expert interviews are with people who are not current or potential consumers but that have needed information. Intercept interviews are short interviews that are conducted at the location where the needed participants can be found.

- Descriptive questions ask participants to describe their behaviour. Causal question ask for the cause of the behaviour. Consequence questions are the most difficult to answer as they ask the participant about what will happen as the result of a behaviour.

- Different recruitment methods are used for each type of interview. The researcher will develop a participant profile for in-depth interviews. However for expert interviews, having the needed knowledge is the only important criteria. For intercept interviews the profile must be based on characteristics that the researcher can see.

- Interviewers must be patient, have a sincere interest in people and possess excellent communication skills. The location chosen for the interview will vary depending on the type. Expert interviews are usually conducted at the location most convenient for the expert while intercept interviews are held at the location where the participants can be found.

■ References

Bell-Ellison, B.A., W. Loomis, M. Tucci, and G.P. Quinn, (2007) 'Adolescent perceptions of violence: Formative research findings from a social marketing campaign to reduce violence among middle school youth', *Public Health*, Vol. 121, No. 5.

Denzin, N.K. and Y.S. Lincoln, (2005) *The SAGE Handbook of Qualitative Research*, SAGE Publications, Thousand Oaks, CA.

Donnan, S. (2007) 'Breakfast with the FT: John Wood', *Financial Times*, 23 February.

Foddy, W. (1995) *Constructing Questions for Interviews and Questionnaires: Theory and Practice in Social Research*, Cambridge University Press, New York, NY.

Remafedi, G. (2007) 'Lesbian, gay, bisexual, and transgender youths: Who smokes, and why?', *Nicotine and Tobacco Research*, Vol. 9.

Rubin, H. and I. Rubin, (2005) *Qualitative Interviewing: The Art of Hearing Data*, SAGE Publications, Thousand Oaks, CA.

CHAPTER 9

Projective and observational research

Objectives

- Explain the uses of projective techniques and their advantages and disadvantages
- Describe the types of projective tasks that can be used
- Discuss the uses of observational research and the types that can be conducted
- Introduce the steps in the observational research process

■ Introduction

Too many non-profit organizations only include in their research toolbox the basic techniques of surveys, focus groups and interviews. However, adding new tools is not that difficult. Two techniques that are easy to learn to use are projective techniques and observational research. Both of these are creative techniques that should appeal to people working in non-profit organizations. After all, creative people understand that verbal questions and answers are only one of the ways that people can communicate. Observational research is unique because it notes what people do instead of what they say they do. In addition, projective techniques are enjoyed by participants as they are more interactive than traditional research.

■ Projective techniques

Projective techniques are creative tasks that research participants complete. These tasks allow the participants to provide non-verbal answers to research questions. Instead of responding with the spoken word, the participant answers through writing, drawing or sorting of information.

Advantages and disadvantages of projective techniques

There are three reasons for considering using projective techniques either alone or with another research methodology. These reasons include obtaining information from participants of which they may be unaware. When participants answer a question verbally they have time to consider a rationale response. Projective techniques tap into feelings at the emotional level. The information that is written or drawn may reveal feelings or ideas of which the participant is unaware or would have difficulty verbalizing.

Projective techniques also allow participants to respond anonymously to sensitive issues. Rather than have to speak up in front of other participants, their ideas can be written on a card. All the cards can then be collected by the researcher who lists them for the participants to see without attributing the comments to any specific individual. Therefore, projective techniques allow participants to express themselves more freely. This is especially important when participants are expected to reveal information that is negative about their own behaviour. For example, if participants are asked verbally whether or not they are following their prescribed exercise plan, they may all answer affirmatively. It is not that people want to be dishonest; it is just that they have trouble admitting the truth that they have not exercised. If everyone responds in writing and the researcher reads the responses, everyone can feel comfortable discussing the reason why it is difficult to follow the plans and what type of marketing message could be used to motivate people to exercise.

The third reason for using projective techniques is that they are interactive. Technology allows people to multi-task by providing many sources of instant access to information and entertainment. People can listen to their choice of music or watch television while also performing other tasks. The computer allows people to access information in small bits that are quickly read and then people move on to the next topic that strikes them as interesting. As a result people have short attention spans. The idea that participants will be able to stay focused simply discussing a topic for an hour or an hour and a half is unrealistic. This is true no matter how skilled the researcher. People are simply conditioned to expect a high level of stimulation and may find engaging in 'only' a conversation 'boring'. Projective techniques help the researcher engage and maintain the interest of the participants.

Advantages of projective techniques

- Obtains emotional rather than rational responses
- Allows privacy when discussing sensitive topics
- Engages and maintains interest of participants

Of course, there are situations where projective techniques might not work. Some participants might find the idea of drawing a cartoon or completing a story too challenging. Other participants might be reluctant because they believe that they will be judged on their creative abilities. These reluctant participants might be encouraged to participate by reassuring them that projective techniques are not to be taken too seriously. They should be reminded that it is simply a fun way for the participant to provide information. Of course, any participant who objects should be told that their participation is entirely optional.

Disadvantages of projective techniques

- Tasks are too challenging
- Concern about lack of creative ability

Process of conducting projective research

Successfully using projective techniques will take planning. Projective techniques are sometimes used alone but usually are employed along with other methodologies. The researcher might plan to use projective techniques as an integral part of the research process. However, researchers may also want to consider having contingency plans for adding projective techniques to other methodologies when the participants are not responding well to questions. For example, a researcher who is conducting a focus group or interviews may have difficulty getting the participants emotionally involved in the discussion of the promotion of a new arts festival. It is useful to have a projective technique, such as having the participants design an ad, ready to liven up the conversation.

The steps involved in using projective techniques include deciding upon the method, preparing the materials and testing the procedure. When deciding upon the method researchers should consider how the participants will react to tasks that are unstructured and creative. If the researcher feels that the participants may feel more anxiety than excitement with such a task, simple word association can be used. If, on the other hand, the participants would enjoy the interaction, drawing or ad completion can be used to gain additional insights and spark conversation (Seale *et al.*, 2006).

The materials should be prepared and duplicated before the research starts. To help participants with the completion tasks, it is useful to have the task on a form that they can then complete. To simply provide a blank piece of paper can seem intimidating to participants. Therefore, researchers should take the time to produce a handout with the words or visuals attractively arranged. If the date and subject of the focus group or interview is already placed on the form, these will alleviate having to record this information later.

Before using the projective technique it should be tested on people with similar characteristics. The test is not only to determine if the technique works, but also to practice the directions that will be used by the researcher. If the directions are too specific, the projective technique will not be useful in obtaining the participants ideas and opinions. However, if the directions are too vague, the participant will be at a loss as to what is expected.

WORD ASSOCIATION CAN BE AN ONLINE GAME

Researchers wanted to know what the term 'healthy living' actually meant to the people that use it. To obtain this information the researcher decided to use word association because the technique does not suggest any possible answers to the participants. The research project was jointly designed between a university and a marketing consultancy group with the aim to develop new products. Via email, consumers were invited to participate in an online word association game. A single screen asked them to type the word that first comes to mind when the term health living is heard. The researchers then used a computer program to analyze both the frequency and the linkages between the terms. Using this technique they learned that the term means natural, balanced diet, well-being, keeping fit and eating well. Using word association the researchers were able to quickly uncover attitudes that would have taken hours of interview time.

Source: Marsden (2002).

Question to consider: How could we use word association via email to learn more about our customers?

■ Types of projective techniques

There are many established projective techniques that can be used by researchers. In addition, researchers can create their own techniques to obtain information. Many projective techniques involve completion tasks. With these techniques the participants are given the start of a task, such as a sentence, story or cartoon, and asked to finish. Creative tasks start with less direction. The participant is asked to free associate, draw or compose an ad or programme for the organization. Other common projective techniques include thematic appreciation tests and component sorts.

Completion tasks

There are a number of completion tasks that can be used starting from the simple to the more challenging. The purpose of the tasks is to uncover participants' ideas, attitudes and opinions, towards an organization or the product they provide. The task can be constructed so that the participants are expressing their own ideas. For example, a sentence completion might start with 'After I visit the Marine Museum I feel _____'. Or the task can be constructed so that it is expressing the opinions or ideas of someone else such as 'After Sue visited the clinic she felt _____'. The latter form is used when participants may be reluctant to own up to their own feelings. Participants may find it easier and safer to assign their feelings or opinions to someone else.

Completion tasks are a useful means for starting conversations. They can be used in focus groups but they are also useful with other forms of research methodology. For example, a researcher may feel that an in-depth interview on the reason why people are not interested in foreign film festivals is off to a difficult start as participants seem uninterested in the topic. Giving the participant a task to complete, such as sentence completion on why a person chooses not to attend can help the conversation get started as the task provides the participant with more structure. This structure can help to relieve any pressure the participant might feel to say the 'right' answer and allows the participant to feel more relaxed.

Sentence completion

Sentence completion tasks are easy for the researcher to create and can be used alone or with other types of methodology. The sentence can be used to gain information on the participant's opinions about the organization's current users. It can also obtain information on the organization's product, pricing, promotion or location (see Table 9.1). An advantage of sentence completion is that using the same sentence for all participants allows comparability. While the words provided by the participants may vary, the researcher will almost always find common themes.

Table 9.1 Examples of sentence completion task

Topic	Sentence	Possible answers
Other customers	People who visit the senior centre are _____.	Possible responses: friendly, too old, interesting, boring, infirm, lonely, outgoing
The participant	When I visit the senior centre I feel _____.	Possible responses: excited, welcomed, like I am home, one of the gang
Product	The activities offered by the centre are _____.	Possible responses: different, unique, familiar, fun, easy, boring, too limited
Price	I feel the prices charged for lunch are _____.	Possible responses: fair, too high for what you get, rip off
Place	The senior centre building is _____.	Possible responses: too many steps! looks ugly, is nearby, looks like home
Promotion	The ads for the senior centre are _____.	Possible responses: what ads? informative, too brief, interesting

For example, a sentence completion task on senior centres might focus on participants' perceptions of who uses the centre. The sentence might start with 'People who visit senior centres are _____. The sentence might also gauge their opinion of the product such as 'The activities offered by senior centres are _____. Even information on price can be obtained with sentence completion using a sentence such as, 'I think the prices for an evening dinner dance sponsored by the senior centre are _____'. These sentences should not ask for factual information such as what price the centre should charge as this is a simple survey question. Instead the sentences should be aimed to obtain information at an emotional level. Sentence completion tasks could be used in focus groups and in-depth and intercept interviews.

Story completion

This completion task requires more time during the research session and also more effort on the part of the participants. To complete this task the participant will need to have information on the research topic so that they have enough ideas to finish the story. Therefore, this technique works best with participants who have a high level of familiarity with the organization or issue being researched. The story should be constructed so that the circumstances and names used are familiar to the participants. For example, a religious organization that provides outreach to Hispanic youth in urban areas would construct a story using Hispanic names and a city setting. The names in the story can then be changed when working with a different ethnic group.

Example of story completion task

'Maria has just returned home for the Christmas holidays after her first semester away at college. That evening she decides to have pizza with Elena, an old friend she knows from church. Elena asks her if she is planning to attend Christmas Eve services. Maria answers that she stopped going to church because none of her new college friends go. Elena's response is _____.'

Cartoon completion

Another form of completion task has the participant write words in the thought bubble above a character drawn in a cartoon. The advantage of cartoon completion over sentence or story completion is that it provides more information to the participant making it easier to complete the task. The cartoon picture helps the participant visualize the situation as it shows the context, such as the people and surroundings, in which the comment is made. This context can be changed based on who is participating in the research.

For example, a new social services agency that was formed to encourage volunteerism might show a cartoon with one person saying to another, 'I'm spending part of this weekend volunteering, why don't you?' The other character in the cartoon might be saying, 'I don't volunteer because _____'. The cartoon can show two young people at a sports arena when young people are participating in the research. Another cartoon might show older people leaving a senior centre. The ethnicity and gender of the cartoons can also be changed so that the participant can more easily imagine what is being replied. Of course, participants will most likely reply with their own feelings which they will assign to the cartoon character.

Creative tasks

Another type of projective technique is creative tasks. All of these tasks can be used in focus groups or in-depth interviews. In addition, word association can be used as part of an intercept interview as the task can be completed in less time than the others. Tasks that take longer include drawing exercises that can be used to gather details that are difficult to verbalize. Programme or ad creation is a way to have participants participate in designing of the organization's product or promotion.

Word association

Word association allows the participant to respond on an emotional level by asking for the first one, two or three words that come to mind. Word association attempts to get at a 'gut' level emotional response from the participant. The stimulus for this response might be a name, product or photo. What is used will depend on what is being researched. For example, the Smithville Hiking Club, an organization that sponsors mountain hikes, might want to learn more about the perception of their organization. To do so, they can simply ask participants to say the first three words that come to mind when the organization is mentioned.

Sample word association exercise

What are the first three words that come to mind when you hear the name Smithville Hiking Club? _____, _____, _____.

If the answers recorded include boring, old people, dull, dreary and senior citizens the organization knows that they had better create more effective promotion to communicate that they are an organization for all ages that takes people on challenging and exciting hikes.

Word association can also be used to get an emotional opinion of the organization's product by showing the product and then getting a reaction. If the organization is planning to order 1,000 T-shirts as a promotional giveaway to new 'Friends' members this is an effective and easy method to make sure that the design is one that the potential Friends will like. Word association can also use photos. This might be a photo of a product that cannot be physically shown. Or it could be a photo of the outside or inside of the organizations building or lobby.

If this technique is used alone as a research methodology, it is important that a sufficient number of responses are received. However, these tasks are most effective when used along with other methodologies as the researcher can then ask participants additional questions about the reason for their response.

Drawing

A creative task that can be used to add a little fun to a focus group is asking the participants to draw. This is usually a way of getting at underlying perceptions about the organization by asking the participants' view of the current customers. For example, the Smithville Hiking Club might understand that they have a problem with the perception of the current club members. If they decide to conduct a focus group on this issue, they might ask participants to draw a picture of a hiker that belongs to the club. Artistic ability is not required as participants will be asked to explain their drawing. At this time the participant can explain that the stick figure is bent over because he or she is old.

A projective technique such as drawing is used to get people emotionally involved with the topic. If a drawing technique is used, large pieces of paper and colourful pens should be provided to participants. It is important that the researcher create a relaxed setting that communicates to the participants that the exercise will be fun. This setting will help alleviate any concern that the participants may have that they will be judged on their artistic ability.

Programme or ad creation

Even more creative is to ask the participant to help in designing the organization's product or promotion. The product for a non-profit organization is often intangible, such as a list of services or a programme of events. To obtain information on what they might prefer, the participants can be asked verbally. However, this might be met by silence as the participants have not given the subject much thought and may be at a loss of where to start.

Instead an organization that provides musical events might ask the participants to create the programme for one evening. To get them started a list of various performers or pieces of music should be provided. After choosing the performances the participants could then be asked what else they would like to see happen that night, such as lobby entertainment or the availability of special menu items. A blank programme form could be created that the participants working alone or in groups would complete.

Sample programme creation

Enjoy The Music!
Tonight's Programme Will Include:

_____

_____

_____

Lobby entertainment provided by _____

Don't forget to stop by the café for _____

After the programmes have been created each person or group will share what they have created, which should result in a lively discussion as people will agree or disagree with each other's choices. This same technique could be used to create a list of client services that could be offered or a schedule of classes that could be held.

This technique also works well with promotion ideas with the participants asked to create an ad for the organization. The participants are responsible for developing a 'message' that would head the ad and the visuals the ad would contain. The researcher will provide large pieces of paper, colourful pens and pencils and even photos that can be cut and pasted on the ad. By creating such a stimulating environment, the participants' inhibitions should be lowered and they will be able to provide more creative ideas than if they just answered with words. Again, sharing the created ads will help spur conversation among the focus group members. For example the participants would be asked to design an ad that would encourage more families to visit the State Park.

Sample ad creation

Mountain State Park: Our _____!

Mountain State Park: The Place For Families Because _____

While at Mountain State Park You Can _____

(Draw below the visuals that should be used in the ad)

Thematic appreciation test

Thematic appreciation tests were first used to understand what motivated people to achieve. However, the concept is now used to help researchers understand any type of human behaviour. During this technique the participant is shown a single or a number of pictures that show people encountering a dilemma. This dilemma might be a serious problem such as being diagnosed with an illness. Or it can be an everyday dilemma of where to go on Saturday night. While thematic appreciation tests can be used by many different types of organizations, the cards will always focus on a customer's perception of the organization and the choices he or she must make.

For example, a health clinic might wonder about their patients' perceptions of their services when bad health news is given. As part of this research a thematic appreciation test might be used. First a card showing a woman walking into the doctor's office with a smile on her face will be shown to the participant. The next card might show the doctor and woman in serious discussion. The third card would show the woman leaving the office with a serious look. The researcher would ask the participant, 'What is the woman feeling now?' The answers received may range from comments that she is thankful she has a good doctor to take care of her to she is scared to death because she does not know where to turn now. The answers will tell the researcher about the client's perception of the services offered.

The cards shown should be ambiguous enough so that participants can project their own thoughts onto the dilemma being portrayed. However, they should not be so vague that the participant states the woman is feeling hungry and wondering where the nearest coffee shop is located.

Component or card sorts

This technique also attempts to get information on underlying attitudes towards an organization. However, this technique focuses on what participants feel are similarities between products or organizations. Flash cards are prepared that list characteristics of products, types of consumers or the names of organizations. The participant is then given directions on what categories the cards should be sorted into. The researcher then analyses why the participant chose to put a card into a specific category.

This simple technique could be used to help a theatre company assess how people feel about them in relation to their competition. The participants may be asked to sort cards with the names of competitors and competing activities along a continuum of those most like, and those least like the organization. This would include not only direct competitors such as other theatre companies, but also indirect competitors such as formal dining, going to a movie, having a beer in a pub, going to a dance club or playing sports. This categorization will help the researcher better understand how consumers perceive the organization in relation to other available activities. If the theatre company finds that they are sorted with other theatre companies and formal dining, they know that they are perceived as a serious activity. If they are sorted with going to a movie and grabbing a bite to eat, they know that the participants believe they are an informal activity.

Another type of sort can use cards with the names of competitors and also with the names of different market segments. These might include middle class families, working class individuals, the elderly, and teens. The participants are then asked to sort which segment uses the services of which competitor. For example, a social services agency might want to know how its various outreach activities are perceived by the public. They may find that people associate their drug treatment with teens and their shelter with the homeless when in fact this is not true.

DO YOU KNOW WHAT YOUR CUSTOMERS WANT AND NEED – TODAY?

Everyone will agree that new technology, an aging population and changes in people's interests are changing the way people live at an ever increasing rate of speed. These changes are also affecting the marketplace for products. Unfortunately most organizations have an outdated idea of these wants and needs. Of course the organization can use marketing research to ask consumers what they need. However, consumers often have a difficult time expressing these thoughts. Observational research can help discover these facts about consumer behavior of which people may be unaware. For example, Clarks, a UK company that produces shoes, wanted to know how people determine if walking boots will be comfortable. By watching the purchase process, observational researchers learned that customers gauged comfort by feeling the tongue of the boot! By observing customers, nonprofit organizations can also learn how they make their purchase decisions, and, what is important to the consumer may never have occurred to the organization.

Source: Goffin and Rick (2006).

Questions to consider: What behaviour can we observe to determine how people are using our organization to meet their needs?

■ Observational research

Observational research is one of the few methodologies that do not rely on verbal communication between the researcher and participant. Instead of asking people about their consumer behaviour, with this methodology the researcher watches and records what they actually do. This method is used by researchers because what people say they do, and what they actually do, is not always the same. This is not because people intentionally lie. Instead people's words and actions differ because they may not remember the details of their behaviour.

For example, a botanical garden may wonder how people spend their time when visiting. Conducting a phone survey of visitors will not be the best methodology as people will have forgotten the details of their visit. At best they may remember the highlight of the trip, such as the tulips in bloom or a great lunch in the café, but little else. Conducting intercept surveys as people leave the garden will be more successful. However, while they may recall more, they still will not be able to provide details such as how long they stayed at each exhibit. Only observational research can answer the question of what people do when they visit the garden.

Uses of observational research

Observational research is used to gather data on consumer behaviour. Of course, an analysis of this behaviour will also provide insights into consumer preferences. Observational research is used because it is often too difficult for individuals to recall behaviour. However, it is also used when it would be inconvenient to stop and ask people about their behaviour.

For example, visitors to a museum may not be able to provide verbal information on what they saw during a visit. To do so they would have to be both familiar with, and be able to recall, the names of artists and works of art. Another example of participants' inability to recall behaviour would be to ask people how they spent the time waiting in the clinic's waiting room. This question would probably result in an answer describing the length of the wait, rather than what they did. People are not intentionally lying, as the wait may indeed have seemed more like an hour to them then the actual 15 minutes, which they spent watching the video being shown.

Another use of observational research is when asking people questions about behaviour close to the time when it takes place would be inconvenient. For example, a theatre company might want to know how people spend their time during intermission. However, right after intermission, everyone is hurrying back to their seats and is not interested in answering questions.

Another situation where observational research is useful is when people may be inclined to give what they consider the correct answer to a question. Visitors to a history museum, when asked how they spent their visit, might respond by mentioning exhibits they remember seeing. They will rarely respond that they spent most of their time in the gift shop and café. After all, everyone knows that one visits a museum for educational reasons.

Advantages and disadvantages of observational research

As explained above the major advantage of observational research is that it obtains information on what people do rather than what they say they do. However, another advantage is that it can be less costly than other forms of research such as interviews, focus groups or surveys. With this methodology there is no need to hire a professional moderator or interviewer. There is also time savings because there is no need to recruit participants.

Another advantage of observational research is that the organization does not need to gain the permission of the participants as long as the observation takes place in public. Of course, observational research does not mean spying on people. For example, a youth sports organization may need to know more about how young extreme sports fans spend their time. These young people are unlikely to willingly participate in a research study. However, they can be observed in a public place such as a park or parking ramp.

Advantages

- Record behaviour without verbal input from participants
- Cost and time savings
- Involve participants who may not be willing to participate in a study.

There are also disadvantages to the observational research methodology. While there is no need to hire professionals to conduct the research, there is a need for patient and observant researchers to faithfully record the data. These observers must also be supervised as they will be working on their own. Even with supervision they must be vigilant if they are to accurately record details.

Another significant disadvantage is the inability to ascertain if the participant meets the required profile. While the profile for observational research is usually broadly defined using observable demographic characteristics, such as ethnic families with preschool age children, there may still be a problem with observation. It will be left to the skill of the observer to determine the age of people and their ethnic background. It is even more difficult to use psychographic characteristics when defining the participant profile. Sometimes lifestyle can be guessed by clothing or hairstyle, but this is very weak evidence.

Lastly, the research methodology is dependent on who happens to be at the public place. A research study on what types of people attend free concerts in the park can be meticulously planned. However, the research effort might be wasted if the night is cold and rainy and the crowd is sparse.

Disadvantages

- Findings depend on accuracy of observations
- Difficult to profile participants
- Success dependent on who is present

Types of observations

If an organization decides to conduct observational research, its next decision will be what type to conduct. The organization can choose from complete observer, participating observer or complete participant. The choice will depend on the behaviour that needs to be studied.

Complete observer

For some research tasks, it is important that the researcher is not noticed by the participants. With this method the observer will station themselves at a location where they cannot be seen. The reason is not because the organization wants secrecy. Rather the reason is because the act of being observed may change the behaviour of the participants. For example, researchers standing at the side of a theatre lobby with a clipboard making notes on the behaviour of the crowd might find that everyone is avoiding where they are standing. In this example it would be better idea for the researcher to observe the crowd from a balcony.

The best complete observation is when the behaviour is videoed so it can then be studied. Of course, this would not be appropriate in any public setting. In fact, videoing behaviour even at the organization only for reasons of conducting research should not be done without the permission of those being videoed. However, some organizations may have video cameras that are used in public places such as lobbies, which are part of the security system. The tapes can be studied to determine if there is a need to redesign the seating in the lobby based on how easily people can find somewhere to sit while they have their drink before theatre.

Participant observer

Most observational research is conducted with a participant observer. With this technique the researcher does not try to be hidden from view. Instead the observer tries to mix in with those being observed. While the observers do not try to hide from view, they will try to make their observations as unobtrusive as possible. For example, the parks department of a city may want to know how people use the local park. Observers would be asked to record who comes to the park, how long they stay and what recreational equipment they use while they are at the park.

The observer would not try to hide in the park. Instead they would sit on a bench with a book and read while at the same time observing. If the researcher has a good memory, they can watch for a few minutes and then record at another location. This method could also work well for observing how people are using the lobby of a theatre during intermission.

The observer would be dressed similarly to the theatre goers and observe while casually strolling around. Or, an observer at a museum might station themselves by one exhibit and record who stops and how long they view the exhibit.

If someone questions what the observers are doing, they should explain that they are trying to learn more about the organizations customers without bothering them with questions. If researchers are observing in a public place they should have with them a letter explaining the purpose of the research and for what organization it is being conducted. This letter should also contain contact information for someone in the organization who can verify the researcher's identity.

Complete participant

Sometimes the observer is also a participant. With this type of observational research, the observer participates in the same behaviour as the research subjects. For example, if the researcher wants to know more about how people interact during the annual 'Community Clean Up Day' the observer can be cleaning up the public areas right along with the volunteers. This not only allows the researchers to observe behaviour, it also allows them to overhear comments. The researchers do not identify themselves; they simply participate in the activity under study. What they do not do is ask questions as this would be dishonest behaviour. Such questions should only be asked when respondents clearly know that they are participating in research.

RESEARCH CAN BE CONDUCTED DURING INTERMISSION!

Observational research can be conducted by any one in an arts organization every time there is an event. All the person needs to do is take ten minutes to watch the audience. While observing the researcher should ask the questions below. If they watch at a number of events and on different days and nights they can see if the answers vary.

- Who is attending? Singles – Families – Couples – Groups?
- Are they reading the program?
- Are they noticing the art work on the walls?
- Are they discussing the art or other subjects?
- Are they able to get to the bar?
- Is there a line at the restroom?

If there is time the researchers can also conduct intercept interviews with the audience. They can select participants to ask the following intercept interview questions:

- How did you hear about this event?
- Why did you decide to come today?
- Where else do you attend?

Conduct this observational research and intercept interviews at every event, and by the end of the season the organization will have its own internal database about the audience!

Source: ArtsMarketing.org (2004).

Question to consider: How can we combine observational research and intercept interviews to learn more about our customers?

■ Observation research process

The same as other methodologies, to successful complete observational research takes advance planning. While simply watching and recording behaviour seems simple, without preparation no useful data will be recorded. The steps involved in planning include deciding what behaviour to observe, preparing a participant profile, choosing the correct site, choosing the dates and times, preparing the observation form and training observers (Abrams, 2000).

Deciding on behaviour and participants to observe

Research always starts with a question or problem whose answer depends on input from current or potential customers of the organization. Most research will obtain information about facts, attitudes, opinions and ideas using a question and answer format. Observational research can only obtain answers through watching behaviour. Therefore, the researchers must first decide what behaviour they want to learn more about. While the analysis of the behaviour might provide insights into attitudes, this cannot be the purpose of the research. Instead the research must focus on people's actions. For example, an inappropriate research question for observational research would be, 'Do people enjoy intermission at the theatre?' An appropriate question would be, 'What activities do people engage in during intermission at the theatre?'

The participant profile that is developed by the researchers must only describe characteristics that can be determined visually. The profile starts with describing the behaviour, such as theatre attendees, park users or clinic patients. The profile should not ask the researcher to observe participants with psychographic traits, such as 'theatre lovers'. There is no way for the observer to know an individuals emotional involvement with the theatre. Instead the profile should describe demographic characteristics such as age and gender. Other easily observed characteristics that can be used are whether the individual is alone or with others or whether they are disabled or infirm. Some demographic characteristics, such as ethnicity, are more difficult to ascertain.

Observation logistics

A critical step in designing the observation research methodology is to choose the site or sites where the research will take place. The site must be a place where the profiled participants can be found. For current customers this will usually be at the organization's location, whether it is a theatre, school or a public place, such as a park. Choosing a site is much more difficult when trying to observe the behaviour of people who are currently not customers of the organization. Sometimes the location chosen is one that is used commonly by people for the behaviour the organization wants to observe. For example, if an organization wants to serve the needs of the infirm elderly by providing adapted living spaces, they could observe the elderly at senior centres.

Once the correct site is chosen, the researchers must decide what are the best days and times to observe the behaviour. Using the theatre example, there might be a difference in behaviour between matinees and evening performances, as the audience will differ with more families attending the matinees. If the theatre company wants to know more about how all theatre goers use intermission, they should make sure that they observe both matinees and evening performances. If they want to know more about families, they should then concentrate their observations on matinees. If the organization is studying one narrowly defined group of users, they should focus on when this group will be at the location.

The best method for choosing both location and day and time is for the researcher to scout the location. The researcher should visit the site to determine if it is frequented by a sufficient number of people who meet the participant profile. Then the researcher should visit at various days and times to determine when the observations will be most successful. There is no purpose in scheduling observations when no behaviour can be observed.

OBSERVATIONAL RESEARCH CAN BE CONDUCTED ANYWHERE!

African-American's share of book buying is increasing while the market for books as a whole is stagnant. In fact African-Americans spent $300 million on books in 2003. To meet this demand, publishers are hurrying to sign up new authors. And African-American writers are responding by sending their manuscripts to publishers.

But how do publishers decide what books to publish? According to Malaika Adero, an editor at Atria, part of Simon & Schuster, one tool she uses to get ideas for what new books to publish, is to watch what people are reading on the subway. While on her way to work, she is already at work conducting consumer observational research.

Source: Collier (2004).

Question to consider: What could I research on my way to work?

Preparing the observation form

Even the best observer can only remember a limited amount of detail. Therefore, the researchers will need to prepare an observation form where data can be recorded. For some types of observations, the form can be filled out while the observation is taking place. Other times, the researcher will first observe and then later record the data. This method will be used when recording data at the same time as observing would draw attention to the researcher.

The form should have a place to note the date, time and place of the observation and also the name of the observer. The form should then have a place to record details on who is being observed. At a crowded location, observers cannot possibly note the behaviour of everyone. Therefore, they must choose which participants to observe and then record their characteristics. For example, they may note that they are observing a family with two adults and three children, a same gender couple or single elderly male.

The form will provide time slots where observations will be recorded. Most observation periods will be from 10 to 15 minutes to as long as half an hour. The time will depend both on the time period in which the participants engage in the behaviour and the comfort of the observer. Because the research is dependent on who happens to be at the site when the observation takes place, more than one observation period will be needed. In fact it is best that a number of observations at different days and times be planned. This is to ensure that the research will adequately record the behaviour that is needed to answer the research question.

Choosing and training observers

Like other methodologies the success of obtaining the needed data depends on the skills of the researcher. Observation will take time as a number of observations will need to be made to ensure that the behaviour was adequately observed. This time commitment could be costly except for the fact that conducting observational research does not take a high level of skill. Therefore, the organization may wish to consider using volunteers from their own organization.

However, it is important that the observers be unknown to the participants. If they are known, the participants might come over to strike up a friendly conversation which will end the research. Another idea is to hire college students to conduct the observations. In fact, if the students are in a programme where they are studying research methods, they might find the research not only an educational experience but also something they can put on their resume.

The skills needed by observers are an attention to detail and patience. Observers must use their own judgement as to whether a person meets the participant profile. Therefore, in addition they must be able to make an informed guess as to the observable demographic characteristics of the person. They also need to be able to notice if the person is alone or with someone else. During the observation process they may need to be able to discern if the person being observed seems to be having difficulty, is unhappy or confused.

The observers also must have patience. They must observe the same people over a period of time and then be willing to start the observation period all over again. The behaviour they observe will often be similar. Repeatedly they may record comments such as 'father and child playing on swing set' and 'parents with baby unable to find place to sit'. Alone these observations may not seem all that exciting. However after all the observations have taken place and a researcher analyses the data, it may be found that swing sets are very popular and more are needed and that not enough benches are available in the playground area. These findings can then be used to improve the park.

Once the observers have been chosen it is important to train them properly. The observers should first be instructed on how to identify the proper participants. They then should be trained in the use of the form. To ensure that the observations are successful, the researcher should accompany the observers during the first observation period. This will help the observer with any unanticipated difficulties and also reassure the researcher that the observer will be able to perform the task. It is recommended that the researcher check on the observers occasionally during later observation periods just to ensure that everything is going well.

RESEARCHING THE WORLD OF AUSTRALIAN HIP HOP

Hip Hop culture may have been born in the Bronx in New York City, but it is now global. However, not all Hip Hop cultures are the same and Australian Hip Hop has unique characteristics. How do we know? Marketing research including observation was used to explore the world of Australian hip hop culture. Using observation was necessary as this group of individuals was not interested in helping researchers learn more about their world. Using qualitative techniques the researchers learned that Australian Hip Hopers view themselves as different from the American style Hip Hop culture. While not wanting to be involved in 'commercial' research, interestingly, the Hip Hopers expressed their unique Australian identity through consumption of particular products.

Source: Arthur (2006).

Question to consider: What cultural groups who are uninterested in participating in research could we study using observation?

Summary

■ Projective techniques can be used to obtain emotional rather than rational responses from research participants. They also allow the participants to provide information anonymously. In addition, they can help to make other research techniques more interactive and engaging.

■ Completion projective techniques, which ask the participant to complete a task started by the researcher, include sentence, story and cartoon completion. Creative tasks are more challenging and include word association, drawing and programme or ad creation. Other projective techniques available to the researcher include thematic appreciation tests and component sorts.

■ Observational research is used to watch what consumers actually do, versus asking them what they do. This research method works well when participants do not recall behaviour or it is inconvenient to ask people. Another use of observational research is when the potential participants would not be willing to provide verbal information. Observational research can be conducted as complete observer, participant observer or complete participant.

■ To conduct observations, the researcher must first decide upon the behaviour to observe and develop a participant profile. The researcher must then find a site where these participants can be found and then determine the best times to conduct the observation. An observation form must be prepared and observers must be chosen and trained.

■ References

Abrams, B. (2000) *The Observational Research Handbook: Understanding How Consumers Live With Your Product*, American Marketing Association, Abrams – Chicago, IL.

Arthur, D. (2006) 'Authenticity and consumption in the Australian hip hop culture', *Qualitative Market Research: An International Journal*, Vol. 9, No. 2, p 140–156.

ArtsMarketing.org (2004) 'Practical Lessons in Marketing', Downloaded on January 2006 from www.artsmarketing.org/marketingresources/tutorials.

Collier, A.K. (2004) 'African-American readers and black writers find opportunities in a large untapped market', *Writer*, 1 July.

Goffin, K. and R. Mitchell (2006) 'The customer holds the key to great products'. *Financial Times*, 24 March.

Marsden, P. (2002) 'What "Healthy-living" means to consumers: Trialing a new qualitative research technique', *International Journal of Market Research.*, Vol. 44, No. 2, p 223–234.

Seale, C., G. Gobo, J.F. Gubrium, and D. Silverman (eds.) (2006) *Qualitative Research Practice*, SAGE Publications, Thousand Oaks, CA.

CHAPTER 10

Planning survey research

■ Introduction

Surveys are probably the most common type of research used by non-profit organizations. However, just because everyone is familiar with the method, does not mean that everyone knows how to properly plan a survey. Too often, the questionnaire is put together casually without enough thought as to what topics should be included. In addition, the questions may be written quickly without considering how they will be interpreted by the participant. Lastly, few organizations take the time to test the questionnaire before they start the survey.

If the organization plans to use the results of the survey as the basis for future action or to impress funding organizations, it is important to plan properly. Therefore, taking the time to follow the steps in the planning process is important both to ensure the accuracy of the collected data and also to impress funders with the organization's knowledge of research methodology.

■ Survey research

So far the research methodologies discussed in this book have been qualitative techniques. These methodologies obtain information on consumers' ideas, opinions and attitudes. Qualitative research asks why people act the way they do.

In contrast, quantitative research asks the question of what, where, when, how many and how often. The most common quantitative research methodology is a survey conducted using a questionnaire form. The questions asked are most commonly close-ended with the participant asked to choose from a number of suggested answers. Occasionally some open-ended questions are included where participants are able to supply their own answer.

The survey may be self-administered or be administered by the researcher. A self-administered form may be handed personally to the participant, may be mailed or may be placed online. The survey may also be administered by a researcher either personally or over the phone.

Table 10.1 Use of survey research		
Marketing component	**Issues to researched**	**Sample question**
Customer	Demographic and psychographic facts	What are the age, gender and ethnicity of our current customers? What types of recreational activities do our customers prefer?
Product	Preferences, purchase habits, usage	What type of services do our current customers want us to provide? Where do our customers purchase tickets for our shows? How often do current customers visit our military history museum?
Price	Acceptable, form of payment	What price are senior citizens willing to pay for a bus trip to the state capital flower show? Would the snack bar sell more refreshments if it accepted credit cards?
Place	Location preference, location improvement	What schools should the children's theatre visit during the next academic year? How can the church's recreation center be improved so it is used for more weddings?
Promotion	Choose of media, marketing message, visual impact	Which local newspapers are read by our new target market segment of customers? What benefits should be stressed in our marketing message? What types of colours and pictures most attract the notice of our customers?

Use of survey research

Survey research can be used to answer questions about any aspect of the marketing mix, including the customers and their behaviour. In addition survey questions can be asked about the product, price, place and promotion (see Table 10.1).

Customers: One of the most fundamental uses of survey research is to learn more about the composition of the organization's current customers including both demographic facts and psychographic interests (Corder, 2006). Everyone is familiar with the survey form that is received from an organization through the mail, in person or via email that asks about the customer's age, gender, income, education level and activity preferences.

Product: Another use of survey research would be to learn more about the product preferences of either current or potential customers. The survey form may be designed to ask the customer the brand names of the products they purchase. Or, the form may ask general questions about the benefits customers prefer in a product. Since a product consists both of the actual product or service and also the extended product, the survey might ask what additional products or services the customer would like to see packaged with the product. For example, the survey form might ask what type of food should be served at the snack bar of a theatre or ask if follow up calls from health care providers would be useful for the customer.

Other product issues that could be researched using a survey form include the purchase habits of consumers. A questionnaire could be designed to ask how often the product is purchased, the amount purchased and who does the purchasing. For example, an organization that provides art classes for teenagers would want to know if the teens attend classes regularly or infrequently. The organization would also want to know if they attend one or many classes and if it is the parents or teens that make the decision to attend.

The organization might also use a survey to determine how the product is used. A summer day camp for young children conducted by the local history museum would want to know if the main reason parents send their children to the camp is an interest in history, to get them out of the house, or as inexpensive daycare.

Price: There are also price issues about which a survey can be used to gather data. First the acceptability of various price levels can be asked in a survey question. The question could be written as open-ended such as, 'What price would you be willing to pay?' Or, the question could give a price and ask if the price is too high, too low or about right. In addition a survey could gather data on how people would like to pay. For example, a museum might ask if visitors would like to pay a flat fee for yearly entrance, pay each time they visit, or buy a pack of five tickets that could be used at any time.

Place: Place, or distribution, can also be researched using surveying. For example, the questionnaire might ask about location preference. Questions could be asked about the location for distributing the service or product that would be most convenient for current or potential customers. In addition, a survey form might be designed to ask how the location of the organization can be improved to better meet the needs of the customers.

Promotion: Survey research can also be used to improve the effectiveness of the organization's promotional efforts. A questionnaire could ask what media is used by current or potential customers. This information would help the organization better place their advertisements, both print and broadcast, so that they will be heard by the target market segment. In addition, survey research can be used to help develop the marketing message, or the words that communicate the products benefits to the consumer. For example a question could ask which of several messages the current or potential customer finds most attractive.

Advantages and disadvantages of survey research

The most important advantage of survey research is that it can be used to disprove or support a hypothesis. To do so requires that the organization first construct a statistically valid sample by including a sufficient number of participants in the survey study. Once the survey questionnaire has been developed, it can be easily reproduced and distributed to many participants. In addition, a survey form has the advantage of being able to be self-administered. Asking participants to complete the survey on their own saves the organization researcher time and, therefore, money.

Another advantage of survey research is that the methodology can be adapted to be used in an online environment. While there is some use of the online environment for other methodologies such as interviews, it is survey research, with its factual questions, that best utilizes online technology.

Advantages of surveys

- Can disprove or support a hypothesis
- Can involve numerous participants
- Can be self-administered
- Can be distributed electronically

The disadvantages of survey research include the fact that the survey must be carefully designed with correctly written questions and answers. Writing a good question is not as easy as it may first appear. A poorly written question will get a response that does not accurately address the research question. A vague question will leave the participant confused without any opportunity to have the question clarified.

Survey research results will also need to be tabulated and analysed. When the responses from a large number of questionnaires need to be analysed a software program must be used. While learning to use the software to enter the data can be quite simple, analysis is not. Researchers will need to have some basic understanding of statistical analysis so that they can both manipulate the data to answer the questions and understand the meaning of the tabulated statistics.

Disadvantages of surveys

- Must be carefully designed
- Tabulation may require knowledge of software

IF YOU DON'T HAVE THE EXPERTISE, ASK!

Many nonprofit organizations understand the importance of conducting marketing research but feel they do not have the time and expertise to do so. According to a study conducted in the UK, they should consider asking for professional volunteer help. A survey of nonprofit organizations found that 20% thought that receiving help with marketing from sponsoring companies would be useful. However, only 5% of organizations actually receive such help.

The survey was conducted using a panel of 500 nonprofit groups. The participants were chosen so that they provided a balanced representation across nonprofit sectors. These organizations often use corporate volunteers. Except they use them for mundane tasks such as painting the building. How much better to do the painting yourself, while marketing experts write your survey!

Source: Kilby (2006).

Question to consider: What individuals or organizations could we ask for help with designing a research study?

■ The survey research process

Too often non-profit organizations will simply decide at a meeting to 'let's do a survey!' without adequately understanding the need to follow a process. Just because people are familiar with surveys does not mean they understand the development process. If a survey is to effectively help answer the research question, time and thought must be put into planning. The planning process starts with a meeting between employees of the organization who have knowledge of the research problem and those with the knowledge of research methodology. This meeting will be held to determine the research topics.

Only after this meeting will a draft survey be written. This draft will then be reviewed by management. Once the needed changes have been made to the questions and answers and any additional questions have been added, the draft will again be reviewed. After the draft is acceptable, the answers will be coded and the layout finalized. Then the survey will be ready for testing.

Questionnaire development process

1 Meeting with management and researchers
2 Write draft survey form
3 Management reviews draft
4 Researchers make adjustments
5 Management reviews draft (repeated as necessary)
6 Answers coded
7 Layout designed
8 Survey tested
9 If necessary, changes made
10 Survey again tested

Meeting with management

Once the research question has been finalized those who will be designing the survey form and those in management who have knowledge of the issue that gave rise to the research question must meet. Of course in a small organization, these two groups may be the same people. However, whether the organization is large or small, it is critical that everyone discuss what topics need to be included on the questionnaire. For almost all survey research the topics would include what demographic, psychographic, and in some cases, geographic information should be gathered.

The next decision would be to break down the research question into specific topics that need to be covered. For example, the research question might be, 'Why is attendance declining at senior centres?' The questionnaire on the use of senior centres might be designed to address a number of issues. These must be prioritized so that only three or four remain. It is important that this list not become too long. Each topic area will take more than one question, so if too many topics are covered, the final survey form will be too lengthy.

Sample survey topics

- What do participants believe is the purpose of senior centres?
- Why do participants not visit senior centres?
- Are there positive changes that they could recommend that would entice them to visit a centre?
- How would the participant rank these changes in importance?

Writing and review of the draft survey

After this meeting, it will now be time to start writing the questionnaire. At this stage, the questions will be rough. It may take many repeated efforts before each question is stated in exactly the right words to obtain the needed information. In addition, a first draft of the suggested answers must be written. Most of the survey questions should not be close ended. This means that suggested answers from which to choose must be written. The researchers may be surprised that what at first seems a simple task is actually quite difficult.

Once the questions and answers are written, they need to be reviewed by everyone involved in the process. Possible issues that may arise include having too many questions so that some must be deleted. In addition, it may now be noticed that an important topic area was not included and, therefore, new questions must be added. In addition, questions will be found to be confusing and must be rewritten. The suggested answers may also not be the ones that may most often be chosen by the participants. In this case, the answers must be rewritten.

Potential problems uncovered when reviewing drafts

- Too many questions so that some must be deleted
- Topic area not included so that new questions must be written
- Problem or confusing questions must be rewritten
- Improper or unclear answers must be clarified

Once the draft survey has been modified it must again be reviewed. It is not unusual for a survey to go through the writing and review process several times. However, each time there should be fewer modifications.

While the researchers may have felt the first draft asked exactly what was needed, they may be amazed by how much improvement will result from the review and rewrite process.

PROBLEM OR OPPORTUNITY?

The Theatre Arts Marketing Alliance (TAMA) in Boston wanted to know more about their audience. Specifically they wanted to know who they are, how they make theatergoing decisions and how to best communicate with them.

Many interesting facts were discovered including that the larger, better-established theatres attracted the older, more affluent theatergoers. It was also found that except for one theatre that specialized in family productions, 87% of theatergoers did not have children under the age of 18!

As a result of the discovery of this fact, the theatres realized there was a huge untapped pool of potential theatergoers they could potentially attract.

Source: Frieze (2005).

Questions to consider: Should we consider conducting research to discover untapped groups of consumers?

Coding the answers

After the questions and answers have been finalized, the researchers must code the answers. This coding is done to simplify the data entry task. When data is entered from a survey form it must be numerical as words cannot be manipulated statistically. For example, a question might ask if the participant reads the Sungazette, PennySaver, Daily News or Times. The data entry clerk will not enter the name of the paper that is read, instead they will enter a corresponding number. These directions could be given after the survey is completed by telling the clerk to enter the number one for Sungazette, two for PennySaver and so on. However, it is easier if the number to be entered is already on the form.

Sample answer coding

Please check which of the following newspapers you read daily:

1 ___ Sungazette   **2** ___ PennySaver

3 ___ Daily News   **4** ___ Times

Designing the layout

For both self-administered and researcher-administered surveys, the layout and physical appearance of the form are important. A questionnaire form that is difficult to read, unattractive and confusing may stop a potential participant from completing, or even starting, a survey. Simple issues such as font size, use of white space and the spacing between questions will communicate to the participant whether the form will be difficult or easy to complete.

Layout is important for researcher-administered surveys even though the participant does not see the form. A survey form with unclear markings for where to check the answer may result in a researcher wrongly marking a response. The layout is even important for the data entry clerk. Data entry is tedious and repetitive work. The form must be designed so that the coding of the answers can be quickly and correctly read and entered.

Testing the questionnaire

After the survey questions and answers have been written and approved and the layout designed, the survey is ready to be tested. The testing should be done with people who will be similar to those described in the participant profile. For example, the form should not be tested on the organizations employees if the research participants will be of a different education level or ethnicity. Even age can be a factor as use of terms used by young people may be different from what is used by those from an older generation (Presser, 2004).

The testing should also be conducted using the same survey method. Therefore a self-administered survey form should be tested without the researchers providing assistance. An online survey should also be tested by participants completing the form online. Whatever delivery method is going to be used should be duplicated as closely as possible during testing.

The last issue in testing is to test data entry. The completed forms should be entered into the software package that will be used to analyse the data. This testing will help to uncover any needed corrections in the coding of answers. It is better that errors be caught at this stage rather than after 500 or more forms have been printed.

SURVEYS ARE EVERYWHERE!

How many surveys does a person need to be asked to complete before he or she says – no more! With the ease of creating online survey forms, more and more companies are surveying to learn their customers preferences. If you have stayed in a hotel, had your car serviced or visited the dentist, you may well get a survey form asking about the quality of the service. Companies use these surveys because it is easier and cheaper to keep a current customer happy then to have to find a new customer. And it isn't just companies sending out the survey forms, government agencies, service providers such as law firms, and business to business enterprises are also using surveys more often.

> Is it worth it? Comcast, the US cable TV company, surveys 10,000 to 15,000 customers a month. The findings revealed, inflexible service call schedules were the number one pet peeve. Wells Fargo, the financial company, surveys 50,000 customers a month. They learnt that people hate to stand in line. While these may seem like common sense findings, the companies needed to know if these issues bothered enough people to justify large scale structural changes in how the companies do business.
>
> *Source*: Schellhorn (2006).
>
> *Question to consider: Are we over surveying are customers, and if so, what surveys should be dropped?*

Writing questions and answers

The key to a successful survey research study is writing the questions so that they obtain the right information. While this may seem self-evident, it is not as easy as it seems. Communication between two people can always lead to misunderstandings, even when they are face to face. For self-administered survey forms, the researcher will not be present to correct any confusions or misunderstanding that results from reading the questions. Therefore, it is critical that the researchers invest a great deal of thought into the question and answer writing process.

Another reason for taking care when writing questions is that small wording changes can make a large difference in the response received. Unfortunately while everyone communicates, people do not spend much time thinking about how they use language. A question such as, 'Do you think you might visit the museum this year?' may get a totally different response from one that asks, 'Do you plan to visit the museum this year?' Anyone can think about something with very little effort while planning means that a decision may already have been made.

Another issue of which the researcher must be aware is using loaded words. Words have literal meanings but they also carry emotional meaning. Unethical researchers know that by using words that are emotionally charged, they can manipulate people to respond in a certain way. For example, the question, 'Should the museum charge a fee for viewing special exhibits?' is very different from the question, 'Should people be forced to pay to visit a museum that has already been paid for with their taxes?'

Guidelines for writing questions

There are a number of general guidelines that if kept in mind will help the researcher write better questions. These guidelines include only asking questions participants can answer, keeping the wording simple, writing the question at the correct reading level, asking only one question at a time and avoiding the use of the passive voice. In addition, the researcher must keep in mind that, if necessary, the questions should be easy to translate into other languages.

Only ask what they know: Survey question should be factual. They should ask the what, where, when and how of current consumer behaviour. They can also ask the consumer to predict future behaviour but only based on facts, such as, 'Would you still drive without a seatbelt if the current fine was doubled?' While participants cannot be absolutely certain about their future behaviour, the fact that fines would double gives them factual information that they can use to assess their future behaviour. A question such as, 'What do you think would make drivers buckle up?' cannot be answered because the participant cannot know about what would motivate other drivers, only themselves.

Keep the wording simple: Researchers who work in an organization will be very familiar with the terminology that is used. Even if they are not familiar with terminology when they start the research process, by the time they start writing the survey questions, they will have become familiar because of meetings and discussions with others in the organization. However, the researchers must remember that the people reading the question will not be familiar with terms used on a daily basis in the organization. For example, an organization involved in international aide will certainly use the term NGO for non-governmental organization. However, not only will most people not know what NGO stands for, they will not even know what is meant by non-governmental. In a question, instead of the term NGO, the words 'organization not involved with any government' should be added.

Writing at the correct level: The researchers should keep in mind the reading level of the participants who will be involved in the study. Reading level involves the choice of words, but also the number of words in the question and the question structure. Questions should be kept short and, if possible, not use any subordinate clauses. For example, a question on funding for cancer research could be phrased, 'During the next budgetary year, what additional percentage should be appropriated for cancer research, dependent upon the criteria of no necessity for additional taxation?' could be written more clearly as, 'What additional percentages should be spent on cancer research without raising taxes?'

Asking one question at a time: In an attempt to limit the number of questions, and therefore the length of the survey form, researchers may be tempted to combine questions. This should be avoided as it can lead to confusion for the participant, which will result in inaccurate findings. A question such as, 'Did you contribute to the Nature Fund where your money was well spent saving trees in our city?' might have been written because the organization believes that anyone who contributed must feel the money was well spent on saving trees. However, this is actually two questions. Someone may have contributed to the fund because it was the only one saving the city's trees and yet still feel that their money could be better used by the organization. The questions should be separated such as, 'Did you contribute to the fund Nature Fund last year?' and Do you feel the Nature Fund should spend funds on saving city trees?'

Avoiding the passive voice: The passive voice does not use direct pronouns. Instead of using you, she, he or they, writing in the passive voice leaves the reader without any knowledge of who is the 'subject' of the question. A question such as, 'How important are community parks?' leaves the participant wondering, important to whom? Instead the question must specify whether participants are being asked if parks are important to them personally or to the community as a whole. After all a participant might not use parks, but still feel they are important for families.

Translation issues: When writing questions that will be translated, special issues need to be considered. Colloquial terms that have a meaning not associated with the literal translation should be avoided. Words such 'buzz' might be fine when used in an English question asking if participants thought the current promotion was effective. While the word can be translated, it will not have the same meaning.

Types of answers

Not only do researchers need to understand the general guidelines for writing questions, they must also learn the different types of answer formats that can be used. The types are differentiated by the way that the question can be answered. Open-ended questions will simply provide a blank where the answer will be written or typed in. The blank line should be long enough to accommodate the words without leaving so much space that the participants feel that they are expected to write a short essay. The advantage to fill in the blank answers is that the participant is allowed to answer in any way he or she chooses. The disadvantage is that each answer will need to be read and coded separately.

However with closed-ended questions there are a number of different ways that the answer can be provided. These include dichotomous choice, forced choice, multiple choice, checklist, rating and ranking questions.

Dichotomous choice: This type of answer makes the participant choose from one of two possible answers, which are usually opposites. This type of question provides answers such as yes or no, or male or female. If the research organization wants a direct answer to a question, this is the type of question to use. For example, an organization might want to know if blood donations would increase if blood mobiles offered evening hours. They could ask how important time of day's when making the decision to donate. Or, instead of asking about preference they can directly ask a yes or no question.

Dichotomous choice question and answer

Would you use a blood mobile donation site in the evening?

Yes ___ No ____

Forced choice: This type of answer is similar to dichotomous choice but with an important difference. With forced choice, the two possible answers are not opposites and, in fact, both might be true. However, a forced choice question compels the participant to state a preference. The choices that are given to the participant may have been included based on the knowledge of the organization's management or employees. Or, they might have arisen during earlier focus group or interview research. The organization knows that both answers might apply but wants to know which is more preferred. This type of question often uses words such as major, most often or most important. An example would be an organization that knows that people recycle because of concern for the environment and to reduce the amount they need to pay to get garbage picked up. While the organization knows that both will be true for many participants, a forced choice question will let them learn which is most important.

Forced choice question and answer

Which is your major motivation for recycling? (check one)

Concern for the environment ___ Reduce garbage pick up fees _____

Multiple choice: Multiple choice is a term with which everyone is familiar. This format is used when the organization knows that the question has a number of different possible answers. For example, an organization that promotes seat belt use might want to know why people do not use seat belts. The possible answers will be determined through information the organization already has, perhaps from conducting exploratory research. It is important that as many of the potential answers be included as possible. However, the list should not be so long that it is difficult for the participant to chose which is the best answer. The usual number of answers provided by a multiple choice question may be as few as three to as many as eight. Of course even these might not cover all possible answers. For this reason a final choice of 'other' may be provided along with a line where the participant can write in her or his own answer.

Multiple choice question and answer

What is the most important reason you do not alwayss use seat belts? (check one)

_____ Wrinkles my clothes

_____ Do not like to feel confined

_____ I am a careful driver so do not need to worry about accidents

_____ Will not be able to get out of car in case of accident

Checklist choice: Of course, everyone knows the frustration of believing that at least two answers on a multiple choice question could be right but only being allowed to provide one response. A checklist choice question and answer is a way around this problem. This type of answer allows participants to check more than one answer. This type of answer also allows for the researcher to provide many more choices than multiple choice, as the participant does not need to do the mental weighing of which is the best answer.

Checklist choice question and answer

Which of the following were reasons you chose to attend tonight's opera performance? (check as many as apply)

___ My spouse made me come   ___ Star soprano

___ I love all opera   ___ I love German opera

___ I am here as a professional obligation   ___ I had free tickets

___ Friend/relative recommended the performance

Ranking choice: A checklist choice can be modified so that even more information is obtained. A ranking choice asks the participant to rank their choices as to their importance in motivating their decision. The participant should not be asked to rank all choices as there are some that will not apply. Instead the participant should be asked to rank all those that do apply in order of importance. Or, the participant can be asked to rank the top three or five. A ranking choice provides more information for analysis. For example, a question might ask what three factors motivate their choice of when to go on a diet. The checklist answers might range from 'clothes do not fit' to 'cannot walk upstairs.' All of these answers are very different and the researcher does not know which to use as the basis for their recommendations. A ranking choice will let the researcher know which answer was most important overall. This can be accomplished by not just counting the responses but weighting each by importance.

Ranking choice question and answer

I know it is time to go on a diet when: (rank from 1 to 3 the three most important motivating factors)

__ My clothes do not fit   __ My spouse comments

__ My doctor tells me to   __ When summer is coming

__ When I finally weigh myself   __ I cannot walk upstairs without panting

Rating question: A rating question allows the participant to choose how strongly they agree or disagree to each answer rather than just respond with a yes or no check or a listing of priorities. A rating question also provides a list of possible responses. However the participant can choose for each whether they agree that the response is true, disagree that the response is true or if the response has no effect. For example, a question that asks about the motivation for enrolling in a class to learn more about historic homes might ask whether the participant is motivated by a love of architecture, the need for professional knowledge, the reputation of the teacher, or a desire to discover decorating ideas for their own home. For each they can say whether the factor motivated their decision, did not motivate or is of no interest. For additional information, the survey question can add 'strongly agree' and 'strongly disagree'.

Rating choice question and answer

Rate how each of these factors affected your decision to enrol in the architecture course:

	Agree	No Effect	Disagree
My love of architecture	____	____	____
I need to learn more for my job	____	____	____
I heard the teacher is great	____	____	____
I need design ideas	____	____	____

RULES FOR DESIGNING THE ONLINE SURVEY FORM

The RAND is a nonprofit organization that sponsors research and analysis. Since so many organizations are using online survey forms RAND decided to take a look at best practice in the new area of online surveying. Many of the suggestions they made to improve online surveying pertained to the layout:

1 List only a few questions per screen
2 Use graphics sparingly
3 Make sure that the graphics will not influence the question answer
4 Make error/warning messages as specific as possible
5 Always password protect Web surveys
6 Provide some indication of survey progress
7 Allow respondents to interrupt and then reenter the survey
8 Take advantage of the media's presentation capabilities

Source: Schonlau *et al.* (2002).

Question to consider: Do we need to learn more about how to create online survey forms?

■ Questionnaire layout

At this point in the survey research process the questions and answers will have been written, reviewed and then adjusted as necessary. Now the researchers must consider the layout of the questionnaire. The design, or 'look', of the survey is important as it actually affects the response rate. A poorly designed survey form can look confusing or intimidating. As a result the participant may decide not to even attempt the survey (Fink, 2006).

Besides the effect the visual design has on the participant, the needs of the person entering the data into computer software also must be considered. The coding must be easy for the data entry clerk to read while at the same time not being so conspicuous that it confuses the participant. The coding numbers should be placed immediately next to the line where the checkmark has been made. Or, the participant can be asked to simply circle the number to the answer.

Visual design

The visual elements that must be considered include the font size and style, the number of pages, the use of white space, the colour of the paper and the use of decorative elements. All of these will affect the participant's first impression of the survey. This first impression may determine whether participants even attempt the survey or, if they start, whether they will complete.

Fonts: Font size is important as it effects the perception of the difficulty of the material. Everyone is familiar with the term 'fine print'. When this term is used it usually is referring to detailed information that may be deliberately confusing. While no one writes a questionnaire with this intent, if the font size is very small, the perception that many people may have is that what is written will be difficult to understand.

Therefore the font should be large enough so that it conveys the impression that not only the words will be easy to read but that they will also be easy to understand. Another issue with font size is that it should be large enough for older participants to read with ease. As eyesight diminishes with age, the ability to focus on small print becomes increasingly difficult even with corrective lenses.

In addition to size, the type of font used should be decided upon based on ease of reading. While it may be tempting to use an 'artistic' font, such fonts can be difficult to read. The Times New Roman font is used so often in documents because of the ease of reading. Artistic fonts should only be used in the title of the survey, if at all. The use of underlining, italics and bolding should also be kept to a minimum as they can make the survey seem too 'busy' and therefore give the perception that it will be confusing to complete.

Number of pages: The researcher in charge of the layout of the survey must achieve a delicate balance between the need to include all the questions to which answers are required and the need to limit the number of pages. A survey form with too many pages will be seen as requiring too long to complete and, therefore, will not be even started. If the survey form will run to more than two pages, the researchers may want to add to the directions the anticipated completion time. This will let participants know that while lengthy, the questionnaire can still be completed quickly.

Use of white space: In an attempt to limit the number of pages while not reducing the font size, the researchers may decrease the page margins or the spacing between questions. However, by cutting down on white space on the paper, the survey form will look more difficult to answer. White space is visually 'restful'. It gives the eyes of the participants a place to rest before moving on to the next question. White space should be thought of as the pause that naturally occurs between sentences when speaking. Its effective use helps the participant to more quickly finish the questionnaire.

Paper colour: The questionnaire does not need to be on white paper. Use of an off white paper, such as an ivory, can make the survey form easier to read because it eliminates the stark contrast between the black type face on white paper. The researcher may also want to use coloured paper to better grab the attention of the participant. Having the forms on coloured paper can also make the management of the forms easier. After all, it is more difficult to lose a form in a busy office that is pink or yellow! However, bright or dark colours should be avoided as it can make the printing difficult to read.

Decorative elements: While it is important that a survey form be easy to read, there is no reason it needs to be boring. Adding visual interest can help attract and keep the participants attention. For example, the organizations logo can be added to the first page. In addition clip art that corresponds to the question can be added. For example, a survey form designed to be completed at an art gallery opening asking if the visitor finds the art easy to comprehend or confusing, can show a drawing of a person looking at a painting. Such clip art is included with word processing software and is also available online. The researcher should not add so much decorative details that the form will start to look confusing. However adding some interest will make the form more appealing.

Question order

The researcher must decide the order in which the questions should be listed. The factors that must be considered include both the ease of answering, and also the importance of keeping questions on common topics together. The questionnaire should start with questions that are easy to answer. These will be factual questions using a dichotomous or forced choice format. For example, simple yes or no questions on usage are appropriate as they require little thought. Questions on motivation that require more thought should be left for later in the questionnaire.

Sensitive questions that participants may be reluctant to answer should also be included later in the questionnaire. Of course, participants can always choose not to answer a question that they may find objectionable or too personal. However, if they come across such questions early in the survey, they may simply not continue.

The last questions in the survey form should be the demographic questions. Because such questions are easy to answer, they are sometimes placed at the beginning of the survey form. The reason for listing at the end of the form is that people are becoming more sensitive to any question that could be used for promotional purposes. This is true even when the form does not ask for the name of the participant. For this reason, not only should the demographic questions be placed last, the researchers should add a disclaimer stating that the questions will be used for research purposes only.

Routing questions are used when the answer will determine what questions will be asked next. For example, the first question on a questionnaire might ask if the survey participant is a current user of the organization's services. If they are, they will be directed to answer questions two and three that ask when they first started to use the services and how often they currently use the services. If they do not, they will be directed to skip the next two questions and start the survey again on question four.

Adapting the form for electronic use

Surveys can now be placed online. While this may seem to be a radical change, in fact, it is only a new means of creating and distributing the survey. There are many software packages available that will allow the organization to create a survey to be posted online. However, the same thought and care must go into the writing of the questions. For example, just because the use of word processing programs has made typing easier; it has not made people better writers. The same is true of survey software. It simply makes it easier to write a bad survey question.

If it is planned to use the survey form online, some of the issues for layout design change. While the researcher will still need to choose an easy to read font, font size is no longer a critical issue. This is because the researcher no longer needs to worry about the number of pages the survey will contain and the use of white space. The electronic form can even be designed to limit the amount of information that is shown on the screen at one time. In fact the survey can be designed so that only one question can be seen at a time. This does not mean that the researcher no longer needs to consider the issue of survey length. A survey that takes too long will still not be completed even if the participant can only see one question at a time.

An electronic survey form can more easily be made attractive than a paper survey form by adding decorative elements and colour. However, the researcher must still remember not to add too many decorative elements or the participant may become distracted from answering the questions.

One of the major advantages in electronic survey forms is that the routing of the questions becomes automatic. For example, the survey form might ask the participant a multiple choice question on how they travelled to an event. The answers provided might have included walking, taking the bus, riding a bike and driving. If the respondent answers the question by checking 'driving' automatically the next question will ask about the convenience of parking.

Other issues that will change when designing the survey for online use are coding and the manner of answering the questions. When using an electronic form, the data is entered automatically into a software program. Therefore there is no need to code the answers by adding numbers so that the person doing the data entry can enter a number rather than words. While the types of answers such as multiple choice or rating will not change, how the answers are presented can be altered. The answers can be listed just as they would be on paper with a radio button or dot that is checked next to the chosen answer. Of the answers can be shown via a drop down menu where respondents indicate their choice of answers.

Summary

- Survey research can be used to learn factual information about any aspect of the marketing mix. Its advantages include that the data can be used to support a hypothesis. Other advantages include that many participants can be involved and that the form can be self-administered either through the mail or online. However, to be useful a survey must be carefully designed and the tabulation of the results from a large survey will require a software program.

- Questionnaires must go through a development process that starts with a meeting between management and the researchers to determine the research topics. The drafts of the questions and answers must be reviewed by management and changed where needed until everyone is satisfied that the survey will obtain the needed information. Finally the form should be tested on people similar to the participants.

- When writing the questions, the researcher should make them answerable, simple and readable. The researcher should avoid the passive voice and also use wording that will translate well into other languages. Writing the answers is just as important as writing the questions. There are a number of different formats available. Each format differs in the type of information it will obtain. The right format must be chosen for each answer.

- The layout of the questionnaire form is important as it can affect the completion rate. Design issues that should be considered include font size, the number of pages, and paper colour. The researcher might consider using decorative elements to make the form appear more attractive. An advantage of placing a survey form online is that the layout can be easily modified.

■ References

Corder, L. (2006) *The Snap Shot Survey: Quick, Affordable Marketing Research for Every Organization*, Kaplan Publishing, New York, NY.

Fink, A. (2006) *How to Conduct Surveys*, SAGE Publications, Thousand Oaks, CA.

Frieze, D. (2005) 'Boston's TAMA explores audience demographics', *Back Stage*, Vol. 46, No. 12.

Kilby, N. (2006) 'Charitable marketing: money isn't always what talks', *Marketing Week*, 18 May.

Presser, S. (2004) *Methods for Testing and Evaluating Survey Questionnaires*, Wiley Publishing, Indianapolis, IN.

Schellhorn, E. (2006) 'A tsunami of surveys washes over consumers', *Christian Science Monitor*, 2 October.

Schonlau, M., R.D. Fricker Jr. and M.N. Elliott (2002) *Conducting Research Surveys via E-mail and the Web*, RAND, Pittsburg, PA.

Conducting surveys

■ Introduction

Once the survey questionnaire is completed, more decisions will need to be made. It is not as easy to conduct a survey as might be thought. One issue that researchers face is that people are becoming increasingly hesitant to participate in survey research. This may be due to concerns about privacy, or it may be that people are simply too busy. Another possibility is survey 'fatigue'. The ease with which online surveys can be prepared and sent means that people can feel inundated with requests to complete questionnaires. Therefore, they are more likely to say no. As a result careful thought must be given to how the survey will be distributed. The method chosen should not be the one most convenient for the organization; instead it should be the method that will have the best return rate.

■ Survey research methods

When considering conducting research, surveys might be the first, or even only, type of research that comes to mind. This is because most people have had the experience of completing a survey form. While researchers may understand that care must be taken to determine what survey questions to ask, they may not have considered the fact that as much care needs to be taken when deciding how the survey should be conducted.

One option is for the survey to be self-administered. With this method the participant may be handed a survey form, that they are then asked to complete. Or, the participant may find the form in a programme, on their seat, or at a reception or service desk. In addition, the participant may have the form mailed to them. A newer form of self-administered surveys is sent electronically.

Not all survey forms are self-administered. With some survey research, the researcher or assistant asks the questions verbally and then completes the form. The researcher will either ask the questions in person or over the phone.

Advantages of self-administered surveys

There are several advantages to the organization if the decision is made to use a self-administered survey methodology. These include cost savings and the ability for participants to complete the survey at a time and place that is most convenient for them. In addition, self-administered surveys eliminate bias that might result from the researcher leading the participant to answer in a certain way or the participant answering the question with an answer they feel will be acceptable to the researcher.

There are cost savings that result from using a self-administered survey, such as not having to pay for someone to administer the questionnaire. Of course, in the case of telephone or personal surveying the person assisting the participant does not need to have research skills. This will save costs as they can be paid less than a skilled researcher. However, the organization still must factor in the costs of hiring, training and supervising the employees conducting the survey.

A self-administered survey can be more convenient for the participant. Because they do not need the assistance of a researcher, they can complete the form at the location and time that is best for them. For example, a survey form that is placed at the reception desk of an organization can be completed once the participant has returned home. An online survey can be completed during lunch break at work. A participant may choose to answer the questions on a mail survey form when they are going through the monthly bills.

While having a researcher or other employee help with completing the form may seem beneficial, there are also drawbacks that a self-administered survey eliminates. With a self-administered survey there is no way that researchers can suggest an answer to the participant. While an ethical researcher would not do so intentionally, their body language or just the way they ask the question can lead the participant to answer in a certain way. Another advantage is that the presence of the researcher might result in the participant being less than truthful. With a self-administered survey form, the participant has the privacy that will allow them to answer sensitive questions without concern for the researcher's reaction. Table 11.1 summarizes the advantages of each method.

Table 11.1 Comparison of advantages	
Self-administered	**Researcher-administered**
Cost savings	Provides means of clarification of questions
Completion at convenience of participant	Researcher can motivation participant to complete
Eliminate researcher bias	Encourage participation by disenfranchised groups

Advantages of researcher-assisted surveys

There are also advantages when an organization chooses to have researchers or other employees help participants with the survey questions. With a researcher-assisted survey, someone will ask the questions verbally and then record the answers. A major advantage of this method is that participants can ask for clarification of any difficult or confusing questions. Even simple survey questions such as, 'How often last year did you visit our organization?' may prompt questions. For example, the participant might ask if this includes the times they just gave their neighbour a ride to the organization. Without the researcher's explanation the participant will have to guess whether these occasions should be counted as 'visits'.

Survey completion is always an issue. With researcher-assisted surveys someone is present to encourage participants to complete the entire questionnaire. Even the most motivated research subjects starting a survey in their own homes, may then get interrupted by the telephone or doorbell. Unfortunately, when this happens there is no guarantee that they will return to complete the form. A researcher-assisted survey eliminates these distractions and ensures the form is completed. With a self-administered survey participants may completely skip questions they find sensitive or difficult to answer. A researcher-assisted survey allows the researcher to encourage participants to not skip these questions.

A final advantage of using researcher-assisted surveying is when working with disenfranchised groups. Members of these groups may feel that they have no stake in the decision-making process. Or, the members may not have the language skills or cultural knowledge to understand the research process. Whether the reluctance to participate is from a feeling of being outside the system or a lack of understanding of the process, it may take the persuasive skills of the researcher before participants will cooperate and complete the survey.

**DON'T JUST ASK WHAT THEY BELIEVE,
ASK WHAT THEY ACTUALLY DO**

When considering how to market their brand, arts and other nonprofit organizations might want to consider the 'snob' factor. According to a survey, people will buy books just to impress others. A survey of 2,100 people about their book purchase habits was conducted by British Airports Authority and Expedia. They found that one of eight young people have bought a book because it either won or was a runner up for a literary prize. However when asked whether they had read the prize winning books, the percentages dropped considerably. In fact some participants admitted they buy two types of books, ones to impress people and others they actually will enjoy reading.

> So when writing survey questions about an organization, it is important to ask about the participants' attitudes. But also be sure to ask if they actually do visit your organization.
>
> *Source*: Ezard (2005).
>
> *Question to consider: Do we phrase our survey questions to ensure that we are obtaining accurate information on our customers' behaviour?*

■ Self-administered survey methods

If the organization decides to use a self-administered survey method they must decide on the form of distribution. The questionnaire can be personally handed to the participant or left at some obvious place where it can be readily seen. The questionnaire can also be mailed to the home or work address of the participant. A self-administered method that is growing in popularity is online delivery of the questionnaire form. PDA's and cell phones using text messaging are also now being used to deliver survey questions.

Mail surveys

Mail surveys remain in use despite the growing popularity of electronic delivery formats. An advantage of conducting a mail survey is that almost everyone has an address and they are usually easy to obtain. If the organization is surveying current or past customers, they will probably already have addresses in their files. For people who are not customers, the addresses will most likely be publicly available either from a phone book or by searching online. Mailing lists can also be purchased from companies that supply address lists. In addition, voter registration lists can also be used.

Mail surveys are usually mailed to the potential participant's home address. However, a work address can be used if appropriate. Work addresses would be used when the research question relates to the participant's work responsibilities. For example, a research study on life-work balance for professionals could be sent to a work address. However, most surveys will be sent to home addresses. The survey form is usually sent in an envelope that includes the name of the organization so that the receiver will be motivated to open and read the material. A cover letter explaining the purpose of the research study with contact information will also be included along with a stamped return envelope.

Of course, with mail surveys, the completion rate will depend on the quality of the addresses. If the population that is to be surveyed moves often or lives with relatives, it will be more difficult to find current addresses. Voter lists are limited to those who register to vote, which in the US would limit the list to US citizens. It is also known that voters tend to be older and better educated than the population average. Another problem is that there may not be money in the organization's budget for purchasing commercially available mailing lists.

Survey forms left to be picked up

If the organization wants to survey current customers, the forms can be personally distributed to the potential participants at the organization. The advantage of this method is that the person handing out the survey form can make a personal appeal to the potential participant to complete the survey form. For example, clients who have just completed a clinic appointment may be handed a form while explaining that completing the survey will help the clinic provide better service in the future.

If it is not possible to hand out the survey form personally, the forms can be left on seats at a theatre, included in programmes that are distributed, left at a front reception desk or placed on a waiting room table. In this case, information must also be provided as to the purpose of the research so that the customer will be motivated to complete the survey.

It is important that participants understand what they should do with the survey form once it is completed. They should be instructed to return the form to an individual such as the receptionist, an usher or to place the form in a designated box. The organization must also make sure that the person who has been designated to receive the forms retains them until they can be picked up or that the forms are collected from the box.

This type of distribution is rarely used to research people not associated with the organization. This is because it is difficult to control distribution to people who meet the participant profile. If survey forms were just handed out in public or left at public places it would be difficult to ensure that the people who see the form and complete the survey are the ones that meet the profile. Without any direct tie to the organization, it would also be the rare person who would be motivated enough to take the time to complete the survey form.

Electronic delivery of survey forms

Delivering survey forms online is increasing in popularity. The reasons for this popularity include the low cost of delivery, the ease of completion for the participant and the fact that the software can automatically tabulate results. The cost of a mail survey include postage for both mailing the survey and for the return envelope. With the increase in postage rates, this can be a substantial cost that is eliminated with online surveys. While personally delivered surveys do not need postage, there is still the cost of reproduction that is also eliminated with online surveys. Online surveys are also easy to complete and return for the participant. Another advantage for the organization is that the researchers can track completion rates on a daily basis. The software will also tabulate results automatically, eliminating the need for data entry, which is also another cost savings (Sue and Lois, 2007).

However, electronic delivery is not appropriate for all populations. It works best when the profile describes a younger, better educated participant. First, the participant must have an email address and access to a computer for their personal use. Second, they must be frequent computer users so that are they comfortable with online completion.

Electronic forms are not sent out via email either in the body or as an attachment. This method does not work well as the size of the form may be a problem for the participant's computer. Instead the electronic survey form is housed on the organization's website and the participant is given the link that will gain access. An email is sent to participants with a link, information on the research study and an invitation to participate. The link will bring the recipient directly to the form for completion.

Of course, before sending the email the organization will need to design the online survey form. There are several free or inexpensive tools available to help the organization with this task. Having the survey form online in no way shortens the questionnaire development process. The same process of writing and reviewing draft survey questions must be followed. When the layout stage is reached the questions and answers will be typed into the survey software instead of into a word processing program.

Once the survey process is started, electronic forms have several advantages. The researchers can monitor the completion process by checking how many forms have been completed. The researcher can then send follow-up reminder emails to encourage completion. The researchers can also monitor if specific questions are not being answered or are eliciting confusing answers. If necessary, these questions can then be changed for future participants.

Other forms of electronic delivery of survey questions are now being tried. A limited number of survey questions can be delivered via text messaging. This method is most often used with a group of individuals who have already agreed to this form of contact.

IF YOU WANT THEIR HELP, WHY SHOULDN'T YOU PAY?

Theatergoers, who went to see the Lord of the Rings production in Toronto, were given a handout as they left the theater. They were offered $5.00 or a Rings souvenir if they completed an online survey. The production company's purpose was to learn more about the behavior of the audience. They found that a large proportion of their audience do not attend other theatres. The information on where the audience members live allows the production company to better target their promotions. But the theatergoers are also asked about their opinions of the production and the company listens. Changes have been made to the show based on audience feedback.

Source: Posner (2006).

Question to consider: What type of incentives can we provide participants when we ask them to complete a survey?

■ Researcher-administered survey methods

The organization may decide that it would be best if a researcher or other employee helped with administering the survey. This method would be chosen if it was believed that the potential participants might not be sufficiently motivated to complete the survey on their own. The questionnaire can be administered personally or over the phone.

Researcher-administered methods have the advantage of personally persuading the individual to participate in the study. While the research study is very important to the organization, potential participants may see no reason why they should stop what they are doing to give even five minutes to answer survey questions. It can take a personal appeal with the researcher explaining how the public will benefit from the study before participants are willing to participate.

Personal surveying

Personal surveying has the advantage of face-to-face contact. This allows the researcher to explain the purpose of the research and how participation will be helpful. Personal surveying can be conducted where individuals who meet the participant profile are located. For current customers this will most likely be at the organization. For individuals who are not users of the organization this will be at other locations. For example, if the organization wishes to survey mothers with children they may decide to conduct the survey at a local day care centre. If young women and men are the targeted population the organization may conduct the surveys at sports facilities or shopping malls where they may naturally congregate. Of course, the permission of the business or organization where the surveying will be conducted must be obtained. Non-profit organizations have an advantage in gaining permission, as the research will be used for a social benefit and not just to sell more products.

When conducting personal surveys the researcher can use visual prompts that can assist the participant in answering the question. For example, if the organization wishes to learn more about the effectiveness of promotional material, they can show participants sample ad copies that have been produced. They can then ask the participants to rank them on their appeal. They could also show photos of art work, park designs or even have them listen to short clips of music. All of these methods need to have a researcher present to explain how these prompts relate to answering the question.

When at the location where the survey will be conducted, the researcher must first ascertain that the potential participant meets the profile characteristics. Even if the survey is held at the organization's location, not all customers may meet this profile. Some characteristics may be visually verified such as gender, family status or age range. Others, such as lifestyle or religious background cannot be so easily seen. The researcher must first ask the potential participant screening questions to see if they fit the profile.

Before asking these questions the researchers should introduce themselves and quickly explain the purpose of the survey research. They then should explain what type of participant is needed and why. For example, the survey research may have been designed to determine whether an art school is meeting the needs of parents or if childcare should be provided. However, the researchers will have no way of knowing which student is a parent. By explaining the purpose of the study first, the potential participant will not be offended when, after having stated they do not have children, they are not asked the survey questions.

Telephone surveying

The disadvantage to personal surveying is that the researcher must be at the same location as the research participants. This is not a problem when the potential participants can be found at the organization. However, this is often not the case. For many organizations the potential participants will be non-users of the organization or members of the general public. In this case, telephone surveying can be conducted. Telephone surveying has the advantage of the researchers being able to motivate the individual to participate and complete the survey even though they are not physically present. In addition, the researcher can explain any confusing questions. The advantage of telephone over personal surveying is that the participants can be geographically dispersed. In addition, telephone surveying is useful for groups that may not be easy to find in public places such as the elderly or infirm.

Another advantage that telephone surveying has over personal surveying is privacy. With a telephone survey, the participant may be more willing to reveal sensitive or negative information. For example, a survey conducted by an organization promoting mental health may ask if the participant has ever suffered from depression. The participant may be more willing to answer this question affirmatively if they are not face-to-face with the researcher.

Everyone has experienced receiving a telemarketing call right at the dinner hour. This was not an unfortunate coincidence as these calls are made at dinner time exactly because that is then people are home. The same is true of telephone survey calls. They are made in the evening after people have returned home, but not so late as to disturb someone who has already retired for the night.

While telephone surveys have long been one of the most popular methods of surveying, there is a growing concern whether this method will survive. First, technology has made telephone surveying difficult. As people switch from land lines to cell phones, obtaining usable telephone numbers for the general public has become more difficult. This is an especially critical issue if the potential participants are younger as they may not ever have had a land line phone in their home.

Another issue for organizations is no-call lists. These lists may not apply to the organization if it is a non-profit. However, most people may not understand the distinction and will be unhappy that they are called. Even for those who still depend on land line phones and are not on no-call lists, Caller ID allows them to screen calls resulting in the organization not even having their call answered.

TIPS TO REMEMBER WHEN USING ONLINE SURVEYS

There are a number of different survey tools available online. SurveyMonkey, Zoomerang and QuestionPro are probably the best known. Some of these companies offer free services for small surveys. All charge for longer surveys with many participants. The most frequent use of online surveys is to gauge the level of customer satisfaction. When using surveys for this purpose there are some guidelines that can help ensure success. First understand what you want to know. Second, make sure that the survey is delivered to the customer as soon after they visit the organization as possible. Third keep the survey short and simple. When reviewing the responses don't be tempted to discard any that are unfavorable. Finally, be sure to thoroughly analyze the answers.

Source: Campanelli (2007).

Question to consider: How can we implement an online survey process for determining customer satisfaction?

■ Surveying process

The process of designing and conducting a survey is similar for both self-administered and researcher-administered surveys (see Table 11.2). Both will start with a meeting between the researchers and the management of the organization. After the research question has been determined the organization must decide on both the participant profile and the research methodology. If the organization decides to conduct survey research, they then must decide if they wish to conduct a self- or researcher-administered survey. They then must decide on the delivery method.

While the same process of writing and reviewing questions must be followed the form will be tested using the decided upon delivery methods. Besides testing, there are other steps in the process that change

Table 11.2 Process of conducting surveys				
Self-administered			**Researcher-assisted**	
Mail	**Drop off**	**Online**	**Personal**	**Telephone**
Obtain list	Determine sites	Obtain software	Determine site	Phone list
Mail surveys	Pick up forms	Send emails	Hire/train	Hire/train
Compile	Compile	Monitor	Conduct	Conduct
Analyse	Analyse	Analyse	Compile	Compile
Report	Report	Report	Analyse	Analyse
			Report	Report

based on the delivery methods. For example, with researcher-assisted surveying, the organization must hire and train those who will conduct the survey. In addition, with telephone surveying, the organization must procure the needed telephone numbers. With online surveying, the organization must obtain the needed software.

Hiring surveyors

If the survey is to be researcher assisted, the organization must find a sufficient number of individuals to conduct the survey. The number of people who will be needed will depend on the number of surveys that must be completed. For a small personal survey of current customers that will be conducted at the organization, one or two individuals should suffice. For a large scale telephone survey requiring several hundred phone calls, a dozen of more people will be needed over a period of several days.

For small surveys, people who already work at the organization can be used as surveyors as long as they have the interest and skills. For larger surveys, the organization may be able to use volunteers or members of a 'Friends' organization. Using volunteers or friends will help to keep the research costs down.

However, there may be occasions when the organization must use outside assistance. A large organization may contract with a call centre to conduct the survey. Call centre employees are trained to conduct survey work for many different types of organizations. Of course, only the largest non-profit organizations would be able to afford such an option. Instead, most organizations may need to pay individuals to conduct the survey. A good source of such short-term employees would be a local college or university. College students often do not mind making the phone calls and are often in need of extra money.

The individuals who will be conducting the survey must have strong oral communication skills. The manner in which the survey taker speaks will make an immediate impression on the potential participant. In addition they must be personable, as their tone of voice must communicate an interest in both the research and the participants' responses. This does not mean they need to comment on what is being said but rather that they communicate through their personality and tone of voice that the research is important and that the research process will not be overly onerous. Surveying is hard work in that it requires repeating the same process numerous times. The survey taker may find the responses from the first few participants of interest. However, they must keep at the process long after this interest has waned. Finally, the survey taker must be honest. Otherwise they will be tempted to start to skip difficult questions and fill in the answer themselves. In fact some survey takers might be tempted to fill in the entire survey. This is especially true if the survey takers are paid by number of forms completed. To decrease this temptation, the workers should be paid on an hourly rate and be supervised.

Skills and characteristics

- Ability to communicate
- Personable and enthusiastic
- Hardworking
- Honest

Training surveyors

The success of a researcher-assisted survey will depend on the skill of the survey taker. Hiring survey takers with the needed skills and characteristics is important. However, the organization must also provide training, whether the survey takers are volunteers or paid. Of course, if they are being paid, they will also need to be paid during training, as they cannot be expected to attend for free. When there are only a few individuals who will be conducting the survey they can be trained individually. Larger groups can be trained in a classroom setting.

The first step in the training process is to explain the organization and its mission. The organization will be relying on the fact that it is non-profit and contributes to the public good to motivate participation. Therefore, the survey takers will need to understand the work of the organization. The training should then explain both the research topic and the benefits that will result from the survey data. Besides providing information that they can communicate with the participants, the survey takers will feel better about making the calls when they know the good that will result from the research findings.

Once this background information has been covered, the person conducting the training will go through the survey form question by question. The survey takers will need to clearly understand each question so that they can clarify any confusion that a participant might have. In addition the trainer should review directions on how the questions should be asked.

The survey takers should then role-play administering the survey. The 'participants' can be other trainees or the trainer. The first time through the role-play will be just to let the surveyor have the experience of asking the questions and recording the answers. Then the trainer should role-play difficult situations that might occur so that the survey taker learns the proper way they should be handled. This includes potential participants who want additional information to confirm the legitimacy of the caller and hostile participants.

Finally, the first surveys that are administered should be monitored by the trainer. The trainer needs to be present to help with any unforeseen difficulties. They also need to monitor and correct, if necessary, the attitude of the survey taker. As they are representing the organization, it is important that they handle all situations professionally.

Training of survey takers

- Introduce organization and its mission
- Explain the research topic
- Review the survey form and directions
- Practice role playing of survey taking
- Supervise and monitor first surveys

The survey taking process

Both personal and phone surveys follow an established process with which the survey taker must be familiar. This process should be covered during training and should be reinforced with role playing. Ensuring that the process is followed is one of the reasons that the first few surveys taken should be monitored by the researcher (Gwartney, 2007).

Either in person or over the phone, the conversation should start with an introduction of the organization. The survey taker may also use their first name if it is felt to be appropriate and helpful in established a friendly atmosphere. However, what is most important is that the participant immediately knows that the call is coming from a non-profit organization. The first concern most people have when being approached either in person or over the phone is that someone will try to sell them something.

The introduction should include both the name and, in case the participant is not aware of the organization, a few words on the mission. For example, all that needs to be said is, 'Hello I am calling from Hope House an organization that works to provide better lives for disabled children.'

After the introduction of the organization, the next step is to explain the reason for the call. Again this can be quickly stated such as, 'We are calling tonight to learn more about the community's opinion of services for disabled teenagers.' The survey taker will then explain why the individual is being called. This is important as after allying the individual's fears that the call or conversation will involve sales, the next concern will be why he or she has been singled out. Therefore, the survey taker should explain how the participants have been chosen. They may explain that city residents are being randomly called, that the names are on a list of previous donors, or that they were stopped as part of a random sample.

If there are any eligibility questions that need to be answered, they should be asked at this time. For example, the survey taker may want to confirm that the person called has teenage children, is over a certain age or has used the services of the organization. If the answers provided by the individual meet the participant profile requirements, the survey can proceed. If not the survey taker should thank participants for their time and go on to the next call.

If the participant does meet the profile the next step would be to explain the time requirements. For example, participants should be informed that the survey should take five to seven minutes of their time. The participant should then be informed that their answers will not be associated with their name and that the data will only be analysed by the organization. The individual should also be told what will happen to the results. This would be a statement that the final report will be available for review at the organization's office or posted on their website.

Once these preliminary steps have occurred the survey taker will ask if they can continue with the survey questions. The survey is then conducted and the participant is thanked at the conclusion.

Survey process

- Introduction of organization
- Explain purpose of research
- Explain how sample was choosen
- Determine eligibility with screening question
- Explain time requirements
- State privacy policy
- Inform what will happen with results
- Obtain consent
- Conduct survey, clarifying questions when needed
- Thank for participation

■ Motivating participation

While the organization may understand the need for the research to be conducted, this will not necessarily be true of those individuals who will be asked to participate. In fact, obtaining cooperation from potential research participants is becoming increasingly difficult. This disproportionately affects survey research because with surveys more participants are needed.

This reluctance to participate may stem from two sources. First, the rapid strides in communication media means that people can be contacted easily and in multiple forms. Individuals may receive mail at their work address or at home. They will have a work phone number, a home land line number and a cell phone. They can both be called and text messaged. They can also receive emails at work and at the email address on their home computer. As a result individuals will receive sales solicitations and survey research requests via all these media. Therefore, it is not surprising that when asked to participate in a survey their first instinct is to respond no.

A second reason for the reluctance to participate in a survey is privacy concerns. Although the non-profit organization would not do so, other organizations may state that they are conducting research while the call is really about making a future sale. This is unethical behaviour, but it does occur. Therefore, individuals will be careful about with whom they communicate. In addition, people wonder what will happen to the information they provide. They may be reluctant to participate in even bona fide research studies because of the concern that they will then receive additional phone calls from the same or other organizations.

Motivation for survey participation

However, there are still people who are willing to participate in research studies. One of the reasons is they do so is to assist an organization or cause that they support. Therefore, the potential participants who are most likely to cooperate will be current or past users of the organizations products and services.

However, others will be willing to participate because they have an interest in the research subject. For example, if an environmental organization is conducting a research study on people's awareness of global warming, those who have an interest in the subject are much more likely to participate than those who are not even aware of the issue. Of course, it is difficult to determine who will have an interest in the research subject before the call is made, which is why the surveyor should introduce the organization, its mission and the research topic early in the research process.

Some people who are not interested in the organization or the research topic, may be motivated to participate when they understand how the research findings will benefit others. These altruistic individuals will respond once it is explained how the public will benefit from the results of the research.

Non-profit organizations have an advantage over for-profit businesses in that few people will respond to a survey on orange juice consumption to support the orange juice company, an interest in the 'pulp versus no-pulp' issue, or because they want the world to have more pulp choices at breakfast. Therefore, businesses must often rely on financial incentives.

Non-profit organizations may also want to consider offering some type of incentive to those who participate in the survey. Because of budget constraints it is unlikely that the organization could offer an incentive that would motivate the participation of someone who would otherwise be uninterested. However, a small incentive is a way of thanking the person for taking the time to participate. After all, almost everyone enjoys receiving a gift. The incentive does not need to be costly. In fact, it could be a product or service of the organization. For example, free tickets or a free CD of a performance could be offered. Products with the organization's logo, such as pens, mugs or T-shirts, are a way of saying thanks while also promoting the organization. If the organization cannot afford to give out free tickets to everyone who participates they could hold a drawing for a pair of tickets to a sought after event.

Motivation for participating in surveys

- Support of organization
- Interest in research subject
- Altruistic concern for others
- Product incentive

HOW TO BUY AN ONLINE SURVEY TOOL

Online survey tools can be easy to use. But they are not always easy to buy. Here are some suggestions about questions to ask when buying a software tool. First ask the total cost. Then ask about the company's customer service and how long they have been in business. Check the company's references. Make sure that all data will be kept confidential. Determine the speed of the software. Ask what happens when an email message to a participant about the survey is bounced back. Find out about the software's reporting function. Finally don't forget to ask if the software will provide design guidance.

Source: Muldoon (2005).

Question to consider: How can someone in our organization become familiar enough with the various software packages so that we can choose the right one?

Cover letters or emails

For self-administered surveys, the information that will motivate participation will need to be in written form. This could be a cover letter sent in the mail with the questionnaire, or an email regarding the online survey. For survey forms that are left to be picked up, the information will need to be included in the form itself.

The letter, form or email should contain information on how to contact the organization that is conducting the research. A name of a specific contact should be included along with their phone number. It is not enough to just provide the main or central phone number for the organization as the person answering the call may not even be aware of the research project. The letter should be on official letterhead to reassure the participant of the legitimacy of the form. If the contact information is included in the form of an email, if possible, the organization's logo should be included. The contact information is provided so that if the recipient is still in doubt, the legitimacy of the survey can be verified.

The letter, form or email should then contain a very short description of the organization and the purpose of the research. It is critical that this be stated in as few words as possible; otherwise the recipient will not take the time to read the information. Information on why they were chosen to receive the request should also be included along with information on confidentiality. This is even more important with a self-administered mail or email survey as the participants may wonder if the returned form will in some way be coded so that it can be traced back to their name and address.

The letter, form or email will then explain how the information will benefit the public in general, not just the organization. Printed surveys will often be more than a single page because of the space needed for providing the many potential answers. Individuals looking at the form may decide it will take too long. Therefore, information on estimated completion time should be provided, such as "This form contains 20 questions and should take five minutes to complete." For online surveys the number of questions and the estimated time should be provided as the individual will be unable to gauge the length of the questionnaire visually.

For mail surveys a stamped, return envelope should be included. While this can be expensive, providing the envelope and stamp can increase the likelihood that the form will be completed and returned. If the organization feels that the response rate will be low and therefore too many stamps wasted, the mail can be metered so that the organization is only charged if the stamped envelope is used. For surveys that are to be returned to a drop-off location, the organization must clearly state where the form should be returned. To increase likelihood that it is returned, more than option can be given. The directions might state the form can be left at the reception desk, given to any organization employee or mailed.

For online surveys the email should include a link where the form is located. The recipient should be able to simply click and reach the form. In case the recipient has difficulty reaching the form in this manner, the website address where the form is located may also be included. The organization should consider adding information on what the recipient should do if they encounter technical difficulties. There may be recipients who will have difficulty accessing the form because they do not often work with computers. Such individuals also might have difficulty understanding how to use the form, such as handling the drop-down menus, once they start the survey. Therefore a name and number they can call for help would be useful. Another reason for including contact information in case of technical difficulty is that there might be problems with the website hosting the site of which the organization may be unaware. An email or phone call from a participant would notify them of the difficulty so that it could be addressed.

Cover letter or email components

- Use official letterhead or use logo
- Provide contact information
- Introduce organization and purpose of research

- Explain how the sample was selected
- Assure confidentiality
- Describe how public will benefit
- State length of form and time to complete
- Include mailing instructions and envelope or website link
- Provide contact information for online surveys in case of technical problems

Summary

- Surveys can be self-administered, where the participant completes the survey on their own, or, the survey may be administered by a researcher. The advantages of self-administered surveys include cost savings and the fact that a researcher cannot influence the answer to a question. However, researcher-administered surveys have the advantages of providing participants with assistance if they are confused by questions and also encouragement to complete the survey form.

- Self-administered surveys can be sent through the mail, left to be picked up or delivered electronically. Mail surveys are useful for participants who are not current users while survey forms distributed at the organization target current customers. Online, or electronic survey forms, are becoming increasingly popular but also have limitations.

- Personally administered surveys allow the researcher to motivate disenfranchised groups to participate. Phone surveying is still in use but is becoming increasingly difficult due to use of cell phones, no-call lists and disgruntled potential participants.

- The surveying process differs depending on the delivery method. For mail and phone surveys, the researchers must obtain a valid list of contacts. Electronic surveying will necessitate the purchase of specialized software. For researcher-administered surveying people to administer the survey must be hired and trained.

- The organization should provide information about the purpose of the survey and how the findings will be used in order to motivate participation. It may also be necessary to provide a financial or product incentive. However, non-profit organizations will usually receive more cooperation because they are mission based.

■ References

Campanelli, M. (2007) 'Survey says: Do them right, and online surveys can be very revealing', *Entrepreneur*, January.

Ezard, J. (2005) 'One in three has bought a book just to look intelligent', *The Guardian (London)*, 24 October.

Gwartney, P.A. (2007) *The Telephone Interviewer's Handbook: How to Conduct Standardized Conversations*, Jossey-Bass Publishing, Hoboken, NJ.

Muldoon, K. (2005) 'Hot tip: It's the research, stupid', *Direct*, April.

Posner, M. (2006) 'Mister, will you help us fix this show . . . for $5', *The Globe Review*, 4 April.

Sue, V.M. and L.A. Ritter (2007) *Conducting Online Surveys*, SAGE Publications, Thousand Oaks, CA.

Analysing qualitative and quantitative data

■ Introduction

At this stage in the process the organization has results. They either have a pile of completed questionnaire forms or tapes and notes from focus groups, interviews or observations. Now the issue is to use analysis to turn these results into recommendations. While quantitative and qualitative results will be analysed differently, both should result in useable recommendations for the organization. The recommendations might describe new consumer segments the organization should target. They might also make recommendations on improving the price, distribution and promotion of a product. The recommendations should not just be 'good ideas' on which the organization might wish to take a 'chance'. Instead they will be ideas for action that are backed with research results.

■ Unique aspects of analysing data

The organization will have spent a considerable amount of time planning the research process. They will have determined the research question that expresses what the organization needs to learn that they currently do not know. They will then have decided upon the research methodology that will best provide the answer. After these two major decisions, the organization then faces the task of developing the participant profile. Finally, the organization can proceed and conduct the research.

After conducting the research the next step in the research process is to analyse the research findings. Without this step the entire research process would be wasted. The analysis process varies dramatically depending on whether quantitative or qualitative research has been conducted. The process of analysing quantitative data uses mathematics and statistics. In contrast, the researcher will use coding and development of themes and categories during the process of analysing qualitative data (see Table 12.1).

Analysing quantitative data

If the research was a descriptive study using a quantitative methodology, such as a survey, the organization will be left with a pile of questionnaires.

Table 12.1 Differences in analysis	
Quantitative analysis	**Qualitative analysis**
Basic analysis requires only counting and math Sophisticated analysis requires knowledge of statistics Numbers are used to describe consumers and behaviour Can be used to disprove or support hypothesis Analysis of quantitative data occurs after research has been completed Numbers are compared and contrasted for new meanings	Coding for concepts Coding used to develop themes and categories Analysis of data occurs while research is still being conducted Methodology may be changed based on findings Data is repeatedly analysed by researcher for new insights Recommendations based on analysis of data and skill of researcher

The responses on these questionnaires will be counted and the results will be the number of participants that responded to each question by selecting a particular answer. These numbers can then be analysed by turning them into percentages or ratios. Everyone is familiar with research findings that state 62% of the audience is male or that people prefer purchasing their tickets online by a three to one majority.

Simple quantitative analysis using only counting and basic math can describe both consumers and their behaviour. For example, a quantitative study can state that 22% of the audience for the opening performance was under the age of 30 years. Numbers can also state that 37% of the audience recalled seeing the advertisement for the opening night in the local newspaper. In addition math can be used to calculate the variation in the behaviour of members of a group.

However more sophisticated quantitative analysis requires knowledge of statistics. While software programs will do the calculations that result in the statistics, the researcher will still need to understand how the statistics should be interpreted. These statistics are used to disprove or support the hypothesis that was stated when the research began. For example, analysing the research findings will allow an organization to state, 'With 97% confidence over 50% of city residents prefer to have their tax dollars fund recycling.'

The analysis of quantitative data only occurs after the research has been completed. After all there is no reason to analyse findings when only half of the forms that are expected to be returned are in. It would be a waste of effort since the exact same analysis will need to be completed once all the forms are available. However, once the analysis of findings does begin the numbers can be continually compared and contrasted for new meanings. For example, a survey on recycling habits of local residents can first examine how many people recycle. Later someone may ask the question if senior citizens recycle more than people in their twenties. The data can then be re-examined for an answer to this question.

Analysing qualitative data

Analysis of qualitative data is a completely different process. Rather than a pile of completed questionnaires whose responses must be counted and calculated, the researchers will have tapes and written material. This raw data will be coded for concepts that are repeatedly present. These concepts will then be studied to find common themes that will then be categorized into relevant issues (Patton, 2002).

Also unique to qualitative research is the fact that the analysis of findings does not wait until the end of the research process. The research has started with a research question but not with a hypothesis. This is because qualitative research is used to explore an issue of which little is known. Because of the lack of knowledge the organization is unable to even generate a hypothesis. For example, an organization such as a pre-school may be experiencing low enrolment. They therefore decide to conduct focus groups on why enrolment is declining with an assumption that it is being caused by a lack of awareness of the organization. During the first couple of focus groups they may instead learn that the participants are aware of the pre-school but are unhappy with the school's curriculum. Therefore the organization may decide to change the focus of the research to learning more about the parents' preferences for a pre-school education.

Once the research has been completed the researchers will have multiple transcripts of focus groups or interviews. They will also have written material produced during the focus groups such as lists of preferences or concerns. They will also have material produced as a result of projective techniques. All of this raw material will be repeatedly analysed looking for meanings that may not be apparent at first. For example, interviews conducted with parents of troubled teens may contain many references to the parents' fears for their children's future. However, careful listening to the tapes or reading the transcripts will find comments on the fact the parents do not know how to communicate their concerns to their children in a way they will hear.

Recommendations will then be built from this analysis and the knowledge of the researcher who conducted the interviews. With quantitative research someone other than the researcher can conduct the statistical analysis. With qualitative research it is the knowledge that the researcher brings to the analysis process along with the findings that result in the recommendations. For example, after learning that parents care about their children's futures but do not know how to talk to them, the research might recommend that social workers at the organization run joint sessions between teens and parents.

■ Organizing qualitative data

The need to analyse the data after the research has been finished should always be in the mind of the qualitative researcher. Conducting focus groups and interviews can be an emotionally draining process as it requires intense concentration. It would not be surprising for the researcher to simple want to take a break as soon as the last participant has left. However, before the researcher leaves it is necessary to organize the data that has been collected during the research.

If the interview or focus group has been recorded the tape must be removed and labelled. If a digital recorder has been used a notation to the tape should be added that identifies the date and topic of the interview or group. After this task has been completed, any written material that has been put onto the walls should be taken down and labelled. During the process the researcher will have been so emotionally involved it may be hard to imagine that they will forget the meaning of the list. However, it frequently happens that by the next day or week, the list or words may no longer make any sense at all to the researcher.

Therefore added to any lists should be the date and topic of the research along with the question that was asked that inspired the list. For example, a list may have been have generated on why teens feel alienated from the community. The words 'why alienated' should be added so that this list can be differentiated from the list that resulted from the question of what can be done, which would be labelled 'solutions'.

In addition to lists the researcher may have asked participants to place ideas on cards. These should have been collected during the research process and set aside. They now can be clipped together by topic and labelled. Handouts such as cartoon completion should be similarly handled. While these may seem mundane tasks, in fact they are just as important as not losing completed questionnaires when conducting survey research. The material is what will be analysed and if it is not collected and organized, the researcher is left with only memories.

Back in the office the researcher will face the task of transcribing the tapes. In addition the information on the lists and cards should be typed. Any information on handouts such as cartoon completion, or ad creation should also be typed or scanned. Once the information has been typed, the original material should still be kept, because the written or drawn material will contain information other than just the written words. For example, a participant in a focus group on community development may write in large letters with a red marker the comment 'more police'. The fact that the participant wrote the words larger than any other comments and in red communicates the intensity of the feeling in a way that the typed list can never do. Therefore the original material should always be kept for reference.

RESEARCH IS MOVING ONLINE – OR AT LEAST QUANTITATIVE RESEARCH IS

The transition from using mail surveys to using phone surveys took ten years. The transition from phone to online is moving much faster. In 2006 online surveys accounted for almost one-third of total spending on surveys. In 1996 $3.8 million was spent, while in 2006 the amount rose to $1.35 billion. Why the move to online? It is both cheaper and faster. It is cheaper because there is no need to hire researchers to administer the survey and it is faster because the participants enter the answers directly into software that automatically conducts the analysis. However, despite the advantage of conducting survey research online, only 1% of qualitative research is conducted online and this amount is not increasing.

Source: Johnson (2006).

Question to consider: How much of the research we are planning to conduct can be done online?

Transcribing taped material

After all the material has been organized by being labelled and dated, the next step in the analysis process will be the transcription of taped material. These tapes will have been produced during both focus groups and interviews. With quantitative analysis the routine task of data entry does not need to be done by the researcher. This task can be performed by anyone with computer skills. However, with qualitative research the act of transcribing the tapes is not a routine task but part of the analysis process. Therefore the researcher should do the transcription because it is not just the words that are important but also how the words are said. These nuances of tone of voice will have meaning to the researcher who will remember them in the context in which they were made. This information would be lost if someone else transcribed the tapes.

The transcription should take place as soon as possible after the conclusion of the research. At best it should be done the same or next day. When listening to the tape, the speakers will not be identified by name and the researcher, who may be conducting more than one focus group or interview, may quickly forget who is speaking. Of course the actual name of the speaker is not important, but the researcher will want to remember if the comments were made by the older women who was quiet but intently listening throughout the group session, or the older women who was quiet because she seemed bored.

If time allows, it is recommended that the researcher simply listen to the tape before the transcription process is started. During focus groups or interviews, researchers are so focused on the process that they may miss some of the underlying meaning of the words that are being said. For example, a researcher may initially miss the anger in someone's statement that they are tired of always being put on hold when they call for an appointment. While during the focus group the researcher may have thought of this simply as a matter of inconvenience, listening carefully to tape might make the researcher realize that the person making the statement sees being put on hold as indicative of an overall uncaring attitude.

A word for word transcription of the tape would be ideal, but is not necessary. Instead as the researcher listens to the tape, he or she will make a note of all comments with a form of shorthand. For example, a long statement about the inconvenience of the organization's location and the amount of money it costs in bus fare can be simply typed as 'location inconvenient – bus fare too expensive'.

However, the researcher may also want to add their own comments on the speaker's statement. The tone of voice and whether they spoke eagerly or reluctantly should be included. For example, the researcher could add to the statement above the notation that the speaker 'interrupted, angry' which would be a very different notation than 'speaker reluctant to speak, seemed ashamed because cannot afford'.

A method of handling these types of comments is to type the transcripts in columns. The first column would include the words that are stated, the second column would be used to add any notes about what is being said. A third column should also be added. This column will be used to add the coding after the transcription is done.

The typing of the transcript should not be an onerous task. There are parts of a focus group or interview, particularly at the beginning, when little of importance is being said. These notes can be made at the same speed as the tape is playing. However, other portions of the tape will be rich with material that needs to be typed. At these times the researcher will need to stop the tape in order to type all the necessary comments or even go back and listen again.

PARKS AND PEOPLE – A PERFECT MATCH OR A PROBLEM

What is the first step that should happen when a city plans to redesign their parks? They could call in park designers who would be happy to redesign parks to the latest standards with expensive amenities. Or, they can first conduct research to determine what people actually want in their neighborhood parks. The City of Williamsport, PA decided that rather than start with the experts; they would start with the people.

How do you design a study that would gather opinions in a city of almost 30,000 and with six parks to study? Using knowledge of marketing research methods, a study was designed that would gather opinion using more than one method. The study:

- Surveyed 1,000 citizens over the phone
- Held five focus groups of people who lived near the parks
- Conducted 60 intercept interviews of park users
- Held 30 observations of people using parks

Did the marketing research cost money? Absolutely, but what it discovered could actually save the city money. It was found that people did not want new and fancy sports or recreational equipment. What they wanted most was better maintenance, lighting and activities. These amenities the City could afford to supply but they wouldn't have known about these basic needs unless the research had first been conducted.

Source: Williamson and Kolb (2007).

Question to consider: How would you present recommendations that seem to be common sense and yet took six months of research to confirm?

■ Coding transcribed material

At the end of the transcription process the researcher will have typed lists, the transcript and perhaps drawings or photographs. The researcher will already have been thinking about the meanings of what has been said. However, the researcher should not just go with his or her first insight, such as 'cost is the problem' or 'location needs to be changed'. Instead the researchers will now start a process called coding. This is a systematic way to go through all the typed material looking for common concepts.

For example, reading through the transcripts and lists that resulted from a focus group on museum attendance, the researchers may notice that the concept of costs repeatedly emerges. It may be stated directly as, 'the ticket price charged is too high' or indirectly such as, 'cannot afford to pay both our bills and take the family on outings'. Each of these statements would be coded as 'cost'. Other cost comments might be about the cost of transportation, the cost of babysitting, or the cost of having lunch in the cafe. At this point in time, the researcher does not differentiate but simply codes them all as cost issues. Other issues that might be coded from such a focus group might be 'type of art', 'not fun' or 'do not know enough to enjoy'.

Coding process

The researcher can code the material by simply using a different coloured highlighter for each type of issue. As the words are highlighted, in the third column any other issues are noted. The researcher will find that different comments will have the same coding because the participants may state the same issue in different ways.

The researchers will need to review the same transcripts more than one time before they are sure that the coding is complete. For some focus groups or interviews the issues will become plain early in the coding process. For example, interviews of parents who bring their children to a museum may quickly reveal that the parents are concerned about educating their children. This is not a surprising finding and hardly worth the trouble of conducting the interviews. Repeatedly going through the transcripts might also reveal that each of the parents state, although using very different words, that they tell their friends about the experience.

The researcher may then start thinking that besides educating their children; another motivation would be to gain status as a 'good' parent.

Developing issues and themes

Once the coding is completed, it is now time for the researcher to consider the connections between the codes. At this stage the researchers might realize that codes they thought were separate are common themes and need to be combined. For example comments on inconvenient location of bus stop, lack of parking, and cost of subway all are part of the same theme of transportation problems.

The researcher may find they need to separate some coding into different categories. For example, the researcher might separate issues of cost into those concerned with the fees directly charged by the organization and those related to other issues such as dining, transportation and childcare.

At times a new theme will need to be created by the researcher. For example, a focus group on perceptions of senior centres might have resulted in coded material grouped under separate themes of 'cliquish' and 'no one greets'. After some thought the researcher might realize that all this coded material is connected by a single theme of 'unwelcoming'.

This type of insight could then lead directly to a recommendation that the management designate 'greeters' at special events who will make sure that everyone feels welcome when they come in the door. This type of insight is why the analysis of qualitative data requires a skilled researcher and is more of an 'art' than the statistical analysis of quantitative data.

WHAT'S HIDING IN YOUR AVERAGES?

Calculating the mean or average of a response on a survey may be one of the first steps in analysis but it should never be your last. For example a study was conducted of how much people spend on gifts at Christmas. The survey found that Americans are the most generous at $1,528 with the British second at $1,200. What is misleading about these figures is the assumption that every American spends around $1,528. Obviously some spend lots less, which means there must be a group that are spends lots more! Here are three reasons why marketing researchers should not depend on averages:

- Averages over simplify the consumer marketplace
- Averages ignore marketing segments
- Averages focus on mass consumption rather than targeting

Source: Ritson (2005).

Question to consider: When we conduct statistical analysis what target groups should be analysed separately?

■ The process of quantitative data analysis

Once quantitative survey research methodology has been completed, the researcher will be left with a pile of questionnaire forms. To turn these forms into findings from which recommendations can be made, a standard process should be followed (see Table 12.2). The process includes a pre-analysis stage where the forms will be reviewed, coded and the data entered. The data can then be analysed using descriptive statistics. Inferential statistics can then be used to determine statistical differences and also hypothesis testing.

Table 12.2 Qualitative analysis process	
Stage	**Task**
Pre-analysis	Review data for validity, completeness and accuracy
	Code open-ended questions
	Enter data into computer software program
Analysis of responses using descriptive statistics	Frequency
	Central tendency
	Dispersion
Analysis using inferential statistics	Statistical difference
	Hypothesis testing

Pre-analysis of survey forms

A great deal of time and effort has gone into conducting the survey. The researchers will now have before them a pile of questionnaires and it is understandable that they will be excited to discover how participants responded to their questions. Therefore, they may be tempted to immediately start to enter the data into a computer program. However, they first must take the time to review the questionnaires for validity, completeness and accuracy.

Review: Validity refers to whether the forms were actually completed by the participants. If the researchers conducted the survey themselves, this is not an issue. If someone else conducted the research, the forms need to be checked to ensure that the assistants did not complete all or some of the forms without actually surveying participants. Assistants might be tempted to complete the forms themselves because of greed, laziness, or frustration with the survey process. It is impossible to know for certain if a researcher took shortcuts, which is why careful hiring and training of assistants is important.

However the researchers should check for validity by reviewing the forms while looking for random or nonsensical answers. For example, it would be extremely odd if the researchers found that almost all forms had 'married with children living at home' checked when the participant profile called for a study of university students.

While problems with validity should be rare, what is more common is the issue of completeness, especially with self-administered surveys. It is not uncommon for participants to not complete every page in a survey or every question. This might be because they did not notice a page in the survey or they found some of the questions confusing. The researchers will have to decide how many or which of the questions can be skipped and still have the survey form be useful. For example, if the survey was designed to determine if there is any difference in preference between males and females, and the gender question is unanswered than this survey form may be discarded.

Lastly, the survey forms must be checked for accuracy. Before data entry the researchers should review each forms to determine if all answers are clearly marked and legible. This must be done before data entry because if the data entry clerks are unable to easily distinguish which answer has been marked, they might just make their best guess.

Coding: After the forms have been reviewed, they are now ready for data entry. All the data will need to be entered as numbers rather then words, which should not be a problem as all answers will have been pre-coded with numbers. However, the researchers will now need to code the answers to any open-ended questions. For example, if a question was asked for the main motivation for attending an art opening, the answers will need to read and then grouped by theme just as is done when analysing qualitative data. Once the themes are found each will be given a number and the numbers will be placed by the words on the forms. Once the coding of open-ended questions is complete, there is no reason why the data entry cannot be done by someone other than the researchers.

Data Entry: If a spreadsheet program such as Excel is used to enter data, columns will be designated for each answer with each row corresponding to one questionnaire. After entering the data, the number of the row will be recorded on the questionnaire so that the data entry can be checked for accuracy if needed. Excel will allow the researchers to analyse for frequency, central tendency and dispersion.

If more sophisticated analysis is needed, a specialized computer software program will be needed such as SPSS. With this program a form for data entry will need to be constructed with a separate field for each answer. The form can even be constructed so that it looks similar to the questionnaire, which should speed data entry. If the researcher has not worked with such a program SPSS has a tutorial feature.

Analysis using descriptive statistics

Once the responses from the surveys have been entered in the software program, the researchers are now ready to being analysing the findings. The easiest way to do so is using descriptive statistics. These methods, which include frequency, central tendency and dispersion, look at the responses alone or in comparison to each other. Using descriptive statistics, such as frequency, the researchers should be able to find patterns in the behaviour. Using cross-tabulaion they can then analyse if certain groups of people behave differently from others.

Of course, the behaviour of the individuals that participated in the survey will differ. However, it will not be completely random. Central tendency can look at all the participants in the study to determine what behaviour is the usual or normal of all the individuals participating in the survey. Besides what is the usual or normal behaviour, the researchers will want to know how much individuals vary from this norm. Statistical measures of dispersion can provide this information.

Determining frequency

One of the easiest statistical methods to calculate is frequency distribution. This is simply counting how many participants responded to a question with each possible answer. For example, frequency is simply stating how many participants are male versus female. Or, how many participants noticed the organizations recent ads on pet adoption. The first statistic the researcher should have the computer calculate (or count by hand) are the frequencies for all possible answers to all questions.

Besides just counting the number of responses, the researchers should also calculate the percentage of each response group. The researcher probably planned to conduct an even number of surveys such as 100, 250, 500 or 1,000. However not all survey forms will have been useable because of problems with validity, completeness and accuracy and as a result some will not used. The usable survey forms will be a number such as 81, 412 or 98. Because of this it will be difficult for the readers to mentally calculate percentages. Therefore the percentages should be included with the frequencies. Instead of just stating 39 respondents were male and 42 were female out of a total of 81, the percentages of 48% male and 52% female should be included. The frequencies will be much more meaningful to the reader when the percentages are included.

However, frequency statistics can be used to provide much richer information. For example, the organization may have found that only 43% of participants were aware of the promotional campaign on pet adoption. Of course this might be a matter of concern for the organization, but this finding provides no information on how to solve the problem of low awareness. Perhaps the organization would like to know if more men or women heard the promotional message. Cross-tabulation can be used to answer these types of questions. Cross-tabulation can be calculated by hand if the number of survey forms is very small. However with a large number of surveys this type of calculation will require a computer program.

Cross-tabulation can split the responses into two groups such as male and female. It will then calculate the number of positive and negative responses separately for each group. Using this method, the researchers may learn a larger percentage of males then females responded that they had not heard the promotional message. The organization might then speculate that the campaign message was not placed in the media read by males. However, the organization might also want to cross-tabulate responses on awareness by geographic area. The computer can be asked to calculate the number of positive and negative responses by zip code. This result may find that specific zip codes have a much higher negative response rate than others. Perhaps the issue is not male or female, but where people lived. The computer can then be asked to run a cross-tabulation by males versus females and zip codes at the same time. This will tell the organization which factor, location or gender, is resulting in the negative response rate.

Central tendency

The researcher can use the computer to calculate the mean, mode and median of the total responses for each question. Some questions provide only two possible responses, such as male or female, or, yes or no. The central tendency that will be calculated for these types of responses is mode. The mode is simply the answer that received the most responses.

The statistical concept of median is used to calculate the mid-range of all answers. It is not the same concept as the 'average' of all responses. It is used when a selection of possible answers is provided but the responses are not quantifiable. Perhaps an organization promoting pet adoption asked participants a question on how important is the issue of stray animals in their town. The answers provided might have been 'extremely important', 'very important', 'important', 'neither important or unimportant', 'unimportant', 'very unimportant' and 'extremely important'. The median response might have been 'unimportant'. This means that just as many participants responded with answers above this response as below this response.

The statistical concept of mean is what is usually referred to as the average. Of course to have an average, the computer must have numbers to calculate. Using the example above, the researchers know that just as many participants responded in the range above 'unimportant' as below. However, it makes a difference if most of these participants checked 'neither important or unimportant' or if they checked 'extremely important'. By providing numbers from one to seven for each of the possible responses the researchers can have the computer calculate the mean response. This will have more meaning than just the median response which is only the midpoint of the responses but does not take into consideration how far all the individual response are from the midpoint.

ONLINE SURVEY SOFTWARE AND THE RIGHT INCENTIVE PRODUCE RESULTS

A company that provides electronic content to libraries wanted to know more about their digital needs. The company produced a survey form using the Survey Monkey online software that was distributed to librarians at 2,600 libraries around the world.

A total of 552 libraries responded. This is an astonishing return rate of 21%. Was it the ease of completing the form online? Or was it the incentive that every librarian who responded received a year's access to the company's Library Center and also illustrated guides from the US Library of Commerce? Or, perhaps it was both.

Source: Brynko (2007).

Question to consider: How can we research what incentives will result in the highest response rates?

Statistical measures of dispersion

To obtain more information on how the individual responses are distributed from the mean, the researchers will need to use statistical measures of dispersion. These include range, variance and standard deviation.

The easiest measure to use and understand is the range of the responses. For example, the organization may have asked the survey question, 'How much would you be willing to pay to adopt an animal in a shelter if you knew that the money would be used to save other animals from euthanasia?' Perhaps 232 participants responded to the question and the researcher calculated the mean response as $56. As the mean is the average response, the next question that needs to be answered is what were the highest amount and the lowest mentioned. This would be the range of the responses. The researchers might find that the lowest amount given was $20 and the highest was $150.

The reason it is important to calculate the range, is that the researchers need to know if the mean or average has been affected by extreme answers on either side of the range. Perhaps they will find that someone has given the unrealistic amount of $500. The researchers might find that the next amount listed in descending order was $150. The possibility of having more than one person who is willing to pay $500 to adopt a cat is extremely unlikely. However, this amount is skewing the mean of all responses much higher. Therefore the researchers may want to drop this response and recalculate the mean.

The variance of the set of responses to the question on how much someone is willing to pay helps the researcher to understand how dispersed each individual response is from the mean. While the researchers may have dropped the one response that was way outside of the usual range of responses, they still do not know how dispersed all the responses were from the recalculated mean of $45. One way to calculate this number would be to subtract each individual amount from the recalculated mean of $45 and then add the differences. However, this will not work because the negative numbers and the positive numbers will always cancel each other out and the answer will be zero. The total amount of dollar amounts listed below $45 is exactly the same as the total amount of dollars listed above, which is why $45 is the mean.

To solve this dilemma, the difference between each individual data number and the mean is first calculated using subtraction. However, the answer to each subtraction is then squared and these squared answers are then added together. The final step is to divide the sum by the number that is one less than the number of responses. This step allows the researcher to compare the variance between data sets that have different numbers of responses. The final number calculated is the variance. (Of course the computer can calculate this number for the researcher.)

The researchers might look at this number without a great deal of excitement. After all what does a variance of 2.5 really mean? Actually it will not mean much on its own. Its value is in allowing the researchers to compare the variance between two sets of numbers. For example, the researchers may calculate by gender the mean of the amounts people are willing to pay to adopt an animal. They may find that the means are different, with the mean for males being $48 and the mean for females being $37. The question facing the researchers is if the dispersion of responses is greater or less for males versus females. If the variance for males is 4.05 while the variance for females is 3.72 then the amounts that males are willing to pay varies more widely than for females. It would be interesting to cross-tabulate and find out if males expressed an interest in adopting dogs more often than cats. If the question was asked on the survey, and it was found that men were more likely to adopt dogs, this might be the reason that they have a wider dispersion. The potential dog adopters may be willing to pay more.

Standard deviation would be the next calculation made by the researchers. The researchers know that the higher the variance, the more dispersed are the responses in the set of data. They have found that the amount males are willing to pay is more dispersed. The problem with the variance number is that being squared; the number no longer has any meaning on its own. If the square root of the variance is calculated, the answer is the standard deviation, which is in the same units, dollars, as the original numbers.

If the standard deviation is added and then subtracted from the variance, this tells the researcher that this range is where the most responses will fall. The standard deviation for the females is 2.72 and for the males is 4.05. Therefore the responses provided by males are varied more widely. While this is easy to see visually in a small sample of 10 responses, it would not be easy to see when the researcher has a list of 150 responses.

If these standard deviation numbers are then added and subtracted from the mean, they will show where most of the responses lie. For females, this is between $34.28 and $39.72. For males, it is $42.95 and $53.05. The deviation is much larger with males and so it will be harder to determine what price to charge.

Descriptive statistics and data analysis

- *Frequency*: One way, cross-tabulation
- *Central tendency*: Mean, median, mode
- *Dispersion*: Range, variance, standard deviation

A NEW RESEARCH TOOL FOR THE YOUTUBE GENERATION

How do you learn about the lives of young people so that you can design a message that will motivate them to use your organization? One of the newest research tools is ethnographic research. This research involves detailed observations of day-to-day life using video. Rather than ask questions about preferences, the organization watches to learn the likes and dislikes of its target market. While an older generation might have been astonished at the thought of someone recording their every move, the YouTube generation takes it in stride. Below are five rules when conducting ethnographic research:

- Have an idea of what you are looking for
- Don't tell the subjects this idea until the end of research
- Don't bother the subjects with questions while filming
- Get to know the subjects so they will be relaxed
- Encourage subjects to work with you on the process

Source: Hoare (2007).

Question to consider: How could we analyse video behaviour (filmed with the permission of the research subjects) to learn more about our customers?

■ Hypothesis testing

The other type of statistical analysis that the researcher can conduct uses inferential statistics. These statistical methods go beyond just describing the data discovered during the research. Of course, no marketing research study that uses a sample can 'prove' anything with absolute certainty. What the analysis of quantitative research data can do is indicate whether a hypothesis is most likely to be true or false. Using inferential statistics, the researcher can perform statistical tests to determine if the responses from the sample can be used to draw conclusions about the entire population (Levine and Stephan, 2005).

Statistical testing process

The first step in using statistical analysis to support the truth of a hypothesis is to state the hypothesis, or guess, about some characteristic of consumers or their behaviour. For example, this could be the average fee that people will be willing to pay to attend new programming at an arts centre or the percentage of people interested in new services at a clinic. The research will then be designed to measure this characteristic.

Once the research study has been completed and the data entered into the computer, the percentage from the sample of participants will be compared with the expected outcome stated in the hypothesis.

Of course they will never be exactly the same. The issue is if the difference is so insignificant that it could be the result of random error or if the difference is significant and the hypothesis is wrong. The z-test is used to determine if the differences in percentages or averages are statistically significant or not.

Stating the hypothesis

A hypothesis is a guess that is made by the organization conducting the research. Perhaps a theatre company would like to offer early evening performances. The organization needs to know if there will be sufficient attendance so that they should spend the money to offer the performances. The theatre's finance department has stated that at least 20% of current attendees will need to plan to attend to make it financially viable to offer early evening performances.

This first hypothesis is the null hypothesis and will be stated as what the company does not wish to be true. (The symbol H_0 is used to designate the null hypothesis.) This null hypothesis is considered true until proven false. For the theatre company the null hypothesis is: less than 20% of current attendees will be interested in attending the early evening performances. The alternative hypothesis would be that 20% or more will be interested. (The alternative hypothesis is designated H_1.) One hypothesis is the opposite of the other and, therefore, both cannot be true.

There are no statistical tests that can prove a hypothesis true. This is impossible as the only way to know with 100% accuracy if the hypothesis is true is to survey the every current attendee of the theatre. However, if the null hypothesis is proved false, then the alternative hypothesis, that more than 20% of attendees will be interested, can be accepted as true. Therefore the null hypothesis needs to be expressed so that its rejection, leads to the acceptance of the preferred conclusion – offering evening performances.

Let us say that the theatre company surveys a sample of 1,100 attenders (more than the sample size of 1,024 that are needed to make the study valid at 95% confidence) and found that 22% stated they were interested. While this is over the required 20%, the researchers know that a sample is never as accurate as asking everyone. However, the question remains if 22% is so close that it is simply random error that made it over 20%.

The organization needs to determine whether the difference between the results stated in the hypothesis and the survey results are statistically significant. While the word 'significant' usually means important, in statistics it means 'true'. A statistical formula can be used to mathematically calculate this number. However, it is no longer necessary to do so, as the test to find if the difference is significant or just random error, or z-score, can be automatically calculated by a statistical computer software program such as SPSS.

This calculated z-score (sometimes referred to as the p-value) can be compared with the numbers found on a table of z-scores to determine if it indicates that the null hypothesis is not true.

It is standard procedure to have the computer software both calculate the z-score and compare the scores. The results will vary depending on whether the organization wants to be 90%, 95% or 97% confident that the results are accurate. However, the researcher can make a rough calculation by remembering the standard numbers for confidence levels. For a 95% confidence level the number was 1.96. The computer software calculated the z-score for the example of the survey of theatre goers as 1.658, which tells the researchers that they cannot with 95% confidence say the null hypothesis is not true. The percentage of 22% from the sample is just too close to the needed outcome of 20%. After all not everyone was asked the question. Therefore the null hypothesis remains true and the company does not go ahead with offering evening concerts.

Interestingly, if the survey sample returned a result of 23% of theatre goers being interested and the computer calculates a new z-score, it would be 2.48 which puts the results within 95% confidence so the null hypothesis is proved false, the alternative hypothesis must be true and, the company starts presenting evening performances. The same type of calculations can be done for comparing a hypothesized average and the average that was found by surveying the sample.

Steps in analysis process

1 State hypothesis
2 Conduct research
3 Compare measured results with expected results
4 Decide necessary level of confidence
5 Have computer calculate z-score for significance
6 State conclusion and recommendations

Summary

■ A very different process must be followed when analysing qualitative data versus quantitative data. Quantitative research will result in completed survey forms. The responses to each question on the form must be tabulated. Statistics can then be used to determine averages, percentages and distribution along with testing of hypotheses. Qualitative research will have resulted in tapes and written material that must be transcribed and coded.

■ The first step in the qualitative analysis process is to gather and label all written material. This will include lists of issues from focus groups and also the results of projective techniques. The taped conversations must then be transcribed by the researcher. The transcription does not need to be word for word but can summarize the information.

- The typed transcripts are then coded using a method such as coloured highlighting pens. Different issues will be highlighted with different colours. Some of the issues can be gathered together under common themes. These issues and themes will be the basis for the recommendations for change made by the researchers.

- The process of analysing quantitative data includes a pre-analysis of the questionnaire forms. The forms must be checked for completeness, validity and accuracy. Once the responses from the forms have been entered into the computer, they are tabulated. The results are then analysed for frequency, central tendency and dispersion.

- The results from quantitative research can be used to disprove a null hypothesis. A statistical computer program will perform the calculations of whether the results from the survey are significantly different from the hypothesized results. The organization can use a 90%, 95% or 97% level of confidence.

■ References

Brynko, B. (2007) 'Global survey offers insight into libraries' use of Ebooks', *Information Today*, July/August.

Hoare, S. (2007) 'Big brands turning to big brother: Questionnaires and focus groups aren't enough', *The Daily Telegraph (London)*, 29 March.

Johnson, B. (2006) 'Forget phone and mail: Online's the best place to administer surveys', *Advertising Age*, 17 July.

Levine, D.M. and D.F. Stephan (2005) *Even You Can Learn Statistics: A Guide For Everyone Who Has Ever Been Afraid of Statistics*, Pearson Prentice Hall Publishing, Upper Saddle River, NJ.

Patton, M.Q. (2002) *Qualitative Research and Evaluation Methods*, SAGE Publications, Thousand Oaks, CA.

Ritson, M. (2005) 'On average, market research is flawed', *Marketing*, 14 December.

Williamson, J. and B. Kolb, (2007) '*Lycoming/Clinton Bi-County Office of Aging Senior Center Planning Project: Final Report*', Center for the Study of Community and the Economy, 13 June.

CHAPTER 13

Written report and presentation

- Explore the importance of the written report and the types that can be produced
- Introduce the structure of the formal written research report
- Explain the steps in the process of writing the report
- Discuss how to make a professional oral presentation

■ Introduction

At this point in the research process it is not at all unusual for the researchers to be more than ready to finish and move on. While the researchers may have been very excited about the findings and found the process of making recommendations rewarding, they have been working on the research for weeks if not months. It is hardly surprising that they are ready to move on to a new task. However, there is still one important step in the research process remaining, which is to report the findings. Both a written report and oral presentation need to be prepared so that all that has been accomplished will not be wasted. Writing the report is never as interesting as conducting the research and yet the researchers must maintain their enthusiasm and finish the process or all the preceding effort may be wasted.

■ After the research

The completion of the research methodology is too often seen as the end of the research process. However, all the effort that has gone into conducting the research effort will be wasted if the organization does not understand the importance of the final step in the process. The recommendations that have resulted from an analysis of the research findings must be presented in both a written report and an oral presentation. After all recommendations that are not communicated, cannot be implemented.

When reporting the recommendations the researchers must also present information on the methodology, the participants and the findings. This background information gives credibility to the recommendations. The reporting can be communicated in more than one format, however the most traditional is the formal written report. Such a report has a standardized format that is adapted from both business and social sciences processes. However, the recommendations should also be communicated through either a formal or informal oral report. This report could be to the management of the organization, the employees, the customers, the board or other external stakeholders. In addition, the report may be in a nontraditional format, such as a video. Researchers will choose the formats that work best for communicating with the organization, not the format they would prefer.

Reluctance to produce a written report

Even if a video or oral presentation is the primary means of communicating the recommendations to the organization, there is still a need for a written report (Wolcott, 2001). The researchers may wish to skip the step of preparing a written report for a number of reasons. First, writing clearly is a skill that not everyone possesses. Therefore, writing a many page report is difficult. To write clearly is a very different process from speaking as written English is much more concise than spoken. With spoken language, the speaker is watching the listener. When the speaker notices that the listener looks confused, the speaker can immediately clarify the message using additional and different words. With written English writers must ensure that what they are communicating clearly the first time and therefore every word is important.

Not only is writing clearly difficult, the report must be organized logically. To have this logical order the writer must clearly understand every step of the research process. If the organization of the report is incoherent, the reader will not find the research process credible. Confused thought will be evident in a confused organizational structure.

Another reason for reluctance to prepare a written report is when the researcher does not have any recommendations. It is easier to fake your way through an oral presentation with poorly developed ideas. With writing it will clearly become apparent that the author conducted the research, but does not know what it means.

Lastly, preparing the written report comes at a time when the researcher's initial enthusiasm is running low. What seemed like a worthwhile research project has now been going on for weeks, if not months. The researcher is ready to move on to something else at the very same time that a significant amount of energy needs to be put into writing the report.

Reasons for not preparing a written report

- Writing is difficult
- Organization requires knowledge
- Writer has nothing to say
- Time and effort when researcher is tired of process

Purpose of the written report

While all of the above reasons for not preparing a written report may be present, the researchers should still write a report. There are a number of reasons why they must make the effort and take the time to do so. First, the report will be read by people in the organization and especially outside the organization that may not have any knowledge of research methodology. The written report will provide the reader with background information on how the research was conducted. This would include details on the methodology that researchers could not present in an oral presentation, as people without research knowledge would have difficulty understanding the information.

Another purpose of the written report is that it is a means of documenting the actions that will need to be taken to implement the recommendations. Of course, these recommendations can be communicated orally. When they are presented the organization may be very enthusiastic about the recommendations. However, that enthusiasm may quickly fade because of the routine challenges of running the organization on a day-to-day basis. If this happens the organization can always go back to the written report to again go over the steps that will need to be taken to implement the recommendations.

In addition, the written report is there to clarify any misunderstandings. It would not be unusual for two people who listen to the same oral presentation to come away with different recollections of what was said. If this happens, the written report is available for examination. Finally, the written report is there to preserve the research findings for future employees. This includes information on the methodology and sampling as well as the recommendations. It may well be that in the future the organization may again decide to conduct research using the same methodology. This is not just a matter of convenience, as the organization may want to use the same survey questions or focus group script to see if the answers have changed over time. If they do conduct similar research, the report will have all the needed information to both conduct the research and analyse trends.

Purpose of written report

- Explanation of research terminology and methodology
- Action plan for recommendations documented
- Clarification in case of misunderstandings
- Preservation of knowledge for future employees

Types of research report

More than one type of research report may be needed and produced during the research process. This fact should not unduly alarm the researcher, as additional reports do not mean that each is entirely unique. What differs is the type of information and the amount of details that is needed by the reader of each form of report. Therefore, the length of the reports will differ with some information being contained in all reports while other reports will include less detail (see Table 13.1).

Preliminary report: Even before the research process is completed, the researchers may consider the necessity of preparing a preliminary report. This report would be prepared for those in management who are responsible for commissioning the research. This group will be concerned with the success of the research process. The preliminary report will include any problems or concerns that have been noted by the researchers during the early stages of the process. For example, the preliminary report may note that some focus group participants seem hesitant to speak in front of other participants about their usage of the organization's services. As a result, management may decide to include some individual interviews in the research process.

Table 13.1 Types of research reports

Type of report	Recipient	Form of report	Reason for report
Preliminary	Commissioners of research	Notes and explanation	To inform on progress or problems so can adjust methodology if needed
Full	Management and commissioners	Formal document	Documents methodology, sampling, findings and recommendations
Condensed	Stakeholders	Letter or memo	Highlights findings and recommendations with short description of methodology
Recommendations	Employees	Email	Informs of recommendations that may affect organization
Summary of findings	Research participants	Posted on website	Describes important findings but not recommendations

In addition, the preliminary report may present initial findings, even though they have not been substantiated by all the research methodology. For example, initial findings from interviews may include the fact that the community has a negative perception of the organization. Therefore, the organization may decide to conduct additional focus groups to learn more about why this is so.

Full: After the conclusion of the research the organization will prepare a full report for the organization's management. This report will include all the details of the methodology, the selection of participants, the research findings and the recommendations based on these findings. This will be the report that will be kept as a reference in the marketing department.

Condensed: However, not everyone who needs information on the research project will want all of these details. A condensed report should be prepared for those who have an interest in the findings and recommendations but are not interested in all the details of the methodology and selection of participants. These individuals may include trustees and other stakeholders. They are willing to trust the organization that the right decisions were made on methodology and participants. What they want to know is what was learned from the research.

Recommendations and summary of findings: There are two additional reports that may need to be prepared. A recommendations report may be written for employees of the organization. These are the people who will be most directly affected by any change in the organization. It will help with implementation if all employees understand that the recommendations were made as the result of the research. The participants may be sent a summary of findings. This report would cover the issues that were discovered during the research. Since it is the willing participation of these individuals that made the research possible, they are entitled to know what issues were raised during the research process. The participants do not need to be sent information on the recommendations. At this stage the plans of the organization may not be finalized and ready to be made public.

Not all of these reports need to be presented as a formal written report. The preliminary report can be in the form of notes along with an unofficial conversation at a meeting. The condensed report may be written in the form of a letter or memo but also may be presented orally at staff or board meeting. The recommendations report may be sent out to employees via email. The organization may consider placing a summary of findings for participants on the organization's website.

■ Structure of the written report

The formal full and condensed written report should follow a prescribed structure (see Table 13.2). The reason is that individuals familiar with standard business practices will read the report and this is the type of structure that will be expected. It may be that the researchers will find this highly organized approach confining, or even boring. They are free to be more creative in their approach to writing reports that are for their own employees and the participants. However, reports that will be seen by trustees, funders or the management of the organization should follow a standard format.

Table 13.2 Components of research report

Component	Contents
Introductory material	Title page Table of contents Executive summary
Research methodology	Research question Research objectives Sample selection Methodology
Findings and recommendations	Quantitative data or qualitative findings Recommendations
Appendices	Biographical information on researchers Further details on sampling procedure Examples of methodology Full data

The structure should start with introductory material including a title page, table of contents and executive summary. The purpose of this section is to set the stage for the information that will follow. The methodology section will include information on the research question, the objectives of the research, how the participants were selected and the details of the methodology. The findings and recommendations section will now tell the reader what was learned during the research and what it means for the organization. Finally, the appendices will contain all the supporting information.

Introductory material

The purpose of this section of the report is to provide legitimacy to the report's contents. The title page should include the name of the organization along with any logo, if possible. In addition the name of the head of the organization or the person who commissioned the research should be included. The names of the researchers along with their official titles should be placed at the beginning of the report. If the researchers do not work for the organization, the name of the company they work for along with contact information should also be stated. The table of contents is prepared after the report has been completed. The purpose of the table of contents is to allow readers to quickly find needed information. This is especially important when the report is being discussed in meetings. For example, if questions are raised about the participant profile, everyone will be able to quickly find that section without any need to stop the conversation.

The purpose of the executive summary is to 'sell' the report to the reader. Everyone is busy and only those people involved in the research are going to be willing to read the full report. Other readers might intend to read the report but instead it will sit on a shelf or desk until they have the time – which often will never happen. The executive summary is a very condensed version of the report that will state in a page or less what research was conducted, the findings, and the recommendations. Hopefully after reading the executive summary, the reader will be interested enough to read the full report. The executive summary also helps as a convenient review of the contents to refresh the memory of the reader.

Research methodology

This section of the report will provide the background information that adds legitimacy for the findings and recommendations that are to come. The section will first address the research question. It is important that readers understand what organizational problem or concern was to be addressed by the research. After a brief explanation, the research question should be directly stated. If the research study was quantitative the research question should be stated in the form of a hypothesis.

The research objectives should also be stated. These are more action oriented than the research question. While the question concerns what the organization needs to know, the objectives are why the organization needs to know this information. For example, the report may discuss that the city government was concerned about a lack of economic development in the downtown core leading to a loss of tax revenue. The research question was what kinds of stores are desired by local residents. The objectives might include the organization's plans to use this information to recruit new businesses.

Of course, the findings and recommendations will not have credibility if the reader is not convinced that the research participants were properly selected. After all an easy way for the researchers to obtain the research findings they want is to ask people that they know will answer the question in a certain way. Therefore, the report should describe how the participants were selected to remove this potential bias.

Finally, the methodology will need to be discussed. First, the writer should explain why a specific methodology was chosen. It should not be assumed that the reader will automatically understand why a focus group rather than a survey was the proper method to gather information. Then the writer should explain the details of the methodology. For example, this would include the numbers of focus groups, interviews or observations that were held and the number of surveys conducted. For surveys the method of distribution would be explained. Of course, the dates the research was conducted should also be provided. General information about the questions that were asked or the topics discussed in focus groups or interviews should be included. There is no need to describe every detail as a copy of the survey form, examples of projective techniques, the focus group script and the interview guidelines can be included in the appendices.

Findings and recommendations

This section is the heart of the report as it provides the information on what was learned during the research process. It will also provide ideas on what actions should be taken as a result of what was learned. It is the information in this section that is the payoff for the time and money that was spent on the research.

This section of the report cannot contain all the information that was learned during the research process. It is up to the researcher to make the judgement about what is important enough to be included. This is especially true of quantitative surveys. The numbers that result from surveys can be statistically analysed in many different ways. Using the example of the types of stores preferred by local residents, it may be very important to include the results of a separate analysis of the preferences of college students if they make up a significant proportion of the population.

The researcher might have found the preferences of older residents of interest, however if this population is not large enough to affect the decision making of the city, it should not be included.

While the earlier material in this section is simply a reporting of findings, the next material will cover what action should be taken by the organization based on these findings. Not all researchers are comfortable making recommendations, preferring simply to report findings. However, the trend in marketing research is to help the organization see the implications of the research by making recommendations. Of course, the organization is free to ignore the recommendations and make their own decisions. Even so the recommendations can spur the organization to think about changes that should be made. If a report does not make recommendations, there is a risk that after if it is read, it will end up simply sitting on a shelf, which would be waste of research time and effort.

The recommendations must be based on the findings and not simply the researchers own ideas. For example, the researcher who is analysing the findings from the economic development survey might personally feel that a shoe store is needed. However, if a shoe store does not rank highly in the data, the recommendation should not be included.

There may be recommendations made by the researchers that result from seeing patterns in the data. These surprising findings may not have been foreseen by the research question. For example, the researcher may have decided to analyse the data from the economic development study by ethnic groups. As a result it was learned that a specific group expressed no interest in what stores were downtown. When cross-analysed with frequency of shopping it was learned that this group rarely shopped downtown. Based on these findings the researchers may recommend that the city develop a promotional campaign to motivate members of this group to shop downtown.

PARTNERSHIPS ENCOURAGE IMPLEMENTATION OF RECOMMENDATIONS

So how do the researchers make sure that management implements their recommendations? The answer involves the working partnership between the researchers and management of the organization. This partnership involves trust, risk, contact and acceptance.

First, the partnership must be based on trust. This means that management must trust more than the numbers. Of course a good market researcher will produce accurate findings; management must also trust the recommendations made by the researchers.

Second, management must be willing to risk making changes based on the research findings. This risk taking approach must start at the research proposal stage. If the research proposal is written to allow only a conservative research approach, no breakthrough findings can possibly result.

Third, the researchers must be in contact with other departments throughout the company as the recommendations that result from the research will impact more than the marketing department. If the finance, production and even human resources departments do not trust the marketing researchers, they are more likely to argue against taking action based on the recommendations.

Fourth, management must accept that research findings are based on the consumer's viewpoint, which can be surprising and sometimes uncomfortable for management to hear. It is not the responsibility of the researcher to only bring good news.

Source: Focus Research (2006).

Question to consider: How are we establishing a relationship of trust with our management?

Appendices

Included in this final section will be relevant information that is important but too lengthy to include in the body of the report. The researchers will need to decide based on personal judgement what should be included. The purpose of this information is to increase the legitimacy and credibility of the findings and recommendations. For example, if the researchers may be unknown to the report readers, the appendices could include more information. A short statement on the researchers' previous research projects could be appended along with their educational background. Or, if appropriate a full resume might be added.

If the researchers believe that the readers might question the sampling procedures, additional detailed information on the process can be included. In addition, examples of the research methodology can be added. For example, a copy of the complete survey form or a copy of the focus group script could be included in the appendix. After all it is much easier to add this information in the appendices than to describe every detail in the body of the report.

Finally, the complete data set of all the findings should be included. This would mean the answers to all survey questions will be provided. As explained earlier, it is not possible, or recommended, that all the findings be discussed in the report. Only the most important findings on which recommendations are based will be discussed. However, in the appendices all the answers to survey questions will be reported. In addition, a copy of the transcript of focus groups and interviews should be included.

RESEARCH ABOUT RESEARCH PRESENTATIONS

If you want to give a strong oral presentation on your research findings using PowerPoint slides, here are some research findings that can help. A research survey asked people the three most annoying mistakes presenters make when using PowerPoint. The winners were:

● Reading the slides during the presentation
● Using a font so small the words couldn't be read
● Writing in full sentences rather than in bullet points

Source: Nonprofit Briefs (2006).

Question to consider: How can I learn to use PowerPoint more effectively?

■ Writing the report

Just as important as what the report contains is how the report is written. There are general report writing guidelines that, if followed, will ensure that the report is well written (Harvard Business School, 2006). To achieve this standard the writer will need to write more than one draft of the report before it is finished. In addition, the writer must know how to present numerical information visually.

Report writing guidelines

The final report should be concise, readable and interesting. One of the issues that the report writer must balance is the need to include all relevant information with the need to keep the report as short as possible. It is important for the writer to understand that more is not necessarily better when writing a report. This is true because people are busy and do not have the time to read an unnecessarily lengthy report. Also, if the report looks too long, some people may be intimated by the length and never read it at all.

Of course, if the research process was lengthy or involved more than one methodology, it will be difficult to keep the full report short. Therefore, it is very important to add headings and subheadings in the body of the text. Of course, each section listed in the report structure discussed previously, should have its own heading. However, other headings and subheadings should also be added to help readers move through a long report by informing them of what material is coming next. The writer must decide where it is appropriate to place these divisions. However, there should rarely be a page in the report that only has text with no headings.

The final report should be easily readable. The factors that make a report readable include the style and level of language used and also the visual layout. The report should be written at the appropriate reading level, which includes the length of the sentences and the types of words used. The best way for the researcher to get a feel as to whether the reading level is appropriate is to read other marketing research reports. These can easily be found online through the local arts council or other professional associations. The report should not contain any jargon that will not be understood by a reader without a marketing research background. If a term needs to be used, such as participant profile, the first time it appears an explanation of its meaning should be given.

Another issue with readability is the visual layout of the report. The report should use a traditional font face such as Times Roman with a minimum 10-point font. This is a commonly used font because it is easy to read. More creative font styles can be difficult to read quickly if used in the body of a report and should be saved for use in the title page. In addition, the text should be double spaced or at least printed at one and half line spacing. Single space type takes the eye considerably longer to read. The margins should be adequate and extra line spacing should be included right before a new heading. All of these technical details will allow the reader to concentrate on the content without being distracted by any difficulty in reading the report.

Lastly, the report should be interesting. A boring report may not be read. This does not mean that the writer has to be creative, after all the report is factual. However, there are ways to add interest to the report. Rather than just state facts, the report can also describe incidents that give the reader a flavour of what it was like to conduct the research. The report can discuss the eagerness of potential participants to participate in interviews. For example, it may describe a participant who took two buses and the subway in order to be involved. Such descriptions will also remind the reader that the participants are not just statistics but real people whose opinions need to be taken seriously.

Photos of the research process could also be included. This, of course, would include any photos that were generated by participants as part of the research process. However, there could be photos of the research process that might be included such as participants involved in a focus group or of someone completing a survey. If it is not possible to include photos of participants because of privacy issues, the report might include a photo of the researchers and management during a preliminary meeting at the organization. Another idea might be photos of the locations where the observational research took place or even just of the organization's building.

Another way to enliven the report is to include quotes from participants. These of course would be anonymous. Quotes of statements made in interviews or focus groups or comments made in response to an open-ended question in a survey can provide the readers with a feeling of involvement in the process that just reporting findings can never accomplish.

Writing the drafts

To write a professional report the writer should follow the report writing process. The first step is to create an outline. This outline will provide a roadmap for writing the report. Just as the writers would not start out on a journey to a destination through unknown territory, they should not start writing without a plan of where they want to go. The outline will contain the components of the report but will also include more detail. For example, under the heading of 'Sample Selection' there might be subheadings of 'Snowballing' as the method chosen and 'Organizations and Associations' where the information on where they found participants would be included. If appropriate there might be a section on 'Incentives' if the organization used incentives to increase participation. Writing the report will be much easier once the outline has been completed as the writer will have a starting point rather than just be facing a blank piece of paper.

After the outline has been completed, the first draft will be written. Unfortunately a professionally written report will take more than one writing. The first draft is just the start of the process. The draft will be mainly edited for content and should be reviewed to ensure that the organization is correct. Topics that are discussed should fit under the proper heading so the reader does not need to hunt for information. At this point in the process the writer may decide to change the report's organization to one that will make more sense to the reader. In addition, the writer will see if there are redundancies in the report. If topics have been covered at too great a length, they should be edited down. Finally, the writer should check to ensure that all topics have been adequately covered. If not, the writer will need to add more detail to the report.

Once these changes have been made, the structure of the report should be complete. It is now time to edit for wording. At this stage the writer will slowly read through the report noting where wording or sentences should be changed or improved. This can seem to be a tedious process but it is the process that results in a professionally written report.

With these changes made, the report will now be ready for proofreading. This is the process that will catch any spelling, grammatical or punctuation errors. It would not be surprising if the writer is so tired of the process that it is difficult to look at the report with the attention that is needed to catch these errors. The writer may want to ask someone else to take a fresh look at the report and do the proofreading.

The report is now ready for layout. This means that the writer will check to make sure that all the headings and subheadings are formatted consistently, that page numbers are attached and that the pagination breaks between pages make sense. Again, this can be time consuming and the writer may well want to just print the report and be done. However, it is the layout that provides the first impression of the report and the writer will want this first impression to be professional.

Report writing process

1 Prepare outline
2 Write first draft
3 Edit for content

    a Reorganization
    b Redundancies
    c Missing material

4 Write second draft
5 Edit for wording
6 Proofread
7 Check layout

Presenting numerical information

If the research was quantitative and the methodology chosen was a survey, the writer will have many numbers and statistics to be included in the report. There are two problems when the written report includes many numbers. The first problem is that reading numerical information can be tedious. The reader will quickly start skipping over the material if they are faced with sentences such as, 'Of the total of 100 park visitors interviewed, 22 were below age 18, 15 were aged 19–30, 12 were aged 30–45, 25 were aged 45–60 and 26 over 65'.

The other issue has to do with the relationship between numbers. It is easy for the reader to visualize the relationship between numbers when information such as 40% of participants were male and 60% were female is presented. However, when more percentages are added, understanding the relationship becomes difficult. A sentence such as, 'Twelve percent of the participants were Catholic, 42% were Protestant, 27% were Muslim and 19% were Jewish' makes it difficult to understand the relative relationship between the numbers. For these reasons numerical information is often presented visually. The human brain finds it easier to read numbers that are presented either in rows and columns in a table, or in a chart or graph format.

IT'S ABOUT THE FOREST – NOT THE TREES

Too often researchers will add unnecessary details to research reports in order to impress. The belief is that a report that is dense with numbers must mean that the researcher's impressive intelligence deserves respect from the reader. However, excessive detail will not only confuse, it will actually mislead. Qualitative marketing research can never predict consumer behavior with absolute accuracy. Just think about this example.

A researcher interviews 205 people to ask if they will visit a particular store and 23 said they would do so. The 205 people are part of a population of 678,900. The researcher could project the 23 people onto the total population and say that 76,169 will visit the store. Why doesn't this type of projection work? Each of the 205 people interviewed represents 3,312 of the total population (678,900/205). This is not enough precision with which to predict behavior. What does the researcher do with this type of result when writing a report? They should take the big picture and provide a rounded estimate of 75,000. Using the number 76,169 in the report implies a precision that is not warranted with qualitative research.

Source: Semon (2000).

Question to consider: How can we use tables and charts and graphs to present numerical information not only for ease of reading but also honestly?

Tables: If the writer is faced with a series of numbers that all pertain to the same topic, the simplest and the most easily understandable way of presenting the information is in a table. For example, a presentation on the number of park visitors can be quickly understood if presented in columns that show both the total number and the percentage of each age group. As a result in the body of the report the writer no longer needs to mention every number. Instead the writer is now free to highlight what the most important numbers mean. For example, the writer might point out that visitors cover a wide range of age groups but that children are over 25% of total visitors. Therefore, the park is successful in attracting families.

Pie charts: Pie charts are a means of visually presenting information so that the reader can quickly grasp the relationship between the numbers. Even though the percentages may be given, as in the example of park visitors, the human brain has difficulty in seeing the relationship between the five percentages given. The pie chart will show the percentages visually as a total of 100% using a circle, which is why it is called a pie chart. Each section or piece of the pie will represent a section of visitors. By comparing the pieces of the pie, the reader is actually comparing the percentage of each group of visitors to the entire group.

Bar charts: Another way of presenting visual information is using charts and graphs. These charts and graphs can be automatically created using Excel or another spreadsheet program. If the researchers have used online survey software that automatically counts the responses, it might also have the ability to create charts and graphs. A bar chart uses length to show the numbers in relationship to each other. The advantage of a bar chart is that the brain can quickly grasp the relationship between the numbers. Another advantage is that the bar chart can contain more than one year of data. For example, park visitor figures for last year can be shown next to this year's numbers. The reader will quickly see that the number of older visitors may be down but that the number of younger visitors has increased.

Line charts: Line charts are very useful when comparing numerical data over time. The park management might conduct research of visitors every year. Comparing two or even three years of data can be done using bar charts. However, adding more years makes the bar chart too confusing to be useful. Line charts can compare data over many years. On one axis, or side, of the chart will be a grid of percentages from 0 to 100. On the bottom of the chart will be years. A line will connect the same data from year to year. For example, the number of older visitors can be tracked over a 10-year period and visually will show with a single glance whether it is increasing, declining or erratic with a single glance.

PREPARATION AND PROFESSIONALISM ARE THE KEYS

If researchers want to wow the audience with a presentation, there are two essential tasks. First, they must prepare the outline, introduction, ending and visuals. Then they must focus on a professional presentation style. Below are suggestions for a successful presentation.

Structure: Tell them what you are going to tell them, tell them, tell them what you told them

Beware the Beginning: It is critical to get the audience's interest

Prepare the Ending: Last chance to sell them the recommendations

Be Visual: Use visuals to increase memory retention while focusing attention

Don't Read: Not only is reading boring, it prevents eye contact with the audience

Speak Up and Be Clear: Trouble understanding the speaker, distracts from the content

Use Your Voice: Varying the voice adds interest and emphasis

Use Body Language: Position, posture and gestures should demonstrate confidence

Be Interested/Enthusiastic: Audience cannot be interested, if the presenter is not

Source: Polonsky and David (2004).

Question to consider: How can we improve our presentation style using the above information?

■ Oral presentation

Besides a written report, the researchers should also be willing to give an oral presentation. There are a number of reasons why it is a valuable use of the researchers' time to prepare and present the information orally. First, not everyone who should read the report will be motivated to do so. For these people the oral presentation may be their first exposure to the information. A strong presentation may create enough interest to encourage them to read the written report. Secondly, an oral presentation gives the researchers the opportunity to better explain the tie between the research recommendations and the findings on which they are based. While this has been done in the written report, there may be still some individuals who do not understand how the recommendations were derived. The oral presentation can explain this relationship more fully.

Once the recommendations have been explained, the oral presentation can be used to create excitement for their implementation. This is the researchers chance to 'sell' to the management of the organization, the employees and other interested stakeholders how the organization can better meet its mission by taking action based on what was learned during the research. Finally, at the end of the presentation, the researchers can ask for questions. This provides the opportunity to clarify any misunderstandings. Some individuals may have read the written report, but may have misunderstood the explanation of the methodology or how the participants were chosen. In addition, they may have misconceptions about the validity of research and what it can, and cannot, achieve. The oral presentation gives the researchers an opportunity to clarify any misunderstandings. These misunderstandings, if not dealt with, might keep these individuals from believing in and implementing the recommendations.

Reasons for oral presentation

- Provide information that will motivate people to read the report
- Explanation of tie between research findings and recommendations
- Create excitement for implementation
- Opportunity to clarify misunderstandings

Presentation structure

The presentation should follow a planned outline (see Table 13.3). All presentations should start by introducing the presenters along with their titles and their role in the research process.

Table 13.3 Presentation outline	
Component	**Content**
Introduction	Identify research participants Describe contents of presentation
Methodology	Statement of research question and objectives Description of methodology Explanation of sample selection procedure
Recommendations	Description of findings Recommendations for action
Conclusion	Thanks and questions

The introduction should also quickly inform the audience of the time limit of the presentation and when questions can be asked. The introduction will then provide the audience with an outline of the presentation. People can better focus on what is being said if they know what topics will be covered and when the presentation will be concluded. This introduction should only take two to three minutes, at the most.

The researchers will then state the research question and the objectives that the organization hoped to achieve with the research. A short description of how the participants were chosen will add legitimacy to the findings and recommendations. Finally, the methodology used will be described. The researchers should not go into these topics in depth because of time limitations. Instead the audience can be reminded that for those interested more details are available in the written report.

The next section of the oral presentation is the most important. The results of the research study, or the findings, are presented. Not all the findings should be discussed, as this would tax the patience of the audience. Instead the most important findings should be highlighted and the audience referred to the written report for additional information. The findings that must be presented are those that resulted in the recommendations for action. These should be discussed in as much detail as possible. After all, the time and effort that has been invested in the research process was done to solve a problem. The recommendations, which are the answer to that problem, are the reason the research was undertaken.

Finally, the presentation will conclude with thanks to the audience for their attention and a call for questions. The presenters must be careful to plan their presentation so that there is adequate time for questions. If the presenters do not allow adequate time for questions, it may be seen as an attempt to evade answering and lead to suspicion. If there are few questions, the presenters can use this time to remind the audience of any important details that the presenter feels might have been gone over too quickly.

Hints for successful presentations

There are a few guidelines that if followed will result in a more professional presentation. First, the report should never be read. After all, the audience can read the report, what they want are the important highlights. Second, if PowerPoint is used, the slides should be useful and readable. Too often presenters will over use PowerPoint as a way of hiding from the audience. The presenter should be the focus of the audience, not the slides. Third, the presenter should interact with the audience. The audience should be warmly greeted and eye contact should be made with audience members whenever possible. Fourth, the presenter should not bore the audience. The best way to maintain the interest of the audience is for the presenter to demonstrate enthusiasm for the information he or she is conveying.

Rules for professional presentations

- Never read the report
- Use well-designed PowerPoint slides
- Interact with the audience
- Do not bore the audience
- Be emotionally involved with the presentation contents

YouTube YOUR WAY TO A BETTER PRESENTATION STYLE

Instead of just watching funny videos on YouTube, you can use what you watch to become a more effective speaker. Watch the presentation style of posted videos from political debates to learn more about what works well when communicating with an audience. Instead of just focusing on the words, watch the body language. Notice how the candidates stand or sit. Also, you should watch how their gestures match what they say and how they make use of eye contact. You can also learn more about how to handle answering difficult questions. Notice how 'bridging' is used to move from a topic that the candidate doesn't want to address to one that she or he does.

Source: Gallo (2007).

Question to consider: Should we post a video of our presentation online for our organization's customers?

Summary

- There is understandable reluctance to prepare a written report. However, it must be done so that the research is clearly understood. The report also provides an action plan for the organization, a source of clarifications for misunderstandings and a means of preserving what has been learned. The types of reports that can be prepared include a preliminary, full, condensed, recommendations and summary.

- The components of the written report include an introduction, methodology, findings and recommendations section and appendices. The introduction provides legitimacy to the report. The methodology section explains how the research was conducted. The findings and recommendations describe what was learned. The appendices contain detailed information that the reader might want but that is too lengthy to include in the report.

- A report should be readable and interesting. It also should have a professional appearance. Preparing a well-written report requires more than one draft. The first draft is edited for content while the second draft is edited for wording. Numerical information should be presented using charts, graphs and tables. Using these tools will make the report easier to read.

- An oral presentation is needed to motivate people to read the full written report. It also provides the researcher with an opportunity to explain the relationship between the findings and the recommendations. An enthusiastic presentation will help to create excitement for implementations of the recommendations and also provide the opportunity to clarify misunderstandings.

■ References

Focus Research (2006) 'Effective research', *NZ Marketing Magazine*, Vol. 25, No. 10 p.42.

Gallo, C. (2007) 'YouTube your way to better speaking', *Business Week Online*, 9 August.

Harvard Business School (2006) *Written Communications That Inform and Influence*, Harvard Business School Press, Boston, MA.

Nonprofit Briefs (2006) 'Time to ax that PowerPoint show?', *Nonprofit World*, Vol. 24, No. 3, p.32.

Polonsky, M.J. and D.S. Walker (2004) 'Making oral presentation: Some practical guidelines and suggestions', *The Marketing Review*, Vol. 4, No. 4, pp.431–444.

Semon, T.T. (2000) 'Research reports show Devil's in (too much of) the details', *Marketing News*, 17 July.

Wolcott, H. (2001) *Writing Up Qualitative Research*, SAGE Publications, Thousand Oaks, CA.

Index

CPSIA information can be obtained at www.ICGtesting.com
Printed in the USA
BVOW10s0140270215

389511BV00001B/1/P

9 780750 687607